Spencer Robert Wigram, M. J. C Buckley

Chronicles Of The Abbey Of Elstow

Spencer Robert Wigram, M. J. C Buckley
Chronicles Of The Abbey Of Elstow
ISBN/EAN: 9783743349629

Manufactured in Europe, USA, Canada, Australia, Japa

Cover: Foto ©ninafisch / pixelio.de

Manufactured and distributed by brebook publishing software (www.brebook.com)

Spencer Robert Wigram, M. J. C Buckley

Chronicles Of The Abbey Of Elstow

CHRONICLES
OF THE
ABBEY OF ELSTOW,

BY THE

REV. S. R. WIGRAM, M.A.
OF BALLIOL COLLEGE, OXFORD:

WITH SOME

Notes on the Architecture of the Church,
BY M. J. C. BUCKLEY.

Seal of the Abbey.

Parker and Co.
OXFORD, AND 6 SOUTHAMPTON-STREET,
STRAND, LONDON.
1885.

PREFACE.

THIS little work would never have been undertaken, had it not been proposed to me that I should re-cast and amplify some rough notes on the subject, which I compiled some time since, with the view that the profits, if any, of their publication should be, in some way, devoted to the adornment of the venerable Church of Elstow, which has recently been restored, mainly at the expense of Mr. Whitbread.

In preparing it I have had two objects in view, namely to produce a book, which should be [1] of some, even if that some be little, historical value, and [2] sufficiently readable to interest those who may take it up. How far I have succeeded, it is for others, not myself, to judge. Beyond this I have nothing to say as regards my own part therein, but I have a heavy obligation to acknowledge to others for the assistance which they have given me. To Mr. JAMES PARKER, of Oxford, I am indebted, not only for the general plan of the book, but for time and trouble freely spent, both in shewing me how to make use of the material which I had collected, and in searching for more;

to Mr. CARY ELWES, of Bedford, for much local information; to Mr. BROWN, Minister of the Bunyan Chapel at Bedford, for calling my attention to Bp. Longland's Injunctions; and to Mr. MADAN, assistant librarian of the Bodleian Library, and Mr. MACRAY, Rector of Ducklington, for help willingly rendered, whenever it was asked.

Of the Illustrations I need say nothing, beyond availing myself of this opportunity of expressing my thanks to those who have so kindly employed their pencils in behalf of my book, a meed of gratitude which I believe others will feel is quite as much due from themselves as from me.

S. R. W.

Ingle Dene, Oxford,
 Dec. 1884.

ILLUSTRATIONS.

        A Benedictine Nun, (A. BOOKER) . *Frontispiece*
        Seal of the Abbey . . . *Title-page*
PLATE I. Tomb of Abbess Hervey . . *to face p.* 147
  „ II. Interior of Church, (Rev. E. GELDART) . 178
  „ III. Ruins of Mansion, (Miss CLARA WIGRAM) 183
  „ IV. North Doorway of Church, (T. J. JACKSON) 187
  „ V. Ground Plan of Church, (F. J. JACKSON) . 193
  „ VI. Interior of Vestry, (Rev. E. GELDART) . 203
  „ VII. Church as restored, „ . . 206

TEXT CUTS.

Norman Capital, (Rev. E. GELDART) . 194
Early English Capital, „ . . 195
Piscina, S. Aisle, . „ . . 198
Window, N. Aisle, . „ . . 200
Font, „ . . 202

CHRONICLES OF THE ABBEY OF ELSTOW.

THE Benedictine Abbey, Convent, or Monastery of Elstow[a], in the county of Bedford, was founded about 1078 by Judith, daughter of Adelaide, Countess of Aumale, half-sister of William the Conqueror, and therefore niece of that monarch. She was also widow of Waltheof, Earl of Northampton and Huntingdon; and, although an inquiry into her motives in founding the Abbey can afford at best, at this distance of time, only a field for curious speculation, it may yet be of some interest to the reader; as there is at least reason to conjecture that she was actuated by a desire to make such atonement as she could for her share in causing her husband's death.

Waltheof, who was the son of Siward, Earl of Northumbria, in 1069, with his brother Cospatrick, joined the Danes in an attempt to subvert the recently established dynasty. This proving fruitless, in 1070 he submitted to the King, who, in the following year, confirmed him in his rights as Earl of Northampton and Huntingdon, and gave him his niece in marriage. In 1074 another conspiracy against the King was set on foot among the English nobles, and great pressure was brought to bear on Waltheof, in order to induce him to join it. This, however, he refused to do, though at the same time he

[a] The name is spelt in many different ways. For these see Index, under "Elstow."

pledged his word to the rebellious barons that he would not betray their design; and it was this which led to his downfall. The plot somehow reached the ears of Judith; she informed her uncle, and he immediately had the unfortunate Waltheof imprisoned at Winchester, where, after the lapse of a year, he was beheaded, 31st May, 1075. Fifteen days later his body was, by the King's permission, obtained through the intercession of Judith, disinterred by Ufketyl, Abbot of Crowland, and buried in the Chapterhouse of that Abbey. During his imprisonment at Winchester he earned a reputation for extraordinary sanctity, and after his death miracles are said to have been wrought at his tomb. His epitaph, by Orderic Vital, from whose history the above particulars are taken, runs as follows, in the translation by Mr. Forester:—

"Beneath this stone a noble warrior lies,
　Earl Waltheof, great in arms, in council wise;
　Stout Siward's son—'twas his an ancient race
　Through Danish Jarls, Northumbrian Earls to trace.
　But honours, power, and riches, counting dross,
　With contrite heart he knelt before the Cross:
　For Christ he loved, His righteous judgments feared,
　His servants honoured, and His saints revered.
　But chief, where Crowland spreads her wide domain,
　And holy Guthlac holds his mystic reign,
　He joyed to tread the cloister's hallow'd ground,
　Her monks he cherished, and her altars crowned.
　On Winton's hill the patriot bowed his head,
　By Norman malice number'd with the dead.
　Ah! fatal last of May! unrighteous doom!
　Now marshy Crowland boasts her patron's tomb,
　Where living oft he came an honour'd guest:
　God rest his soul in mansions of the blest."

With this we may leave the fortunes of the foundress and her unlucky spouse, and return to the history of the Abbey, which is commonly known as that of the Blessed Virgin, and St. Helen, from whose name, in combination with the old English word Stow[b], the designation of the village is thought to be derived.

As then the spot is so generally connected with St. Helen, it will not be out of place to give here a brief sketch of her life, premising, however, that it is a matter involving very considerable difficulty; as there is apparently but one point—that she was the mother of Constantine the Great—for which there is any contemporary authority. The result is that, so little being known about her, much has been written; and it would seem to have been the chief aim of successive chroniclers to invent new hypotheses, or to overthrow what their predecessors had stated.

And first as to the discovery of the Cross, the great point upon which her fame rests. Even here there is great discrepancy, and probably the best plan will be first to give the story of it as told in its entirety by writers of the middle of the fifth century, and then to endeavour to trace the steps by which it was gradually built up. Socrates Scholasticus (about A.D. 450) tells us (Eccl. Hist. i. 17) that:—

"Helen, the Emperor's mother (in whose favour the Emperor willed Drepanum, of which from a village he had made a city, to be called Helenopolis), being

---

[b] The meaning of this term "stow" is perhaps most clearly expressed by "station," or "clearing," as applied to a settlement in the Colonies at the present day.

warned by a vision in her sleep, took her journey to Jerusalem. And when she found that ancient Jerusalem all desert, as an heap of stones (as it is in the prophet[e]), she searched diligently for the sepulchre of Christ, in which He was laid, and out of which He rose again; and at length, although with much difficulty, through the help of God she found it. And why it was so hard a matter to find I will declare in a few words. Even as they which embraced the faith of Christ highly esteemed that monument after His Passion, on the contrary, such as abhorred the Christian religion heaped in that place much earth, and raised great hillocks, and built there a temple of Venus, and having set up her idol, studied to suppress entirely the memory of the spot. When, however, the Emperor's mother was made privy hereunto, she threw down the idol, digged up the place, caused the great heap of earth to be thrown aside, and the filth to be removed. Then she finds three crosses in the grave, one, that blessed one upon which our Lord suffered, other two on which the two thieves ended their lives. Together with which crosses the table of Pilate was found, whereupon he had written with divers tongues, and signified unto the world that Christ crucified was the King of the Jews. Yet, because there arose some doubt which of these three was the Cross of Christ, for which they had made this search, the Emperor's mother was not a little pensive. The which sorrowful heaviness of hers, Macarius, Bishop of Jerusalem, not long after assuaged, for he made manifest by his faith that which was afore doubtful and ambiguous. He desired of God a sign, and obtained his suit. The sign was this: a certain woman of that place, by reason of long and grievous disease, lay at the point of death. As she was yielding up the ghost, the Bishop laid every one of the crosses upon her, being fully persuaded that she would recover her health if ever she touched the precious Cross of our Saviour. Nor did his expectation fail him, for when

[e] Ps. lxxix. 1; Micah iii. 12.

as both the crosses which belonged not unto the Lord were laid to the woman, she continued none the less at the point of death; but as soon as the third, which was in very deed the Cross of Christ, was laid unto her, though on the very confines of life and death, yet immediately she recovered, and regained her former strength. After this sort was the Cross of Christ found out. The Emperor's mother built over the sepulchre a goodly and gorgeous Church, and called that new Jerusalem, which she had founded over against the old and waste. The one half of the Cross she locked up in a silver chest, and left there to be seen of such as were desirous to behold such monuments, the other half she sent unto the Emperor. The which when he had received, supposing the city wherein it was kept to be in great safety, he inclosed it in his own statue, which was set up in the market-place of Constantinople, over a mighty pillar of red marble. Although I commit this to writing, which *I have only learned by hearsay*, yet in a manner all they which inhabit Constantinople affirm it to be most true. Moreover, when Constantine had received the nails, wherewith the naked hands of Christ were fastened to the tree (for his mother had found these also in the sepulchre and sent them unto him), he caused bits for bridles, helmets, and headpieces to be made thereof, which he wore in battle."

Sozomen and Theodoret, who wrote about the same time as Socrates, but evidently independently of him, omit the story of Constantine having inclosed in his statue the portion of the Cross sent to him, but in other respects tell the tale in very similar terms. The former, however, tells us [d] that St. Helen was guided to the Sepulchre either by a resident Jew, or, as he thinks, more probably, by Divine revelation; and also that the Cross was said to have restored a dead man to

[d] Eccl. Hist. ii. 1.

life. The latter[*] ingeniously accounts for the presence of the Empress at Jerusalem by making her the bearer of her son's letter to Macarius.

Now, with regard to this story, it may be observed, to begin with, that Socrates and Sozomen both admit honestly that their accounts were derived solely from hearsay; further, that all three wrote fully a century after the events which they narrate; and thus it is not surprising that, when we come to collate the works of earlier authors, we find the subject beset with difficulties.

Thus Eusebius[f], the contemporary historian, and at times evidently a privileged spectator of the events which he describes, tells us plainly that it was Constantine who caused the temple of Venus to be overthrown, and the mound of earth to be cleared away, thus discovering the Holy Sepulchre. To him likewise he attributes the erection of a church thereon, and he also preserves a copy of the letter from the Emperor to Macarius, Bishop of Jerusalem, giving most precise directions for its construction. The letter is undated, but a passage in it referring to the removal of him who was a common enemy of all, and who must have been Licinius, places it as during, or just after, A.D. 324. The historian then proceeds:—

"In the same country he (Constantine) discovered other places venerable as being the locality of two sacred caves; and these also he adorned with lavish magnificence. In the one case he rendered due honour

[*] Eccl. Hist. i. 18.
[f] Life of Constantine, iii. 25—43.

to the scene of our Saviour's birth, ... while in the case of the second cavern, he hallowed the remembrance of His Ascension to Heaven from the mountain-top. And while he thus nobly testified his reverence for these places, he at the same time eternized the memory of his mother. .... For this Empress, being resolved to discharge the duties of pious devotion to the supreme God .... had hastened to the Holy Land; .... without delay she dedicated two Churches to the God whom she adored, one at the grotto which had been the scene of our Saviour's birth, the other at the mount of his Ascension."

As has been already stated, the digging out of the site of the Holy Sepulchre must have taken place about A.D. 325, the year of the Council of Nicæa, at which Constantine was present. Eusebius finished his *Chronicon* in this year, and began to write his "Ecclesiastical History," at which he probably worked for several years. In May, A.D. 337, Constantine was baptized, and shortly afterwards died; and Eusebius at once began writing his life, so that no better authority could be desired. It is, therefore, worthy of special remark that he says not a word about the discovery of the Cross, nor does he mention St. Helen as being at Jerusalem, until the greater part of the work had been accomplished under the Emperor's directions.

The next authority, in point of time, is St. Cyril of Jerusalem, who, in a letter to Constantius, son of Constantine, dated 7th May, A.D. 351, states that the saving (*salutare*) wood of the Cross was found at Jerusalem in the time of his father, but still there is nothing to connect it with St. Helen; indeed, if anything, the terms which he uses would seem to indicate that Constantine was himself the finder.

We then come to St. Ambrose, who[g], A.D. 395, relates that St. Helen found *at Golgotha* the three crosses and the nails, that our Lord's Cross was known by the title thereon, and that she made one nail into a bit for a horse, and another into a crown, both of which she sent to Constantine. His story is most graphic; indeed the style of it might not inaptly be termed theatrical, and it is remarkable from the introduction of the designation "Stabularia," which he applies to the Empress. This word means literally an ostler-wench, or a hostess of an inn, and St. Ambrose plays upon it, speaking of her as the good "Stabularia" who so diligently sought out the manger of her Lord.

Following upon him we have St. Chrysostom[h] (A.D. 407), who so far makes a retrograde step, that he does not mention St. Helen, but he narrates the discovery of the Cross, and tells us that it was known from those of the two thieves, not only from the title, but from being found between them.

Rufinus[i], about the same date as St. Chrysostom, goes into far more minute detail, and has, in fact, got the story almost exactly as given by Socrates, even to the miracle by which the true Cross was distinguished. There are, however, two points of difference which should be noted: firstly, he states that she inquired of the inhabitants of Jerusalem the locality of the

[g] Oration on the death of Theodosius, 41—48.
[h] Hom. in Joh. 85.   [i] Eccl. Hist. i. 7. 8.

Crucifixion, and found *there*, i.e. on Golgotha, not in the Holy Sepulchre, the temple of Venus, which she overthrew; and secondly, that no mention is made of Constantine inclosing the fragment of the Cross, which was sent to him, in his statue at Constantinople.

Beyond this point it is unnecessary to follow the story, unless it be for the purpose of mentioning sundry embellishments made by later tradition, such as that one of the nails forms part of the so-called "Iron Crown" of Hungary, and that another was cast by St. Helen into the Adriatic, in order to appease the storms which rendered its navigation so perilous; and thus it only remains to guess, as correctly as may be, how the legend assumed the form in which it has come down to us. Most probably, since there is no direct evidence of Constantine having personally visited Palestine earlier than A.D. 335, when he went to the dedication of his Churches, whereas his mother seems to have gone there about A.D. 325, and may well have sent back certain reliques to her son, the credit of all has been given to her, each historian adding a little until the whole was complete. At all events, there is no evidence against the statement that St. Helen was at Jerusalem at the time of the excavations, and her being there would be sufficient to give rise to the whole story.

As regards the nation and origin of the Empress several guesses have been made. The earlier historians are absolutely silent on the point, and the first who attempts her biography, Altmannus, a monk of Hautville, to which monastery her body was removed A.D. 840, asserts that she was born at Treves, but his writings date no earlier than the ninth century. All the same it is impossible, at this distance of time, to question his authority. The conjecture that she was born at Drepanum is due solely to the fact that Constantine ordered that city to be called Helenopolis, in honour of his mother, A.D. 327, as mentioned in the *Chronicon Paschale*, and by Socrates and Sozomen; but this loses much of its weight, when we remember that Byzantium was re-named Constantinople after himself, and a city in Palestine Constantia, after his sister, about the same time.

The theory that she was of British extraction is based upon the fiction of Geoffrey of Monmouth that she was the daughter of a chieftain, Coel by name, and from whom, as he conjectures, the designation of the town of Colchester was derived. This supposition is not worthy of a moment's attention, nor can those who claim her as a native of Britain advance any more solid foundation for their arguments than the words of the Panegyrists, which may be at once dismissed as utterly inconclusive, seeing that in the first place they speak not of her but of her son Constantine, and in the second their allusion evidently is to his proclamation as Cæsar in Britain, and not to that country being the place of his birth. Constantius died at York, and there Constantine was proclaimed Emperor, but not a word is said about his mother having been with him. Doubts have been expressed by some writers as to whether he was born in wedlock,

Bede[k], among others, styling the Empress a concubine, but against this we have the statement of Eutropius[l] that Constantine had to divorce her, A.D. 292, when he married Theodora, stepdaughter of Maximian, apparently as a condition of his elevation to the imperial purple.

St. Helen died in her eightieth year, about A.D. 328—30, but the place of her death is as uncertain as that of her birth. All we know is that her body was brought to Constantinople, and there buried in a royal tomb. Hence the probability is that she died either in the midst of her labours at Jerusalem, or at some place on her way home; most likely the latter, as Eusebius tells us[m] that Constantine was present at her death-bed.

The History of St. Helen, however, though sufficiently interesting, it is hoped, to serve as an excuse for this long digression, is not that of the place and Abbey to which her name appears to have been given, and it is fully time to take up the thread of their story.

The foundation Charters have not come down to our time, even by copy, in any Chartulary, but it would appear that there was some document in existence when Leland wrote, as he gives this note in his *Collectanea*:—

"The Countess Judith, wife of Waltheof, founded the Church in the vill of Helenestowe in the time of William I., and established holy Nuns there."

He adds that the Church was dedicated to the

---

[k] Eccl. Hist. i. 8.   [l] Roman Hist. ix. 22.
[m] Life of Constantine, iii. 46.

Holy Trinity, St. Mary and St. Helen, and in another passage that Milo of Bray was among the benefactors thereof. This Milo was one of the distinguished company who joined the first Crusade, 1096, in which he was said to have lost his life, but Orderic Vital names him among those engaged in the second, 1101.

Leland also gives the names of the following witnesses, Henry of Ferrers, Henry of Beaumont, and Robert of Mellent. Of these the first named, who was the son of Walkelin of Ferrers, was presented by the King with the Castle of Tutbury in Staffordshire, and created Earl of Derby, 1071. He held at the time of the Survey over one hundred and eighty manors in England, distributed over fifteen counties. The other two were brothers, sons of Roger of Beaumont. Robert, named after an uncle, became Earl of Mellent, or Meulan, in the Vexin, was created Earl of Leicester 1103, and died 1118. Henry, created Earl of Warwick, 1068, was one of the great supporters of Henry I. at the time of his accession to the Crown, and lived until 1123.

As these witnesses were living in the reigns of William II. and Henry I., there is nothing to shew whether their names were attached to the original Charter of foundation, or to a later one granting absolutely to the Abbey the property held under the Countess Judith.

The Doomsday Survey, the date of which is 1086-7, runs as follows :—

§ 1. " Bedefordscire, tom. i. fol. 217 a :—LAND OF COUNTESS JUDITH. In the Hundred of Redburnstoke. COUNTESS JUDITH holds in Meldone (Maulden) five hides[n] and one virgate and a half, and the Nuns of Elnestou hold of her in Elemosiny[o]. The land is five carucates[p]. In the demesne are two ploughs, and seven villanes[q] have three ploughs. There are two serfs[q], and one mill of 3*s.* (value). Meadow, five carucates. Woodland (for) one hundred swine. It is worth 60*s.* When received £4. In the time of King Edward (the Confessor) £7. Alwold, thane of King Edward, held this manor, and one Socman[r] had half a virgate there, and could give it to whomsoever he pleased.

§ 2. "The same COUNTESS holds Winnessamestede (Willshamstead) and the Nuns hold it of her. It is assessed at three hides. The land is six carucates. In the

---

[n] The hide of land was no exact measure, but varied according to circumstances.

[o] Lands held by religious houses in elemosiny, or alms, were discharged from all taxes and other secular burdens.

[p] Like the hide, the carucate seems to have varied in the number of acres it contained. The five carucates here named imply land sufficient to employ five ploughs, which are afterwards enumerated, two being in demesne, i.e. in the hands of the lord, three in those of his villanes.

[q] Villanes and Serfs. It is difficult to determine accurately between the different conditions of servitude described in these terms, but it has been supposed that serfs were those who have since been styled by lawyers "villanes in gross," who, without any determined tenure of land, were at the arbitrary pleasure of the lord appointed to servile works, and received their maintenance and wages at his discretion. The villanes seem to have been of a superior degree, so called because they were attached to the vill and glebe, and held some small cottage and lands, for which they were burdened with certain stated servile offices, and were conveyed as appurtenant to the manor to which they belonged.

[r] Socman. One who held of the lord by soccage, a tenure by which a man was enfeoffed freely, or in fee simple, and was exempt from military service, paying only a rent in money or provisions.

demesne are two ploughs. There eleven Villanes have four ploughs, and there are eleven Bordars[t] and one Serf. Meadow, half a carucate. It is worth £7 6s. 0d. When received 45s. In the time of King Edward, £10 10s. 0d. Eight socmen held this manor, and had power to give and sell. COUNTESS JUDITH gave it to S. Mary of Elnestou in elemosiny; but (their) Soc[u] always lay in Cameston (Kempston).

§ 3. "Elnestou is assessed at three hides and a half. The Nuns of S. Mary hold it of COUNTESS JUDITH. The land is seven carucates. In the demesne are two ploughs, and fourteen villanes have five ploughs. There (are) eleven Bordars, and four Serfs, and one mill of 24s. (value). Meadow, four carucates. Woodland (for) sixty swine. It is worth 100s. When received 40s. In the time of King Edward £10. Four Socmen held this manor; they were the men of King Edward; they had power to give and sell their land; but their soc always lay in Cameston."

The next document of note is a Charter[u] of Henry I. (erroneously ascribed by Dugdale to Henry II.) preserved to us in an "Inspeximus[x]" of Edward II., and confirming to the Abbey

---

[t] Bordars, or Bordmen, apparently occupied a grade higher than the villanes, holding a cottage and land, on condition of supplying the lord with poultry and eggs, or other small provisions.

[u] Soc. In this sense, the duty of the socman of attending the lord's court. When applied to the lord, usually as Sac and Soc, his liberty of holding a court, and exercising jurisdiction over the Socmen within his manor,

[u] Carta Regis Henrici Secundi (Cart. 11. E. 2, n. 88, per inspex.)

[x] Inspeximus. A royal Charter, confirming one issued in a previous reign; so called from the body of it commencing with the word "Inspeximus"—i.e. "We have inspected." For a specimen of one of these documents, see p. 96.

the above-mentioned gifts of land, together with sundry other benefactions :—

"HENRY, King of England, to the Archbishops, Bishops, Abbots, Earls, Sheriffs and all Barons, and his faithful French and English, greeting. Know ye that I have granted and confirmed to the Church of S. Mary of Helenstowe, and the holy Nuns serving God there.

§ 4. "The Church of S. Andrew of Hiche (Hitchin) with lands and tithes and all liberties thereto belonging, freely and absolutely, exempt from all customs, as well episcopal as archidiaconal, except that once a year the archdeacon, with seven horses, shall be entertained there.

§ 5. "And the Church of Westune (Weston).

§§ 3, 2, 1. "And, of the gift of the Countess Judith, the vill of Helenestowe, and the vill of Wilsamested, and in Meldone five and a half hides of land.

§ 6. "Of the gift of Richard of Langecote, two hides in Mulesho (Moulsoe, Bucks) together with his daughter.

§ 7. "Of the gift of Ralph his son, three virgates in the same vill, together with his daughter.

§ 8. "Of the gift of Nigell of Staford, ten and a half virgates of land in Erendesby (Arnesby, Leicestershire), together with his daughter.

§§ 9, 10. "Of the gift of Nicholas Basset, four marks of land in Oxineford (Oxford), and two mills in Risendune (prob. Rissington, Gloucestershire).

§§ 11, 12. "Of the gift of Richard Basset and Jeva, land of Ivo Fridai in Avintone (prob. a manor in Middleton, Oxon), and one mill in Dentune (Denton).

§ 13. "Of the gift of Countess Matilda land of William Medicus of Burn.

"Wherefore I will, and strictly enjoin, that they have and hold all these well and in peace, freely and quietly and honourably, exempt from all aids[y] and gelds[z] and

[y] Aids correspond to the later "Tallage," and probably represented in the case of towns the same demand as was met in the country by the Danegeld.

[z] Gelds. Any tax or imposition.

danegeld[a], and assizes[b], and murders[c], and pleas[d], and all occasions[e], and complaints[f], and scutages[g], and warpeny[h], and all customs[i], and all land service[k],

[a] Danegeld. A tribute originally imposed on the English by the Danes as the price of peace, abolished by Edward the Confessor. A tax under this name was levied by William the Conqueror and William Rufus, as often as money was wanted for defence or expeditions; and, temp. Henry I., was reckoned as part of the standing revenue of the Crown. Stephen, on his coronation, promised its total abolition, but it seems to have been continued on extraordinary occasions, until abrogated by time, or superseded by other taxes.

[b] Freedom from assizes would be represented by freedom from serving on juries in our day.

[c] Murders. The duty of apprehending a murderer was one imposed on the inhabitants of the manor or district where the body was found, and if they failed in doing so within a month and a day, a fine of 46 marks (40 to the Crown and 6 to the relatives of the person slain) was levied upon them. Hence to be free from murders was to be free from the duty of seeking the criminal and its attendant penalties.

[d] Pleas. Prosecutions for recovery of land held under Royal Charter.

[e] Occasions. Tribute due to the lord by the tenant on special occasions.

[f] Complaints. To be exempt from complaints was to be exempted from the customary fees paid to the king, or lord of a court, for liberty to bring actions, but, more usually, to be exempted from fines imposed for common trespasses and defaults.

[g] Scutages. All tenants, who held from the king by military service, were bound to attend personally in wars and expeditions; or, in default thereof, a fine termed a Scutage (derived from the Latin *scutum*, a shield) on every knight's fee was levied for the king's use.

[h] Warpeny; Warde-penny. A customary due paid to the Sheriff for maintaining watch and *ward*, payable on the feast of S. Martin (11th November).

[i] Customs. A custom was a day's work paid by the tenant as a customary servant.

[k] Land service. Duty owing by tenant for tenure of land.

and that they have sac and soc, toll and team[1], and infangenethef[m], and all liberties which the free Churches of my land have.

"Witnesses. D[avi]d, King [of Scotland] (1124—53), T[hurstan] Archbishop of York (1119—53), R[oger] Bishop of Salisbury (1107—42), Ph[ilip] Fitzjohn, and R[obert] de Brus (ob. 1141). At Winchester."

The original of this Charter has not apparently come down to our time, but its contents have been preserved to us, firstly, as has been already stated, in an "Inspeximus," in a Charter Roll of 11. Edward II., of which there is also a copy in the Bodleian Library at Oxford[n]; and secondly in a Confirmation Roll of 2 Henry VIII., to which we are further indebted for many other Charters relating to the liberties and privileges of the Abbey.

An examination of the signatures attached to this Charter enables us to restrict its date within very narrow limits, that of David, King of Scotland, being in itself sufficient to place it between 1124, when he came to the throne, and 1135, the last year of Henry's reign. Nor need we alto-

---

[1] Toll and Team. The former of these words signified in Saxon Charters the right of buying and selling, or keeping a market; in later times the dues paid to the lord for his profits of the fair or market, called "tolling pence." The latter a process whereby any one found in possession of stolen goods could be compelled to shew whence he got them, though not beyond a third person.

[m] Infangenethef. A liberty granted by the Crown to some lords of manors, to try all thieves, their tenants, in their own court. Outfangenethef was a similar licence to try all foreigners and strangers apprehended for theft within their own fee.

[n] Dodsworth MSS. vol. xxiv. fol. 80.

gether stop here; for, since we learn from the Anglo-Saxon Chronicle, under the years 1126 and 1127, that in the former David stayed with Henry from Michaelmas to the end of the year, and that in the latter he was with the Court at Windsor at Christmas; further, from Simeon of Durham, under the year 1128, that his residence with the Court was extended into that year; and again, from Orderic Vital°, that he was engaged in prosecuting a case of treason in the royal courts in 1130, when the Pipe Roll tells us that the expenses of his journey to the south were defrayed by the king, it is reasonable to suppose that his signature was attached in one or other of those years.

The gifts confirmed by this Charter may be briefly enumerated as follows:—First we have those of the Churches of Hitchin and Weston, the origin of which is, as will be seen, somewhat uncertain; then the three benefactions of the Countess Judith, exactly as they are given in Doomsday; next certain gifts, or rather payments, made by persons when their daughters were received into the Abbey, not necessarily as Nuns, but, quite as possibly, for educational purposes; and, finally, five offerings, for which no reason is assigned, and which probably were made out of the pure piety and devotion of their respective donors.

As to the first of these gifts, it may be observed that there is at the present time no Church of *St. Andrew* at Hitchin, but there is a local tradition that the dedication was changed to that of St. Mary, on some occasion when the Church was

° Book viii. chap. 20.

rebuilt; and it was certainly known as St. Mary's in the time of Henry VIII., when the patronage was transferred, after the dissolution, from the Abbey of Elstow to Trinity College, Cambridge.

It has been suggested [p], as a cause for this alteration, that a certain Chantry, dedicated to St. Mary, having been founded in the Church, increased in course of time in wealth and importance to such an extent, that its Altar usurped the place of the high Altar of the Church, and thus by degrees the original dedication was lost, but no evidence is forthcoming to substantiate this theory; and it seems more probable that, after the Church was annexed to St. Mary's of Elstow, the only appellation [q] apparently by which the Abbey was known for several centuries, the dedication of the affiliated church was gradually merged in that of its acquired parent; and it might well happen that, from calling it the Church of the Nuns of St. Mary, people would go on to style it St. Mary's Church.

Who was the donor of these Churches and the accompanying property is a question which it is not easy to answer with any degree of certainty. In the Doomsday Survey, which was taken at the end of William I.'s reign, they are entered as the property of the King, and as having previously

[p] Beauties of England and Wales. Hertfordshire, p. 167.

[q] Though Leland tells us that the Abbey of Elstow was dedicated to the Holy Trinity, St. Mary, and St. Helen, this only amounts to that being the dedication existing at the time when he wrote, namely, in the reign of Henry VIII., shortly before the dissolution. In Doomsday (see ante, p. 14) it is styled "St. Mary" only.

belonged to King Harold, while no mention is made of Elstow; in a Charter of Henry II., which will be cited in its place, they are said to have been the gift of King William, though whether of the Conqueror or William Rufus is not there stated; and in her defence to an action brought against her, 9 Richard I., for the recovery of the advowson of Wymondley, the Abbess claims them as having been given by the Countess Judith. The probability is that they were undergoing the process of conveyance, either to the Abbey directly, or to the Countess Judith, who may afterwards have made them over to the Abbey, at the time when the materials of the Doomsday Survey were being collected. This is, of course, merely a conjecture, but it seems to be the only method of meeting the difficulty, which will at once comprehend the three statements, and account for them satisfactorily.

Of the gifts of the Countess Judith it is sufficient to remark that the Charter agrees with the Doomsday Survey, in so far as both state that while she gave the vills of Elstow and Willshamstead, she gave in Maulden only a certain quantity of land, the sole discrepancy being that the earlier authority gives the land at five hides and a virgate and a half, the later at five hides and a half, a variation which would be unimportant, but for the fact that it tends to prove the independence of the two authorities.

Of the three who gave lands with their daughters, namely, Richard and Ralph of Langecote and Nigell of Stafford, all of whom doubtless made their benefactions in the reign of Henry I., little can be said because little is known, our historical material for this period being anything but plentiful. It may, however, be assumed that all of them were men of wealth, and probably of some note in their day. The Langecotes were no doubt ancestors of the Ralph of Langetote[r], who was honoured by King John in being included among the few barons who were summoned to attend the Council held at Bordeaux in 1214. Nigell of Stafford appears among the "tenentes" (land-owners) in the Doomsday Survey, but his lands all lay in Derbyshire.

We next come to the gifts of the Bassets, a family which, from one cause or another, attained great wealth and eminence. Ralph, who may be considered the founder thereof, and who is as well known as the great benefactor of the Abbeys of Ensham and Abingdon, in which last he was buried, as for having held the office of Chief Justice in the early part of the reign of Henry I., is mentioned by Orderic Vital[s] as having been raised by the King to great eminence from the dust. He had two sons, Richard and Nicholas, of whom the former seems to have inherited his abilities, as we find him succeeding to the post of Chief Justice, which he held throughout the reign

[r] See Close Rolls 16 John, memb. 24. The Close Rolls of 1216 and 1217 also contain two or three orders to sheriffs to allow him peaceable possession of certain lands, and in 1223 he is found receiving a licence to keep "running dogs" to hunt foxes and hares, in the Royal forests, in which he holds property. Langetote appears to be the more common reading of the name, but the c and t are so alike in court-hand that it is difficult to say which is correct.

[s] Book xi. chap. 2.

of Stephen, and he is also mentioned as sheriff of the counties of Surrey, Cambridge, Huntingdon, Essex, Hertford, Bedford, Buckingham, Northampton, and Lincoln. The latter was the donor of the property mentioned here, the locality of which is fully identified by the place, which lies in Gloucestershire, being still known as Rissington Basset. The Jeva, associated with Richard Basset, might naturally be supposed to be his wife, but, according to the genealogy worked out by Dugdale[1], this Richard Basset married Maud, daughter of Geoffrey Ridel by his wife Jeva, she being daughter of Hugh, Earl of Chester; so that the grant was not that of Richard's wife but of his mother-in-law. In the Confirmation Charter of Henry II., as will be seen, the two gifts are entered distinctly from one another, the land in Avintone as given by Richard, and that in Dunton by Jeva, which harmonises well with the Doomsday Survey[u], as we learn from it that Dunton (written in the previous Charter Denton) belonged at that time to her father.

As to the Countess Matilda, though more than one lady bore that name and title about this period, there can be no question that it was Matilda, eldest daughter of Waltheof and Judith, who married (1) Simon of Senlis, who obtained through this alliance the Earldoms of Northampton and Huntingdon; (2) David, King of Scotland. She died 1131.

The land of William Medicus, here described as presented by her, appears in the Confirmation

---

[1] Dugdale Baronage, i. 378-82.
[u] Doomsday Survey, fol. 266.

Charter[x] under the gifts of the Countess Judith. Here evidently is some error, and the most reasonable conclusion is that the name of Matilda was accidentally omitted by the scribe. As to its locality, we learn from the Confirmation Charter, and also from some pleas put forward 15 Edward I.[y] (1287), that it was situated at Cameston (Kempston), and valued at 20s. per annum. The name "de Burna" was no doubt given to the doctor from his living in the hamlet of Kempston, now known as "Bourn End," which is separated from Wooten Bourn by a burn or stream; and it may be noted that both in the *Inquisitio ad quod damnum*, taken 11 Henry IV. (1410), and in the *Computus Ministrorum*, taken 34 Henry VIII. (1542), the Abbess is described as receiving rents both from Kempston and Kempston *Bourn*, the latter in either case being entered at 20s., so that there can be no doubt that it was derived from this gift of the Countess Matilda.

The list of privileges and immunities which the Abbey should enjoy is given in the usual form, and their nature has been fully explained in the notes. Two other signatures appear beside those of the King of Scotland and the two prelates from whom we obtain the date, namely, Philip, son of John, whom it is difficult to identify, and Robert de Brus, who was one of the Norman nobles who came over with the Conqueror. In recognition of his services he obtained vast estates in Yorkshire, in which county he founded the Abbey of Gisburne.

[x] Confirmation Rolls, 2 Henry VIII. Part v. No. 8.
[y] Placita quo Warranto, 15 Edward I. Rot. 8. d.

It will be seen hereafter that this Charter plays an important part in the history of the Abbey, reference being made to it on several occasions, when suits were instituted affecting its rights.

The next Charter we also obtain from the same two sources whence our information respecting the land of William Medicus was derived, and it is given in full in the Confirmation Roll of 2 Henry VIII. as follows :—

"HENRY, King of England, to the Bishop of Lincoln and the Justices, Sheriff, and Barons of Bedfordscire, greeting. I grant that the Abbess of Elnestowe have warren in her whole land of Bedfordscir, and that on this no one hunt thereon without her licence, under penalty of £10. Witness, Richard Basset. At Westminster."

There is also evidence that the privilege of holding a fair was granted in this reign, as Henry II. confirms the same, together with safety for comers and goers, as the gift of his grandfather, Henry I., but a copy of the original charter does not appear to exist.

REIGN OF STEPHEN, 1135—54.

But one charter referring to Elstow has come to light during this reign, and that only incidentally. It would appear that, among the benefactors of the Priory of St. Andrew, Northampton, was a certain Roland of Abrincis (i.e. of Avranches, Normandy), whose wife Maud, daughter and heiress of Nigel of Mundeville, had granted to the same Priory the Lordship of Siwell [1] in Northamptonshire, with the exception of certain lands, which she had given to Elstow at the time when her daughter was received there [a]. This we obtain from the following deed, in which her son William, brother of the occupant of the Abbey, confirms his mother's gifts :—

"Let all sons of Mother Church, both present and future, know that the Lady Matilda of Mundeville, for the salvation of the soul of her father, from whom this inheritance proceeds, and of her Lord Roeland of Abrincis, and of her son, hath made this gift and grant to the Church of St. Andrew at Northampton—namely, she has granted to them Siwell, and all its appurtenances, in wood and plain, and the Church, absolutely, except (§ 14) four and a half virgates of land, which she has given, together with her daughter, to the Church of Elstow. Witnesses, Robert Grimbald, Robert of Weston, Warner Grimbald [b]."

Reign of Henry II., 1154—89.

Belonging to this reign we find an important Charter, confirming all the benefactions to the Abbey, which had accrued up to the time when it was signed. The original deed does not seem to be in existence, and we are indebted for a copy

---

[1] The Lordship of Siwell appears in Doomsday as the property of the Earl of Morton, and was granted to Nigel of Mundeville by Henry I. after the battle of Tinchebrai, 1106, in which William, Earl of Morton, was one of the nobles who were taken prisoners, and was condemned to imprisonment for life and forfeiture of his estates.

[a] See Confirmation Roll (p. 27, § 14), where this is named as the gift of her husband.

[b] The deed dates probably about 1147, as two of the witnesses sign a succeeding one of that date.—Dugdale, Monast. v. 190.

of it to the same source whence we have obtained others, namely to the long Confirmation Roll of 2 Henry VIII.

In enumerating the gifts confirmed by this Charter the same plan of numbering has been followed as was adopted with the earlier one, those which were contained in it still retaining their old numbers, so that it will be seen at a glance what fresh accessions of property the Abbey had received during the interval. The period which elapsed between the two Charters may be estimated at about thirty years, the earlier one dating, as has been already seen, from about 1130, while the signatures to the later one enable us to place it about 1160; and during these thirty years it will be found that over thirty gifts were made to the Abbey, i.e., on the average, one per annum.

The Charter runs as follows :—

"HENRY, King of England, and Duke of Normandy and Aquitaine, and Earl of Anjou, to the Archbishops, Bishops, Abbots, Earls, Justices, Barons, Sheriffs, Ministers, and all his faithful (subjects) of all England, greeting.

"Know ye that I have granted and confirmed to the Church of Elnestou, and to the Abbess and Nuns serving God there, all their lands and tenures, which they had in the time of King Henry my grandfather, and which were duly given to them.

§§ 3, 2, 1. "Of the gift of the Countess Judith, in Bedfordscir, the vill itself in which the Abbey is founded; the vill of Wilshamstudia; and in Meldona five hides of land.

§ 15. "With tithes of two sheepfolds of the vill of Offruit and Emifosbia in Bedfordia.

§ 16. "Of the rents of the same vill four pounds, ten

shillings, and one meadow of ten shillings rent per annum.

§ 13. "And in Cameston the land which was that of William Medicus, which yields twenty shillings per annum.

§ 17. "And the mills of the same vill, and five virgates and twelve acres of land.

§§ 18, 19, 20. "Of the gift of William Basset six virgates of land in the vill which is called Mordona; and his tithe of Disburc; and of Middelt.

§§ 21, 22. "Of the gift of Walter de Einecourt his tithe of Sudbrant and one virgate of land; and his tithe of Woborna in Buckinghamscir, and in the same vill the tithe of three knights, namely Gilbert, Humphrey, and Bareng, and one virgate of land.

§ 23. "Of the gift of Simon de Bello Campo two parts of the tithe of his demesne of Upeton, and one acre of land.

§§ 24, 25. "Of the gift of Helgot, son of Diog[enes], the tithe of Cotes and one virgate of land in Hamtonscir (Northamptonshire); and his tithe of Torendona, and one virgate of land.

§§ 6, 7. "Of the gift of Ralph of Langecot two hides of land and three virgates in Muleshou.

§ 8. "Of the gift of Nigell of Stafford ten and a half virgates of land in Legretscir (Leicestershire) in Ardesbia.

§ 26. "Of the gift of Ralph, steward of Gilbert of Gaunt, the tithe of his demesne of Croft, with all its appurtenances; namely of Torp, and Fenechelanda, and Goldelanda, and Biscopelanda, and Suttona, and the tithe of his fisheries, as well of salt as of fresh water, and one virgate of land, and one salt-pit yielding thence twenty sextaries of salt per annum.

§ 14. "Of the gift of Ruelland of Abrincis four and a half virgates of land in the vill which is called Siwella in Northantscir.

§ 27. "Of the gift of David, King of Scotland, one tun of wine from his rent of Toteham.

§ 28. "Of the gift of Roger Murdac, first two parts of the tithe of his demesne and two bovates of land in the vill which is called Haltona, and afterwards the whole Church of the same vill.

§§ 29, 30. "Of the gift of Walter of Buisseia the tithe of his demesne of Stutesforda, of all (things) whence tithe ought to be given, and one virgate of land; and the tithe of Burton, and half a virgate of land.

§ 31. "Of the gift of William Peverell tithe of Mealdon in Essex.

§ 32. "Of the gift of Geoffrey de Tralli two parts of the tithe of his demesne of Lutegareshala, and one virgate of land.

§ 33. "Of the gift of Walter of Buisseia three virgates of land in Wiment, yielding ten shillings per annum.

§§ 34, 35. "Of the gift of Aelasia her tithes of Estmera; and Redewint.

§ 36. "Of the gift of Simon de Bello Campo one hide of land in Herghedona.

§ 11. "Of the gift of Richard Basset the whole land of Ivo Fridei in Avintona.

§ 12. "Of the gift of Jeva one mill in Duntona.

§ 37. "Of the gift of Oliver de Maleverer and Cecilia his wife the Church of Dumeslai and six acres of land in the same vill.

§ 38. "Of the gift of Roger de Chandos, and by grant of Robert his son, the whole land which he had in Dineleshou.

§§ 9, 10. "Of the gift of Nicholas Basset four marks of silver per annum from his rents in Oxenforda; and two marks of silver in Risendona.

§ 39. "And one mill at Mixberia.

§ 40. "Of the gift of Alexander, Bishop of Lincoln, ten shillings per annum, from his rent of Bugendena.

§§ 4, 5. "Of the gift of King William the Church of Hiccha, and the whole land of the priest, namely two hides of land and one virgate, with all tithes and customs to the same Church appertaining; and expressly its Church of Weston.

§ 41. "Of the gift of Roger de Frievill ten shillings [worth] of land in the vill which is called Fernecumba.

§ 42. "Of the gift of Roasia de Creint a third part of the tithe of her demesne in Beref.

§§ 43, 44. "Of the gift of the Countess Judith twelve acres of land at Caldwella, and seven other acres adjoining the same place; and twelve acres in a place called Berchesdich.

§ 45. "Of the gift of William, son of Richard, two parts of his tithe of Rungeton.

§ 46. "Of the gift of Hugh de Bello Campo one mark of silver per annum, from the rent of the mill of Sandeia.

§§ 47, 48. "Of the gift of William de Bochelanda, and G. his sister, one virgate of land in Wescota; (and) of the land of the Burgesses of Bedford twenty-two acres of land.

"Wherefore I will, and firmly enjoin, that they have and hold all these (properties) aforesaid as well, and peaceably, and freely, and quietly, and honourably, as the Charter of King Henry my grandfather testifies; in wood and in plain, in meadows and in pastures, in waters and in mills, in roads and in paths, in Churches and in Chapels, within borough and without, and in all places, with soc and sac, and toll and team, and infangenethef, and with all other their liberties, and customs, and quittances, as well, and as freely, and as quietly, as ever they held them in the time of King Henry my grandfather, and as the Charters of the same King Henry testify.

"Witnesses: T[heobald] Archbishop of Canterbury (1139-61), R[obert de Chesney] Bishop of Lincoln (1148-67), Ric[hard de Beaumes] Bishop of London (1152-62), R[eginald] Earl of Cornwall (1140—1175), R[obert] Earl of Leicester, Ric[hard] of Hum[et] Constable, War[in] Fitz Ger[old] Chamberlain, Man[asser] Biset, Steward, R[ichard] of Dunest[anville], Joc[elin] of Balliol. At Canterbury."

Here we have a long list of gifts, written out

apparently without any attempt at arrangement; but this is by no means uncommon in old Charters, and may probably be accounted for by the supposition that the scribe had all the different documents before him in a heap, and took them up one by one, as they came, without taking the trouble to sort them.

The arrangement is, however, after all a matter of but small moment compared with the identification of the various grants, a task which is one of very considerable difficulty. Of course in some instances everything is plain enough; in many a guess of more or less probability can be made; but some seem hopeless, not a trace remaining of either donor or locality.

To the first of these categories belong §§ 3, 2, 1, which are the original gifts as recited in Doomsday, and confirmed by the Charter of Henry I.; but with § 1 we find associated

§ 15, consisting of the tithes of two vills in Bedford, the names of which seem to have disappeared entirely. It has been conjectured that Emifosbia may be identical with Einesford, a name which is found in the fine rolls of 7 John, as belonging to Bedfordshire, but that gives no assistance, as it too has been lost in oblivion.

§ 16 is the grant of certain other rents in Bedford amounting to £4 10s. and 10s., and though there is nothing to indicate the property from which these were derived, it is at least satisfactory to find them reappearing, as will be seen hereafter, in subsequent documents[e] relating to the possessions of the Abbey in that town.

[e] Especially Inquisitio ad quod damnum, 11 Henry IV. (1410).

§ 13. As has been already observed, the gift of the Countess Matilda is here included under that of Countess Judith; and with it we find in addition,

§ 17. The gift of the (water) mills of the same vill, i.e. of Kempston, and five virgates and twelve acres of land. These mills are mentioned in several deeds later on [d], but the land it is impossible to identify.

§§ 18, 19, 20. In these we have benefactions by another member of the Basset family, William, who was son of Richard, and was sheriff of Leicestershire 10 Henry II. The lands given by him appear to have been situated in three different counties. Mordona is undoubtedly Maid's Moreton, about a mile north of Buckingham, as we learn from the Hundred Rolls [e] that the Abbess of Elstow held five virgates there of the gift of William Basset; and from the same source [f] that the sixth required to make up the whole of his gift was situated in the neighbouring parish of Leckhampstead. Disburc, it is equally clear, must be Desborough, in Northamptonshire, as the family still held property there in 1275 [g]; and Middelt must be Middleton or Milton Ernest, four miles north-north-west of Bedford, as in the Taxation of Pope Nicholas [h], 1290, we find the Abbess holding a portion in Middleton, in the

[d] Taxatio Papæ Nicholai, fol. 49. b, Inquis. 11 Henry IV., &c.
[e] Rotuli Hundredorum, 7 Edw. I. Bucks. fol. 342.
[f] Ibid. fol. 339.
[g] Rot. Hundr. 3 Edw. I. Northamptonshire, fol. 12.
[h] Tax. Pap. Nic. fol. 34. b.

Deanery of Clopham, Beds, while in the Inquisition of the Nones[i], 1340, the place is further identified as Middleton Erneys, in which parish William Basset held land, 1279[k].

§§ 21, 22. The donor of these gifts appears to have been the grandson of the Walter d' Einecourt[l], who came over with the Conqueror, and was rewarded by him with no less than sixty-seven lordships in different parts of England. Amongst these we find him holding three and a half hides in Brandeston[m] in Northamptonshire; and as a portion of the manor was held by the Bishop of Bayeux, d'Einecourt's property may probably have been called South Brandeston (Sudbrant) to distinguish it. The name is now spelt Braunston, and the place lies three miles north-east of Daventry. Woburn is distinctly stated to be in Buckinghamshire, so that it must be the village of that name four miles south-east of High Wycombe, and in the Taxation of Pope Nicholas[n] it is further identified as being in the deanery of Wycombe, but at the same time we have no evidence to connect it with the d'Einecourt family.

§§ 23, 36. Here again we have to deal with a grandson of one of the Conqueror's companions. Hugh de Beauchamp, the founder of the family, had three sons, Simon, who died young, Paganus (of Bedford), who married Roasia, daughter of Alberic de Vere (and widow of Geoffrey de Magnaville, Earl of Essex), and Milo (of Eton).

---

[i] Nonarum Inquisitio, fol. 18. [k] Rot. Hundr. 7 Edw. I. Beds. fol. 322. [l] Dugd. Bar. i. 385. [m] Doomsday Survey, fol. 226. [n] Tax. Pap. Nic. fol. 33.

Paganus had a son Simon, who is no doubt the benefactor here named, and who is better known as the founder of Newenham Priory; in which, however, he only completed a work which had been commenced by his mother. With regard to his gifts, the record in the Taxation of Pope Nicholas[o] that the Abbess had property in Uptone, in the deanery of Burnham, Bucks, may fairly be taken to identify the spot; but Herghedona is not to be found so easily, and we can only conjecture that the place referred to is Harrowden (a hamlet of Cardington parish, two miles south-east of Bedford, in which the Beauchamps held land[p]), which name is found both in the *Valor Ecclesiasticus* and the *Computus Ministrorum*.

§§ 24, 25. Here we are reduced to absolute guess-work, and even of that little can be done, as nothing has come to light to shew who Helgot, the son of Diogenes, was, or which of the numerous Torendones this may be; while, as to Cotes in Northamptonshire, we have our choice between the place now known as Coton under Guilsbro, in the parish of Ravensthorpe, and Cotes, a manor in the parish of Hardingston, part of which once belonged to Countess Judith.

§§ 6, 7. This is again a repetition of gifts recited in the former Charter, the only difference being that here the father's gift of two hides, and the son's of three virgates, are both ascribed to the son.

§ 8. Nigell of Stafford's gift is also stated as before, but with a slight variation in the spelling

---

[o] Tax. Pap. Nic. fol. 33.
[p] Doomsday Survey, fol. 212. b.

of the name of the place, which is now written Ardesbia.

§ 25½. Of this we know but little, except that Ralph, "Gilbert of Gaunt's man," had property, including a salt-pit, in Croft [q], Lincolnshire, near Boston. Torp is doubtless Thorpe St. Peter, an adjacent parish, and Suttona probably Sutton-in-the-Marsh, but the other names could only be recognised, if at all, by some one possessed of thorough local knowledge. This property seems to have been held by the Abbey until the dissolution, as the name Croft reappears both in the *Valor Ecclesiasticus* and the *Computus Ministrorum*. The salt-pit mentioned cannot have been a very extensive one to produce only twenty sextaries per annum, as that measure is about the equivalent of our pint.

§ 14. The record here corresponds exactly with that given above under the reign of Stephen. What became of the property is uncertain, for no name at all corresponding to Siwell can be found in later documents, unless Sibell, in the *Computus Ministrorum*, may be taken to represent it, but that is there placed in Bedfordshire. At the same time it should be mentioned that Bridges [r] states that the Elstow property in Siwell was granted 36 Henry VIII. to James Marshe and Christopher Edmonds, giving as reference, " Pat. 36 Henry VIII. p. 1."

§ 27. There can be little doubt that the Toteham here mentioned is Tottenham in Middlesex, as Countess Judith held land there [s], which

[q] Doomsday Survey, fol. 355. b.
[r] History of Northamptonshire, ii. 148.
[s] Doomsday Survey, fol. 130. b.

seems to have come down to David through his marriage with her daughter Maud, for we find in a Charter given by Dugdale [t] that Robert, son of Sewin, gave to the Nuns of Clerkenwell one hundred and forty acres of land in Hangre de Totham, which Malcolm, King of Scotland and Earl of Huntendon, had granted to him. If, as seems probable, the Malcolm here mentioned was Malcolm IV., the grandson and successor of David, the property in question may be considered to be sufficiently identified.

§ 28. Of Roger Murdac we have no satisfactory account. Henry Murdac, Abbot of Fountains, and afterwards Archbishop of York, 1147-53, was probably of the same family; and a certain Roger Murdac appears as witness in a case of assault committed in Lincolnshire in 1194[u], but there is nothing to connect him with the person here mentioned. Halton is probably West Halton, Lincolnshire, and it will be seen hereafter that the possession of the Church there was the subject of a lawsuit with the Abbot and Monks of Newhouse. The place is then described as Halton super Humber, and in the Taxation of Pope Nicholas[x] it is returned as in the deanery of Jordeburgh (Jedborough).

§§ 29, 30, 33. Walter of Buisseia comes under the same category as Roger Murdac, the only mention that has been found of a person of that name occurring in the record of a suit in Bedfordshire, 1199, when the Abbot of Wardon claimed

---

[t] Dugd. Monast. iv. 83.
[u] Rot. Curiæ Regis. 6 Richard I. Lincolnshire.
[x] Tax. Pap. Nic. fol. 57. b.

the church of that place, as having been given to the Abbey by William, son of Walter of Bussey [y]; but here again there is nothing to shew that this is the person of whom we are in search. As regards the locality of his gifts we are almost equally uncertain, and can only conjecture that Stutesforda is Shutford, Oxon, five miles west of Banbury, and Burton, Steeple, or Great Barton, in the same county, five miles north of Woodstock; the former of which appears in the *Valor Ecclesiasticus* as Shitford, while the two are found coupled in the *Computus Ministrorum* as Shutforde and Burton Magna. Wiment is probably Wymington, twelve miles north-west of Bedford, which reappears three times [z] in the different valuations of the Abbey property, though always as yielding only 5*s.* instead 10*s.* as here stated.

§ 31. It is uncertain whether this William Peverell was the son or grandson of Ralph Peverell of Nottingham, as both bore that name [a], but there can be no doubt that Mealdon in Essex is Maldon, as that was one of the many lordships held by Ralph. No trace of this property in later times has been discovered.

§ 32. Geoffrey de Tralli is no doubt Geoffrey of Trailli, who, with his wife Albreda, daughter of Walter Espec, founder of Rievaulx Abbey, and his three sons, William, Geoffrey, and Nicholas, witnessed the foundation Charter of that house, 1131 [b]. The manor of Ludgarshall, Bucks, about eight miles north of Thame, is found in Dooms-

---

[y] Rot. Curiæ Regis. 1 John, Beds.
[z] Tax. Pap. Nic. fol. 48. b., Inquis. 11 Henry IV., Comp. Ministr.   [a] Dugd. Bar. i. 436.   [b] Ibid. i. 543.

day[c] in the hands of the Bishop of Coutance, who came over with the Conqueror, and fought at Hastings, and whose estates were confiscated by William Rufus. It is said by Lipscomb[d] that Ludgarshall was then transferred to Geoffrey of Trailli, but as authority for this statement is wanting, it must only be taken for what it is worth. This gift, again, appears no more in any of the Abbey Records to which access has been obtained.

§§ 34, 35. Nothing could well look more unpromising of a satisfactory solution than this vague entry of the gifts of Aelasia, but a key to it has been found through Redewint, Radwinter, in Essex, four miles east of Saffron Walden. Here Alberic de Vere held property[e]; and as his grand-daughter, Adeliza, or Alicia, was married to Henry of Essex, successor to Suene, who held East Mersea[f], a part of Mersea Island, which lies between the mouths of the Colne and the Blackwater, it is reasonable to suppose that we have in her the benefactress here referred to. In this case, once more, we have a gift of which no mention is made in any later documents, and we can only imagine that the properties which have thus disappeared were in course of time sold, or exchanged for others.

§§ 11, 12. The gifts of Richard Basset and Jeva are again recited, but separated, as noticed above; nor is there anything to throw any further light on Ivo Fridei and his land.

[c] Doomsday Survey, fol. 145.
[d] Hist. Bucks. i. 306.   [e] Doomsday Survey, ii. fol. 78.
[f] Ibid. fol. 46. b.

§ 37. On this gift information is altogether wanting.

§ 38. Here it is possible to identify the donor, if not the property given, as it seems clear that he was the grandson of Robert Chandos, who came over with the Conqueror; and other instances are recorded of his son Robert ratifying his gifts to religious houses[g]. As regards the gifts nothing can be stated positively, but there is at all events room for a conjecture, and a probable one, that the 'Dumeslai' of § 37, and the 'Dineleshou' now under consideration, both refer to Dynesley, Herts, the 'Deneslai' of Doomsday, a place which figures considerably in the Abbey history later on, and in which it held considerable property; nor is there anything in the benefactions, as described, to prevent their belonging to the same place.

§§ 9, 10, 39. In the two former of these we have the confirmation of the gifts of Nicholas Basset, in Oxford, and Rissington Basset, which have been already described; but they are supplemented in the third by a further gift of a mill at Mixbury, Oxon, seven miles north-north-east of Bicester. The manor of this place belonged at the time of the Survey to Roger Iveri[h], but it seems to have passed shortly afterwards into the hands of the Basset family; as we find Ralph, son of Ralph Basset, giving the advowson of the Church, with others, all of which he had received from his father, to Oseney Abbey[i], in 1107, so that we can trace their connection with the place, although

---

[g] Dugd. Bar. i. 502.   [h] Doomsday Survey, fol. 158. b.
[i] Oseney Register, copied by Dodsworth, MSS. xxxix. fol. 66, p. 95.

we have not the direct grant. From this we gather that Ralph Basset, who is described in the Register as Justiciary of England, had a third son, Ralph, a monk, who would thus be brother of the benefactor here named, and whose gift to Oseney, being attested by Theobald, Archbishop of Canterbury, must have been made 1139-61.

§ 40. In this instance it is easy to trace both the donor and the locality of the grant. Alexander succeeded to Lincoln in 1123, and held the see till his death in 1148, so that the gift must have been made within that period, but there is nothing to determine the exact year. Bugenden is unquestionably Buckden, Hunts, four miles north of St. Neot's, and the benefaction is found entered at the same value in all the principal records of the Abbey property [k], as tithe arising from mills.

§§ 4, 5 are some of the earliest gifts to the Abbey, for, although in the Charter of Henry I. no donor's name is mentioned, and here, as has been observed, they are assigned simply to King William, it will appear, from a document to be noted later on, that they were granted by the Conqueror.

§ 41. Respecting Roger de Frieville and Fernecumba, no information is forthcoming.

§ 42. Were it not for the designation 'de Creint' appended to her name, there could be little doubt that this benefactress was Rohasia, wife of Pagan Beauchamp, especially as his father, Hugh, held land in Great Barford[l] (Beref), five

---

[k] Tax. Pap. Nic. fol. 52. Valor. Eccl., Comp. Ministr.
[l] Doomsday Survey, fol. 213. b.

miles east-north-east of Bedford. Probably she was the donor, and 'de Creint' some territorial or family appellation, which has not come to light. Barford, again, will be found to reappear in all the records [m].

§§ 43, 44. Caldwella is probably Caldwell, in or adjoining Bedford, where the Priory of that name existed; but nothing has been found to shew that Countess Judith was an owner of land there, nor does either that name or 'Berchesdich' occur in any of the later documents.

§ 45. Here again there is no information sufficient to identify either gift or donor.

§ 46. The Hugh de Beauchamp, with whom we have to deal under this gift, is probably Hugh, son of Oliver, who is described [n] as succeeding Milo, third son of the elder Hugh; but it does not appear in what degree they were related, or how the property at Sandy, of which this is the only notice we have, came into the Beauchamp family.

§§ 47, 48. William de Bochelanda is probably William, son of Hugh, of Buckland, Sheriff of Berks (and seven other counties), 1109, and who was himself Sheriff of the same county, 1118 [o]; but beyond this nothing has been ascertained. G., his sister, is not to be found. Wescota we can only conjecture to be Westcott, a hamlet of Waddesden, Bucks, seven miles north-west of Aylesbury, and it is hopeless to attempt to trace the land of the burgesses of Bedford.

The privileges conferred by this Charter are

[m] Tax. Pap. Nic., Valor Eccl., Comp. Ministr.
[n] Dugd. Bar. i. 223. [o] Abingdon Chronicle, ii. 160.

very briefly expressed, but at the same time very inclusively, as they are made to comprehend all that were enjoyed under the former one, with the addition of the words 'in wood and in plain,' &c.

The signatures to a Charter are only valuable in respect of it, so far as they help to fix its date, which in this instance is restricted to the period between 1154, when Henry came to the throne, and 18th April, 1161, the date of Archbishop Theobald's death; but a few brief notes respecting those who attested it may have some interest for the reader.

Of the Prelates who signed nothing need be said, as their lives are matters of general history; and Reginald, Earl of Cornwall, will be at once recognised as the natural son of Henry I., who was raised to that Earldom by Stephen, 1140; but the others, not being so well known, shall be shortly described.

Robert, surnamed Bossu, Earl of Leicester, was son of Robert of Mellent, who signed the first benefactions of Countess Judith. He was Justiciary temp. Henry II., and died 1167[p]. Richard of Humet was Constable of Normandy at the time of the capture of the Castle of Combort in Brittany, 1163. He also appears as a witness to the treaty between Stephen and Henry, Duke of Normandy, respecting the succession to the English Crown, 19th Sept., 1154[q]. Warin Fitz Gerold, Treasurer and Chamberlain to Henry II., signed the same treaty[r]. Manasser Biset was steward of the royal household, and accompanied the King in one of his expeditions

[p] Dugd. Bar. i. 85.   [q] Ibid. i. 63.   [r] Ibid. i. 411.

to France, signing a Charter at Rouen[1]. Robert of Dunestanville (or Dunstanville) was one of the nobles who undertook (2 Henry II.) that the King should maintain the laws and customs of the realm[2]. Jocelin of Balliol has not been satisfactorily traced.

From the same source whence the above Charter is derived, i.e. the Confirmation Roll of 2 Henry VIII., we obtain two others of Henry II., both apparently granted at the same time with it, as they are issued at Canterbury, and are attested by one or more of the same witnesses.

One is found under an Inspeximus of one of the later Henries, and is a confirmation of the free warren given by Henry I. It runs :—

"HENRY, King of England, and Duke of Normandy and Aquitaine, and Earl of Anjou, to the Justices, Barons, Sheriffs, and Ministers under whose jurisdiction the Nuns of Elnestou hold land, greeting. I grant that the Nuns of Elnestou have warren in all their lands, in wood and in plain, and in all places, as well, and as peaceably, and as freely as they were wont to have it in the time of King Henry my grandfather, and as his letters testify. And I forbid any one hunting, or taking a hare upon them, without their licence, under penalty of £10. Witness, Ric[hard] of Hum[et], Constable. At Canterbury."

The other confirms the fair at Elstow, of the original grant of which no copy has been found, and is as follows :—

"HENRY, King of England, and Duke of Normandy and Aquitaine, and Earl of Anjou, to the Bishop of Lincoln, and the Sheriff, and all Barons of Bedfordshire, greeting. I grant to the Nuns of Elnestou that they

[1] Abingdon Chronicle, ii. 221.   [2] Dugd. Bar. i. 591.

may have one fair at Elnestou for four days, namely, on the Vigil of the Invention of the Holy Cross, on the day of the Feast (3rd May), and two days afterwards. And that they hold it well and peaceably. And that all those who come to the same fair have from me sure peace in going and returning, so that no one thereupon offer them injury or insult, under penalty to me, just as King Henry, my grandfather, granted it, and his Charter confirmed it. Witnesses, Ric[hard] of Hum[et], Constable, and Man[asser] Biset, Steward. At Canterbury."

There is also another Charter, apparently of the same date as the above, as it is witnessed at Canterbury by T. (no doubt Theobald), Archbishop, which is referred to, and partially quoted, in certain pleadings in 15 Edward I., which will be noticed in their place. In it the gift of the land of William Medicus, and other rentals in Kempston (§§ 13, 17) are recited, with the addition of certain liberties not previously mentioned. Perhaps these had been called in question, as otherwise it is difficult to see why such a supplement to the chief Charter was required.

Following upon these in point of date is found, again in the Confirmation Roll of Henry VIII., a document, singular alike in its origin and in its contents, which are thus given:—

"HENRY, King of England, and Duke of Normandy, and Earl of Anjou, son of King Henry, to the Provosts and Burgesses of Bedford, greeting. I charge you that you do not molest, or permit to be unjustly molested, men coming to the fair of the Nuns of Elnestou, or returning thence, nor offer them any injury or insult, or permit the same to be offered, either within or without the fair, so long as it shall last, against their liberties, which the Lord King my father, and King Henry, the grandfather of the Lord King my father granted, and by their charters confirmed, to them. And unless ye do it, the Sheriff of Bedfordshire shall see it done. Witness, Ric[hard], Archdeacon of Pict (Poictiers). At Winchester."

The difficulty as to the origin of this Charter lies in the fact that neither Henry II. nor III. was the son of a Henry, both being grandsons of a king of that name; hence the only person to whom it can be ascribed is Prince Henry[*], son of Henry II., whom his father had crowned during his own lifetime, on June 14, 1170. This Prince died, as may be remembered, in 1183, so that the Charter must have been granted between these years, but unfortunately we are unable to fix its date more accurately, as there is nothing to shew how long Richard held the office of Archdeacon of Poictiers, nor does the place, Winchester, at which it was signed, afford any assistance. It will be seen that it relates to the security of people attending the fair at Elstow, and that while his father's Charter is addressed to the Bishop of Lincoln and the Barons of Bedfordshire, this was issued to the Provosts and Burgesses of Bedford. It may further be noted that there is an appearance of urgency about it, especially in the last clause, and from these circumstances it may be concluded that in all probability some grave case of molestation had occurred,

[*] It is worthy of remark that the King, in a letter to his son, announcing his reconciliation with Thomas à Becket, Archbishop of Canterbury, addresses him by the same titles as those adopted by him in this Charter. Rymer's Fœdera, ed. 1816, i. 26.

with respect to which recourse was had to the King's Court, and that, in his absence, the messengers went on to Winchester, met the Prince, attended by the Archdeacon of Poictiers, on his return from one of his sojourns in France, and got him to grant the desired Charter.

Belonging to about the same period as this we have the record of a suit between the Abbot and Monks of Newhouse, Lincolnshire, and the Abbess and Nuns of Elstow, respecting the advowson of the Church of Halton, given to the latter (§ 28) by Roger Murdac. This is very interesting, as shewing something of the course of procedure, as well as the delays, in Ecclesiastical cases at that time, and it is much to be wished that it was complete. As it is, the later stages only have been preserved, but as we possess the original documents of these in the Harleian collection of Charters, we may venture to form a judgment of the earlier ones; and we gather that, after the case had dragged on for a long time in England, it was finally referred to the Pope, who appointed the Abbot of Rievaulx and the Prior of Bridlington his commissioners to inquire into the matter. Their report[x] is the first document we have, and is as follows:—

"S[YLVAN]y, Abbot of Rievaulx, and G[REGORY]z, Prior of Bridlington, to all sons of Holy Mother Church greeting.

[x] Harleian Charters, Brit. Mus. 44. I. 3.

[y] Sylvan, Abbot of Rievaulx, died 1189, Dugd. Monast. v. 277.

[z] Gregory was Prior of Bridlington just previous to 1181. Ibid. vi. 284.

"By the authority of the Bishop of Rome, we determine the cause, which has been in dispute between the Monks of Nehus (Newhouse) and the Nuns of Elnestow concerning the Church of St. Peter at Halton, by the aid of the Divine grace, following exactly in the footprints of the Fathers, and considering the counsel given by honest men.

"Since for a whole year and more the truth of the matter in question has been duly examined and ascertained, and responsible persons from the monasteries have been heard, and the allegations on either side considered, and those documents of the lords of the property, and that of the Bishop of Lincoln, and those of the Roman Pontiffs, which set forth the right of the Monks over the aforesaid Church, and sworn witnesses have been examined—And since all these have proved to us that the aforesaid Monks obtained the Church canonically, We have adjudged the aforesaid Church, with its appurtenances, to be in the lawful possession of the aforesaid Monks for ever.

"And we have imposed silence upon the aforesaid Nuns respecting their complaint as to the aforesaid Church for ever.

"This was done at Beverley, in the year of our Lord MCLXXVI., in the month of January, on the 4th Ides of the same month (January 10, 1176), these being witnesses:—

"Hugh, Abbot of Rivesby, William, Abbot of Crokerst, Philip, Canon of Beverley, Master Alan of Beverley, Master Silvester of Hotingham, Master Alexander Malebisse of Lincoln."

It should be noted that the seal is attached to the document, and is in fair condition.

Following upon this, though at an interval of over a year and four months, the time taken in communicating with Rome and receiving a reply, comes an Injunction[a] of Richard, Archbishop of Canterbury, who was at that time the Papal Legate, in which he recites the Bull of Pope Alexander III., and concludes with his own decree in conformity therewith. The letter runs thus :—

"RIC[HARD], by the grace of God, Archbishop of Canterbury, Primate of all England, and Legate of the Apostolic see, to his venerable brothers throughout the Province of Canterbury constituted, greeting in the saving truth.

"We have received a mandate from the Lord Pope in these words :—

"ALEX[ANDER], Bishop, servant of the servants of God, to our venerable brother the Archbishop of Canterbury, Legate of the Apostolic see, greeting, and the Apostolic benediction.

"From letters of our beloved brothers, the Abbot of Rievaulx and the Prior of Bridlington, to us transmitted, we have gathered plainly that when, by our mandate, they had undertaken to determine the suit, which had been long argued between the Abbot of Newhouse and the Abbess and Nuns of Elnestowe, respecting the Church of St. Peter of Halton—the truth of the matter having been after more diligent inquisition ascertained, namely, that the Monks had become possessed of the same Church at the presentation of the lords of the estate, according to Episcopal authority (and) canonical institution; And that it has been thus sworn on approved testimony by the more ancient and honourable men of the Province; And that it was testified before him who discharged the functions of the Archdeaconry in the Provincial Chapter, that for forty years and more the Nuns never possessed the same Church—they have concluded with an order of judgment.

[a] Harleian Charters, Brit. Mus. 43. G. 24.

"Wherefore We, since it is not fitting that suits concluded by agreement or sentence should be re-opened, and a fresh conflict begun, commit to your fraternity, by the order of the Apostolic writings, that you decree the above-named Church of Halton, which has been assigned, with all its appurtenances, to the same Monks of Newhouse, to be (by them) hereafter undisturbedly possessed, and that you cause them to possess it quietly and peaceably.

"But if by chance the aforesaid Nuns should attempt to contravene the sentence, which the aforesaid judges, to whom we had committed this cause, have promulgated, We firmly enjoin upon your fraternity, that, all occasion and appeal being at an end, you impose by Apostolic authority upon the aforesaid Nuns perpetual silence concerning the same Church, notwithstanding any letters from us obtained, or to be obtained, in this behalf; so however that We shall be able, not undeservedly, to commend the sincerity of your solicitude and obedience; but that the aforesaid Monks may not be immoderately aggrieved by the vexatious prosecutions of the aforesaid Nuns, and may be able to bear the cost of their suit.

"We (further), by precept through the Apostolic writings, command to your fraternity that you enjoin upon your Suffragans, that if by chance, advantage being taken of your absence, the aforesaid Nuns shall presume surreptitiously to molest or aggrieve the aforesaid Monks, they study to punish that excess with due severity, that others may fear to perpetrate the same.

"Given at Venice in Rivo alto, x. Kal. Jun." [May 23, 1177 [b]].

[b] The Regesta Pontificum Romanorum (ed. Jaffè, Berlin, 1851) shew that Alexander III. (1159-81) signed Bulls at Venice in Rivo alto from 14th May to 2nd October, 1177, and at no other time during his Pontificate, so that the year in which this Bull was issued is placed beyond doubt.

"By authority of this mandate we command and admonish your fraternity that, if ever it shall happen that the aforesaid Nuns offer any molestation or grievance to the aforesaid Monks respecting the same Church, you meet them with due solicitude, and restrain them severely from their unjust vexations and presumptions by the Apostolic and our own authority.

"[Endorsed], R[ichard], Archbishop of Canterbury."

Then comes the final settlement in the form of a Decree[c] by the Archbishop, who, in consequence of the submission of the Nuns of Elstow, makes them some reparation, though it could by no means represent the value of the property which they had lost by the adverse judgment.

The exordium, being much the same as in the previous documents, may be omitted, and it will suffice to give the latter part of the mandate, which is couched in the following terms:—

"The aforesaid Abbess and Nuns of Alnestowe have granted whatever right they claimed in the Church of Halton to the Abbot and Monks, free and quiet for ever, and beside this have granted to them the tithes of the demesne of Halton, and all the land which they had in the same vill (whence there was no complaint between them and the aforesaid Abbot and Monks), saving the tenure of those who formerly held the land of the Church of Alnestowe.

"And the aforesaid Abbot and Monks, for the good of peace, and for the tithes and land aforesaid, will pay annually to the aforesaid Abbess and Nuns of Alnestowe iiij marks of silver, namely, two at the Nativity of the Lord, and two at the feast of St. Botulph [June 17].

"This transaction, moreover, confirmed by faith mutually interchanged, that it may for the future remain

[c] Harleian Charters. Brit. Mus. 43. G. 23.

firm and unshaken, we secure by the present writing, and the confirmation of our seal.

"Witnesses. Walter of Bayeux and William of Gloucester, Archdeacons; William and Moyse, Chaplains; Master Robert of Inglesham; Master Roger of Norwich; John, Chaplain; Richard and Geoffrey, Clerks; William of Sotindon; and several others.

"[Endorsed], R[ichard], Archbishop of Canterbury."

This document, again, is an original one, attested by the seal affixed thereto; and the only misfortune is that no date appears upon it, and no means exist, through the witnesses or otherwise, of assigning one, but it is only reasonable to conclude that it followed immediately on the other.

Lastly, among the records of the reign of Henry II., appears another Papal Bull, respecting the Church of Harenkewod (Harringworth, Northamptonshire). At the time of the Survey, the five hides of which the manor of this place was composed belonged to the Countess Judith[d], from whom the property descended, through her daughter Maud, to David, King of Scotland. It would seem that some time during the twelfth century a church had been built there, and the advowson and all its revenues given (§ 49) to the Abbey of Elstow, though when or by whom does not appear. As, however, it is not found recorded in the earlier Charter, it may safely be inferred that the gift was made later than 1161. For some reason or another it was thought necessary to obtain a Bull confirming the gift, and

---

[d] Doomsday Survey. fol. 228.

hence the following[e], granted by Pope Urban III., March 4, 1186:—

"URBAN, Bishop, servant of the servants of God, to our beloved daughters in Christ, the Abbess and Nuns of Alnestoua, greeting, and the Apostolic benediction.

"It is fitting that we should yield a ready consent to the just desires of petitioners, and fulfil those of their wishes which will not interfere with subsequent provisions. Wherefore, beloved daughters in the Lord, since ye agree with willing assent to our just requisitions, we do by the Apostolic authority confirm, and by the protection of the present writing secure, to you, and through you to your Church, the Church of Harenkewod, as ye justly and peaceably possess it. Decreeing that it shall be lawful for no one of all men to infringe this our Charter of confirmation, or to dare rashly to contravene it. And if any one shall presume to attempt this, he shall feel the wrath of Almighty God and His blessed Apostles, Peter and Paul, falling upon him. Given at Verona iiij March."

It should be added, the original of this is preserved in the Harleian collection. It is written in the tall, fine Italian hand, and is perfect, with the exception of the seal, which is wanting, but it is somewhat difficult to read, being in places much faded.

There is little difficulty in fixing the date, as 1186 is the only year in which we have evidence that Urban was at Verona on 4th March; and the "Regesta" shew that he signed several Bulls there on that day, though this particular one is not named among them.

[e] Harleian Charters. Brit. Mus. 43. A. 17.

Reigns of Richard I., 1189—99, and John, 1199—1216.

It is necessary to combine these two reigns, because the principal event affecting the Abbey at this period runs from one into the other.

This event is a suit, promoted by Reginald of Argentain[f], against the Abbess, for the recovery of the advowson of the Church of Wymondley, Herts; and in respect of it fortunately somewhat full details of the point at issue are preserved in various records. The first mention of the suit occurs in the series of documents known as the *Abbreviatio Placitorum*, 1198[g], when the plea is set forth in full; and curiously enough the very same document, word for word, recurs in the Curiæ Regis Rolls of 1199[h]; the only probable explanation of which is that the cause was postponed, and the original plea re-entered verbatim in the following year. Again, in the *Abbreviatio Placitorum*, just previous to the earlier date, the Abbess is found appointing Simon le Guiz as her attorney in the case, while at the later, according

---

[f] Reginald of Argentan was Sheriff of Cambridgeshire and Huntingdonshire 5—9 Richard I., and of Essex and Hertfordshire afterwards. He sided with the rebellious barons (1216), and had a letter of safe conduct to the King (Pat. 17 John) to sue for peace in their behalf. In this he was unsuccessful, but, making his own composition shortly afterwards, command was given (Claus. 1 Henry III.) to the Sheriff of Cambridgeshire to give him possession of all his lands which had been seized for that transgression. Dugd. Bar. i. 614.

[g] Abbreviatio Placitorum, 9 Ric. I. Rot. 26.

[h] Rot. Cur. Reg. 1 John. m. 22.

to the Curiæ Regis Rolls, she is represented by Eustace FitzWalter.

The case itself is one of great interest, as it involves sundry points of considerable difficulty. In the Charter of Henry I. it will be observed that the Church of Hitchin was given to Elstow, with lands and tithes, and all liberties thereto belonging. In the Charter of Henry II. it is stated that King William gave the Church, with the land of the priest and all tithes and customs, and expressly the Church of Weston. Beside these Charters, the Abbess puts in two earlier ones, namely the original grant by William I., and the confirmation by his son. Neither of these seem to have come down to our time, but we may infer that they differed but little in terms from those which we have. The argument, as adduced by the Abbess, seems to be to the effect that " Hitchin was given with its appurtenances, Wymondley was appurtenant thereto, and so Wymondley was given." The fact is that the Doomsday Survey, had it been put in, would have shewn no trace of Wymondley belonging to Hitchin. Of Weston, which was specially given, it is expressly stated that it "jacuit et jacet in Hiz[i]" (lay and lies in Hitchin), whereas Wymondley is described as having originally belonged to St. Mary of Citrez[k], and having been taken by Harold, through whom it naturally fell into William's hands. If, as the plaintiff pleads, this was given to his grandfather with the Church, and that he presented a " Par-

[i] Doomsday Survey. fol. 132. b.

[k] Ibid. fol. 132. Citrez is the ancient name of Chatteris, Cambridgeshire.

son" thereto, there was no ground whatever for the Abbess; but apparently we do not know all the circumstances of the case, for later history definitely shews that Reginald somehow lost his cause, Wymondley re-appearing in the *Computus Ministrorum* as belonging to the Abbey. The record[1] of the suit runs thus :—

"Reginald of Argentain pleads against the Abbess of Alnestowe for the advowson of the Church of Wimundesle as his right, and as that which belongs to his inheritance which he holds in serjeantry of the lord King in Wimundesle, and to which he established his right against Andrew of Vitric, into which Church she has no entrance save by her 'ablator[m].'

"And Simon le Guiz, appearing for the Abbess, comes and defends her right, and says that the Countess Judith, niece of King William the Conqueror, who founded the Abbey of Alnestowe, gave to the Church of Alnestowe the vill of Hiche, with the Church of the same vill, and with the Chapel of Wimundesle, which belongs to the Church of Hiche, by his Charter, which she produces, and which testifies that she so gave it in free and perpetual elemosiny. In which Charter also is contained the grant and subsequent confirmation of King William the Conqueror, and the assent of William, son of the aforesaid King. She produces also the confirmation of King Henry, And afterwards the confirmation of King Henry, father of the Lord King, And later the writings of the Bishops who held the Episcopate at that time, And the testimony of the Archdeacon, which witnesses that the Church of Wimundele was appurtenant to the Church of Hiche, And the testimony of the bishop who dedicated that Church, And testi-

---

[1] Rot. Cur. Reg. 1 John, m. 22. Pleas on the morrow of Holy Trinity (14 June, 1199).

[m] "Ablator," probably equivalent to "Receiver."

mony by the writing of Henry [brother of[n]] the King, who was at that time legate.

"And Reginald says that the Church of Wimundele never was appurtenant to the Church of Hiche, And that King William never held Wimundele in demesne, but that in his time a certain Alfred held that land, and presented a parson to that Church, And that afterwards the lord King gave Wimundele as his Escheat to Reginald, grandfather of the aforesaid Reginald, in serjeantry, And thence he made presentation to that Church of two parsons, of which the last parson was one Osbert, And thence he exhibits his suit, &c. And he offers to prove it according to his view for the consideration of the court, And because the aforesaid Prioress[o] had thence ingress through her ablatores, and thence he has placed himself upon the laws of his country. A day was given to them, the fifteenth day from the day of St. Michael, to have their case heard. Reginald appoints in his place John of Sandon or William of Bosco, to gain or lose."

From the same series of Rolls[p] it appears that another suit against the Abbess was commenced, a few days later than that just mentioned, by William Buniun, very probably an ancestor of John Bunyan, with whose name Elstow is so closely associated.

The nature of the suit is not very clear, the

[n] These words, "brother of," do not occur in either record, but it seems evident that they must have been omitted accidentally, and that the person alluded to is Henry of Blois, brother of Stephen, who was consecrated Bishop of Winchester, 1129, and appointed Papal Legate 1139.

[o] The word "Prioress" is probably here inserted instead of "Abbess," in order that the suit might still lie, in the event of the post of Abbess being vacant at any time during its progress.

[p] Rot. Cur. Reg. 1 John.

entry of it being to the effect that Buniun pleads against the Abbess that William of Willshamstead had sued him in respect of half a virgate of land (§ 2) in that place, as being his right and inheritance, and that the Abbess appointed Simon le Guiz as her attorney. It may be that Buniun was tenant of some of the Abbey lands, and that, a claim having been set up to them by a third person, this was instituted as a friendly suit, in order that the rights of the Abbess might be confirmed by the decision of the court.

In the following Calendar year, though still in 1 John, the same Rolls[q] shew us that some suit was going on against the Abbess, as Nigel Malherbe and others were sent to inquire by what attorney she would be represented against William Peverell. Simon le Guiz was again appointed, and a day was given, &c., but there the record ends. Probably this William Peverell was a descendant of the donor of (§ 31) the tithe of Maldon, Essex; and since this property does not reappear, this may have been the suit in which it was lost.

We next find mention of a suit respecting the right of inheritance to some land held under the Abbey at Kempston, but as the year of the Roll[r] has not been inscribed upon it, all that can be discovered is that the plea was entered on the morrow of the Sunday after Easter, in some year of John.

Last of the pleas which belong to this reign comes that of Nicholas of Tingrith (Beds), who

[q] Rot. Cur. Reg. 1 John, (23 April, 1200).
[r] Abbrev. Placit. fol. 81.

recovers against the Abbess the right of presentation to (§ 50) the Church of that place [s]. The entry is very short, and it seems that the assize was held simply to ascertain who had presented the last Incumbent [t], and that point being decided in favour of Nicholas, judgment was given for him. Here it is worthy of note that as previously we have had the record of several gifts, the subsequent history of which we have been unable to trace, in this instance a certain endowment is found appearing upon the scene, we know not whence, only to vanish immediately.

To complete the records of the time of John, three other brief notices may be added, the first of which is found in the life of St. Hugh [u], Bishop of Lincoln (1186—1293), and is a pretty little anecdote. The story is to the effect that Hubert, Archbishop of Canterbury (1193—1207), brought over with him, from France, a little boy, Robert of Noyon, then aged about five years, who on seeing St. Hugh, who met the party on their landing, at once "clung to him as to a father." On this it would appear that he was entrusted to the care of the Bishop, as we find that "after a short time he sent him to be taught his letters at Alnestou."

The second notice comes from the Annals of Dunstaple, under the year 1213 [x], and is as follows:—

[s] Abbrev. Placit. fol. 81, 15 John.
[t] Coram Rege Rolls, 15 John. Bedfordscir, Rot. 10. in dorso.
[u] Life of St. Hugh, Bishop of Lincoln. p. 146.
[x] Annales Monastici. iii. 41, 42.

"The same year died... the Abbess of Alnestow... the same year, in the month of November, the King granted free election to many of the Monasteries... so that the Monks of St. Alban's elected William to be their Abbot... and the Nuns of Alnestow, with a like liberty, freely elected their Abbess."

It is a pity that the Chronicler omits to mention the name of either the deceased Abbess, or her successor, as a starting-point would thus have been supplied for our list of Abbesses, which, as will be seen, does not commence until a few years later.

The last is an anecdote introduced incidentally into the history of Matthew Paris[y], and as it relates to the Abbess of Elstow, and is moreover a characteristic example of monastic stories, it is worthy of a place in these pages. It runs :—

"Then shone forth the infliction of the vengeance of St. Paul, for Falk, the bloodthirsty betrayer, had destroyed the Church of St. Paul at Bedford, for the construction and fortification of his castle, and so he was held in the prison-like custody of the blessed Paul. Whereupon the Abbess of Helenestue[z], hearing that Falk had outraged the blessed Paul, but had been up to that time unpunished for the same, ordered to be taken from the hand of the statue of St. Paul the sword which it held, and after vengeance (taken) to be duly restored. And thus, as in a moment, the same Falk, reduced from the summit of wealth to the depths of poverty, could be cited as an example to the many who are guilty of grievous crimes."

The story, in a great measure, tells its own tale.

[y] Matthæi Parisiensis Chronica Majora. iii. 87.

[z] This is the first occasion on which the name of the Abbey is found thus spelt, i.e. with H at the commencement.

The hero, or perhaps rather the villain, of it, Falk de Breaute, had evidently roused the wrath of the Abbess, by using the materials of St. Paul's Church for the fortification of Bedford Castle, which had been surrendered to him Dec. 2, 1215; but in justice to him it should be mentioned that he did not in this act upon his own responsibility, as we have a Charter of Henry III.[a] which seems to shift the blame from him to King John; and though in so doing we transgress a little on a subsequent reign, it is best to quote it here and thus see the end of the matter:—

"THE KING, &c. Know all, &c., that We in recompense of the loss, which John our father caused to the Prior and Convent of Newenham, when he caused to be destroyed the Church of St. Paul of Bedford, which was (the property) of the said Prior and Convent of Newenham, at the time when he caused the Castle of Bedford to be fortified, have granted to the same Prior of Newenham the Church of Tindene[b], &c., to be held in perpetual elemosiny. Witness, the King, at Nottingham, 5th February."

REIGN OF HENRY III., 1216—72.

The first few years of this reign are somewhat prolific in historic material, the record of several events affecting the Abbey, and closely following each other in point of time, having been preserved to us in various documents.

To begin with, we have an agreement between Almeric de St. Maur, Master of the Temple, and

[a] Patent Rolls, 1 Henry III. m. 13.

[b] Tindene, in Doomsday Tingdene, later Thingden, and now Finedon, is a village in Northamptonshire.

Mabilia[c], Abbess of Elstow, who is thus for the first time mentioned by name, respecting the provision of a Chaplain for the Chapel of Preston, which was a hamlet of Hitchin (§ 4). This agreement is contained in three Charters, which will be given in their place, but as they bear no date, it is necessary to assign one to them with as much accuracy as may be. In this, fortunately, there is little difficulty, as, though the exact year in which they were drawn up cannot be ascertained, two names occur in them which enable us to place them within a very narrow limit. Almeric de St. Maur died 1219[d], and as one of the witnesses to the two first Charters is William, Prior of Wymondley, which Priory was founded by Richard Argentain[e] about 1 or 2 Henry III., and the three occur consecutively in the Cotton MSS., it is reasonable to conclude that they were all executed about the same time, 1218-19.

The documents need no comment, as they tell their own tale, in the following terms :—

1. "Covenant[f] between the Master and Brothers of the Temple and the Abbess of Elnestowe concerning tithes in Hichene, and the annual payment of one mark of silver.

"THIS IS A COVENANT made between Brother AL-MERIC DE ST. MAUR, Master, and the Brothers of the

---

[c] Probably elected 1213. See ante, p. 57.

[d] Annales Monastici. iii. 55.

[e] Dugd. Monast. vi. 555. Richard Argentain appears to have been a son of Reginald. William, Prior of Wymondley, is probably the William Argentain mentioned, *ibid.* note b, but nothing has been found to shew what relation he was to them.

[f] Cotton. MSS. Brit. Mus. Nero. E. vi. fol. 128.

military order of the Temple in England, and MABILIA by the grace of God Abbess of Elnestowe, and the Convent of the same place; namely, that :—

"The Brothers of the Temple shall with all integrity pay to the Nuns for ever all tithes of corn from lands which they cultivate in the Parish of Hichene, from which the Church of Hichene has been wont to receive tithes (excepting the cultivated land, of which our Brothers of the Temple have hitherto reserved the tithes), and, in addition, [the tithes] of all newly-tilled lands, men [and] assises at the time of this Covenant.

"The Nuns, on the other hand, have granted that the Templars at Preston, in the Parish of Hichene, have a Chaplain, to be selected by themselves, to celebrate divine service for them throughout the year at the appointed hours, according to our rule.

"And the Nuns, for the support of this Chaplain and his office, shall give to our Brothers of the Temple one mark of silver, namely, half a mark at the Feast of S. Michael, and half a mark at Easter, and four pounds of wax at the Feast of S. Michael.

"And the said Chaplain shall do fealty as to all kind of indemnity to the mother Church of Hichene, and the Nuns of Elnestowe present and future, and especially with respect to all things which are contained in this writing; but the Nuns shall receive all tithes, and oblations, and [fees for] confessions of the serving [brothers] of the Templars, who are of their parish, if they hold land. But those who do not hold land shall pay all parochial dues owing to the mother Church of Hichene at the statutable terms, as they ought to do. This only reserved, that all Templars everywhere, who may desire sepulture at their hands, shall receive it, as in their Charters is contained.

"But from the rest, their serving [brothers] who are not parishioners of the Nuns, they shall themselves receive oblations and [fees for] confessions through their Chaplain, and the oblations of their guests, who are not parishioners of the Nuns, the Templars shall receive.

"If, however, the Chaplain ministering at Preston shall not keep faith with the Abbess and Convent of Elnestowe, or shall offend in anything, the Preceptor of the place shall in the first instance admonish him to correct it, and if by chance it be not corrected by means of the Preceptor, the Abbess and Convent of Elnestowe shall claim their right before whomsoever they will.

"These being witnesses, William, Prior of Wilmundele; John of Baldock, Dean; Henry, Priest of Elnestowe; Sir Nicholas Traylly; and others [g]."

2. "Concerning[h] the annual payment of the same mark and four pounds of wax.

"MABILIA, by the grace of God Abbess of Elnestowe, and the Convent of the same place, to [all men] present and future, greeting.

"Know all of you that we are bound to pay, year by year, to the Brothers of the military order of the Temple at Dynesley, one mark of silver per annum, at two terms, namely at the Feast of St. Michael half a mark, and at Easter half a mark; and four pounds of wax at the Feast of St. Michael, namely, for the support of the Chaplain, and for the light for his Chapel at Preston.

"And the Templars for their part shall faithfully observe the Covenant between us and themselves, concerning the said Chapel and the payment of their tithes and oblations to us, as on this understanding is contained in this deed drawn up between them and us.

"But if it happen that we fail to make the appointed payments within the eighth day after the term of pay-

---

[g] Other names beside the above appear as witnessing this and the succeeding deed, but as they do not help to fix the date they have been omitted. Nicholas Traylly is no doubt a descendant of Geoffrey, mentioned above (§ 32).

[h] Cotton MSS. Brit. Mus. Nero. E. vi. fol. 128.

ment, we will give to the aforesaid Brothers half a mark by way of a fine, and will [further] pay what was owing at that term. In testimony of which we have executed unto them this our present Charter, sealed with our capitular seal.

"These being witnesses, William, Prior of Wymundesle; John of Baldock, Dean; Henry, Priest of Elnestowe; Sir Nicholas Traylly; and many others."

3. "Covenant[1] between the Templars and the Abbess of Elnestowe concerning the provision of one Chaplain at Preston for three days in the week.

"KNOW ALL MEN, present and future, that this Covenant has been made between the Chapter of the Temple and the Nuns of Elnestowe, with the assent and approbation of either Chapter; namely that :—

"The Nuns of Elnestowe shall provide for the Brothers of the Temple, who, belonging to Preston, reside at Dynesley, for three days in the week, namely Sunday, Wednesday, and Friday, a Chaplain who shall celebrate Matins, and Mass, and Vespers; unless a Festival shall occur in the week, and then it shall be reckoned for the three days. And the Chaplain of Hichene, whosoever he may be, shall pledge his faith to the aforesaid Brothers for the [due] performance of these services. On the other hand the Brothers of the Temple shall, with all integrity, pay to the Nuns all tithes of corn from all lands which they cultivate in the parish of Hichene, of which the Church of Hichene, or any Church thereto belonging, has been wont to receive tithes, And in addition [the tithes] of all newly-tilled lands, men [and] assises. And if they have recalled into demesne newly-tilled lands in the country formerly let, of them, provided they hold them in demesne, they shall not pay tithes. But if, on the other hand, they have let to men for cultivation newly-tilled land, which they [formerly] held in demesne, of them the Nuns shall receive [tithes] in full.

[1] Cotton. MSS. Brit. Mus. Nero. E. vi. fol. 128. b.

"These being witnesses, Master Robert of Bedford; Gregory of Whathamstudia; William of Kynnefeld; William of Hichene; Richard [of] Dynnesley, Chaplain; Master John of Bedeford; Master Alexander; Richard Cannell; and others."

About this period we have the acquisition by the Abbey of the Church of Westbury (§ 51), five miles west of Buckingham, and although we are unable to fix the date with absolute certainty, nor can we say positively who was the donor, the evidence on both points is yet sufficient to make out a very strong case of probability. Browne Willis[k] says that he has no doubt that Ralph de Hareng was the donor, and there seems to be every reason to believe that he is right, as we learn from the Coram Rege Roll of 1 John[l] that the manors of Westbury and Clanfield, with all appurtenances, the Churches being specially named, were in that year conveyed to Ralph by William of Westbury; and from the *Testa de Nevill*, a register of Knights' Fees in England, temp. Henry III., compiled about 1272, that he "holds the vill of Westbury by one Knight's Fee of Richard, Earl of Cornwall, and he of the King[m]." Now Ralph Hareng, who died 1223[n], was a noted benefactor of religious houses, and nothing seems more natural than that, on coming into possession of new property, should have thus bestowed the Church appurtenant thereto. Further, we have evidence that the Church in question was in possession

---

[k] Hist. Buckingham. p. 351.   [l] Coram Rege Roll. 1 John. No. 7. m. 18. d.   [m] Testa de Nevill. fol. 244.
[n] Annales Monastici. iii. 85.

of the Abbey in 1225, as in that year Robert, Chaplain of Elnestow, was thereto presented by that body [o]. Hence there can be no doubt that the benefaction was made early in the thirteenth century. This property appears to have continued in the possession of the Abbey until the dissolution, and mention of it is found in three of the later records [p]. The advowson was granted, 1542 (33 Henry VIII.), to John Wellesborne, in exchange for the manors of Mixbury and Fullwell; sold, 1642, to Sir Thomas Lyttleton; passed, 1650, to the Price family, and is now held by the Hon. Percy Barrington.

In 1222 a formal agreement [q] was entered at Westminster, apparently after a suit had been tried, between Thomas de Camuilt and Mabilia, Abbess of Aunestowe, who is again mentioned by name, whereby the former surrendered all claim to the advowson of Godendon (§ 52), [Goddington, Oxon, five miles north-east of Bicester] in favour of the latter, who in return undertook that the said Thomas and his heirs should be entered on the roll of the Abbey, to enjoy all benefits and be duly remembered in the daily prayers in the aforesaid Church of Aunestowe. This advowson is mentioned as belonging to the Abbey in the Hundred Rolls only. What became of it in later years does not appear.

Shortly after this we find three decrees in the *Close Rolls*, which are extremely interesting from

[o] Lincoln Diocesan Registers. Bp. Wells' Institutions.

[p] Rot. Hundr., Tax. Pap. Nic., Valor. Eccl.

[q] Pedes Finium. Oxford. 3—20 Henry III. Case 180. No. 18.

the light which they throw upon local history at the period to which they relate. The decrees are as follows, and their bearing will be explained in due course.

1. [r] "In the matter of the Abbess of Alnestowe. THE KING to the Sheriff of Bedford greeting. We order you that, concerning those viij acres of land, with appurtenances, in Bedford, which Falk de Breaute held of Master Adam, Clerk, from which, together with a rent of xj shillings, the Abbess of Alnestowe was wont to receive one mark per annum at the hand of the same Falk, you cause the same Abbess to have the crops of those eight acres of land, this very autumn of our eighth year. Witness, the King, at St. Albans, the xxj day of August, in the eighth year of our reign." [1224.]

2. [s] "THE KING to the Sheriff of Bedford greeting. We order you that, concerning those seven acres of land, and xj shillings and fourpence rent, with appurtenances, which Falk de Breaute held of the Abbess of Alnestowe in Bedford, rendering thence to her one mark annually, you cause the same Abbess to have one mark every year, so long as that land shall be in our hand, and in your custody by our precept. And it shall be allowed you in the Exchequer. Witness, The King at Walingef [Wallingford], the xxviij day of December [1224] before the Justices."

3. [t] "In the matter of the Abbess of Alnestowe. THE KING to the Sheriff of Bedford greeting. It appears to us, from an inquisition which we ordered to be made, that the land with appurtenances, which Falk de Breaute held in Aldemanneby[u] is of the Abbess' fee,

---

[r] Rot. Lit. Claus. 8 Henry III. First Part, m. 6. [vol. i. p. 617].

[s] Ibid. 9 Henry III. m. 16. [vol. ii. p. 10].

[t] Ibid. 10 Henry III. m. 9. [vol. ii. p. 129].

[u] Apparently a district of Bedford, but the name is now

and that the same Falk held it in chief of the same Abbess, and that that land has been in our hand for one year and one day. And therefore we instruct you that without delay you cause the same Abbess to have full seisin of the aforesaid land with appurtenances. Witness, Myself at Undel [Oundle] the xij day of July [1225] before the Justices."

It will be observed that there is in these decrees some discrepancy as to the acreage of the land, and the amount of the rent, but that is a matter of little moment, as they all evidently refer to the same property. How they came to be issued is a point belonging to the general history of England.

From the account given by Matthew Paris[x] we gather that in the spring of 1224 the justices itinerant, holding the King's pleas at Dunstaple, convicted Falk on upwards of thirty[y] counts of unlawful possession of property, on each of which they declared him liable to a fine of £100. This proved so unpalatable to that individual, that summoning his followers, he made a dash on Dunstaple with a view of seizing the justices. Warned of his intention, however, all escaped but one, Henry de Braibroc, whom he imprisoned in Bedford Castle. De Braibroc's wife, on hearing of this, at once made application, 16th June, to the King, who was at that time holding a council on foreign affairs at Northampton, and officers were instantly sent to demand the release of the pri-

---

lost. It will be found recurring later on as "Aldermannesbury."

[x] Matthæi Parisiensis Chronica Majora. iii. 84—94.
[y] Thirty-five. Ann. Monast. [Dunstaple] iii. 90.

soner. To this William de Breaute, who was in command of the garrison, refused compliance without an order from his brother Falk; whereupon the Archbishops and Bishops excommunicated both the brothers and all who were in the castle, and the royal forces laid siege to it, 20th June. On 14th August it was taken, and all the defenders were hanged. Falk in the meantime had escaped to Wales, whence he shortly afterwards returned, and threw himself upon the mercy of the King, who committed him to the charge of Eustace [de Fauconberg], Bishop of London, where he remained until, shortly afterwards, he was deprived of all his possessions and banished.

During the progress of the siege the King, with the view of quartering on the enemy, had seized on all Falk's crops and cattle, and with them naturally the land held of the Abbess. She, however, promptly put the law in motion for the recovery of her rights, and the decrees above given shew that she was speedily successful on all points.

It is not improbable that this property may have originally been assigned to the Abbey, in reparation for some wrong sustained at the time when Bedford Castle was being fortified.

For the next five years history is silent as regards the Abbey, but it is clear that matters had not, during that period, been going smoothly with it, at all events in one quarter; and we are bound to infer that the point at issue was one of considerable moment, in that, like the suit with Newhouse, it was finally referred to Rome for decision. In this instance, however, as will be seen from the subjoined letter[2] of Pope Gregory IX. (1227-41), the Papal fiat was in favour of Elstow :—

"GREGORY, Bishop, servant of the servants of God, to our beloved sons the Archdeacon, the Official of Buckingham, and the Dean of Newport, greeting, and the Apostolic benediction.

"On the part of our beloved daughters in Christ, the Abbess and Convent of the Monastery of Elnestowe, a complaint has been laid before us that our beloved sons the Abbot and Convent of S. Albans, of the Order of St. Benedict, in the diocese of Lincoln, have done them injury, and offered them much and serious molestation, in respect of certain tithes, rents, and other things.

"Hence we have sent our letters to the same Abbot and Convent, to command that they desist entirely from the aforesaid.

"Wherefore we commit to your fraternity, by our Apostolic writing, that if the aforenamed Abbot and Convent of St. Albans neglect to fulfil our command, you, having summoned the parties, hear the case, and, without appeal, terminate it with an order of judgment, causing your decree to be strictly observed under pain of ecclesiastical censure ; and if the witnesses who were named have withdrawn, either through favour, aversion, or fear, that you compel them through the same censure, and without appeal, to give evidence in accordance with the truth. But if you should be unable to accomplish all these things, they shall nevertheless be carried out within two years.

"Given at Reate, xv Kalend. Apr. in the fifth year of our Pontificate." [18 March, 1231.]

Unfortunately this document gives no clue to

[2] Harleian Charters. Brit. Mus. 43. A. 44.

the place whence the tithes and rents in dispute were derived, and thus we can only conjecture that it was either St. Machuts, a manor appurtenant to the Abbey of S. Albans, in which, as we learn from the *Valor Ecclesiasticus*, our Abbey held property, or Silshoe, from which parish, as we gather from the same source, an annual payment of £2 6s. 8d. was due on account of tithes from our Abbey to the Hospital of St. Julian, a dependency of St. Albans.

In the following year is found the settlement of a question respecting certain common rights in the marsh of Flitton and Maulden, which is thus recorded [a] :—

"Our right and that of the Abbess of Aunestowe over the common of the marsh of Flitte and Maldona was declared before them [the justices in Bedfordshire], and these are the words of the King's roll.

"The Abbot (Richard, 1217) of Woburnia and the Monks of Dunstaplia came before the justices, and granted the right of perambulation, as was provided by brief of the Lord King, between the Abbess of Alnestowe and Philip of Flitte; between Maldona, which belongs to the Abbess, and Flitte, which belongs to the said Philip; saving, however, to the same Abbot and Monks the common of pasture over the whole, as they held it."

From this time to the end of the reign our materials are somewhat scanty, the next record [b] which has been found being that of an agreement in 1247, between Hugh Biscop and Agnes, Abbess of Elstow; whereby on the payment by the former of 20s., a certain plot of land, con-

---

[a] Ann. Monast. iii. 130, 131.
[b] Pedes Finium. 31 Henry III. Bedford.

taining one acre, with appurtenances, in Elstow, was secured to him and his heirs for ever, to be held of the Abbey at an annual rent of 2s., payable by equal instalments at Lady Day and Michaelmas.

Here, again, we find an Abbess mentioned by name, and in this case we are able, from various documents, to trace the whole period during which she held office. Her full name was Agnes of Westbury, so doubtless she was a native of the place of that name, the advowson of which had been, as we have seen, recently given (§ 51) to the Abbey. She was instituted in 1241 [c], and resigned in 1250, as is shewn by the following letters [d] :—

1. "To the most excellent and ever to be revered Lord, HENRY, by the grace of God illustrious King of England, Lord of Ireland, Duke of Normandy and Aquitaine, Earl of Anjou, his [servants] ISILIA, Prioress of Elnestowe, and the Nuns of the same place, greeting, throwing themselves at his feet with all reverence and honour.

"Since by the resignation of our beloved mother, AGNES of Westbury, late Abbess of our house, our Abbacy is declared to be vacant, we send to your Lordship Sarra de la Rokele and Cecilia of Chiselhampton, our fellow-sisters, bearers of the presents, to seek from your Serenity license to elect unto us an Abbess, humbly and devotedly supplicating that, of your wonted clemency, in this behalf hitherto accorded, you will mercifully deign to hear them. May your Serenity prosper before the Lord and all people."

2. "To his most excellent Lord, HENRY, by the grace of God, illustrious King of England, Lord of

[c] Linc. Dioc. Reg. Bp. Grosseteste's Institutions.
[d] Royal Letters, Nos. 547 and 548.

Ireland, Duke of Normandy and Aquitaine, Earl of Anjou, his devoted servant R[OBERT ᵉ] by divine mercy, the humble minister of the Church of Lincoln, greeting, and reverence as much due as devoted, with sincere love.

"Be it known to your Lordship that, on the Friday next before the Festival of the blessed Peter, we accepted the voluntary resignation by our beloved daughter in Christ, AGNES of Westbury, late Abbess of Elnestowe, of her office, [the same being] offered to us in our Chair, in Chapter, and before her whole Convent, and into our hands simply and absolutely made, And we released her entirely from the care of the said office, and from the obedience, which by virtue of the same she was bound to render to us. And this, as is fitting, we signify to your Magnificence by these our letters patent. Given at Elnestowe, xij Kal. March, in the year MCCL. [18th February, 1250.] May your reverend Lordship prosper and grow in the Lord for many years to come."

The language of these letters is quaint and interesting, and though no mention is made as to who was elected to the vacant post, we learn from the Lincoln Registers that it was Albreda de Silcampo.

After this date no record comes to light until the year 1257, when we find another Papal Bull [f], granted in this instance by Pope Alexander IV. [1254-61], and confirming to the Abbey the Church of Clanfield, Oxon (§ 53). In respect of this again, it is difficult to say who was the benefactor, but as we have seen that Clanfield passed, with Westbury, into the hands of Ralph Hareng in 1199 or 1200, it is probable that he

[e] Robert Grosseteste, Bishop of Lincoln, 1235-54.
[f] Vatican Transcripts, Brit. Mus. Add. MSS. 15359. fol. 139.

was the donor, and from the existence of the Bull, it seems equally probable that the gift had been disputed by his heirs, especially as the language of that document indicates that some question respecting it had arisen, and would probably be renewed unless decisively settled. The Bull runs as follows :—

"ALEXANDER [iv.] to the Abbess and Convent of the Monastery of Elnestowe, of the order of St. Benedict, in the Diocese of Lincoln.

"The care of the office committed to us warns us that, when specially thinking about religious persons, we should bestow upon them peculiar favour and grace. Sympathising, therefore, in your necessities with paternal affection, and yielding to the prayers of our beloved brother J., Priest, Cardinal of the title of St. Laurence in Lucina, we do, of our special grace, grant to you for ever the Church of Clanfield, in the Diocese of Lincoln, in which, as you assert, you have the right of patronage, to be applied, with all its rights and appurtenances, to the proper uses of yourselves and of those who shall succeed you; further conceding to you that, on the resignation or death of the Rector of the said Church, it shall be lawful for you to enter into possession of the same, by our authority, no consent of the Diocesan or any one else being in any way required, assigning a sufficient portion of the emoluments of the Church to the Vicar, who shall for the time being serve it, to enable him to have fitting maintenance and to bear the Episcopal, Archidiaconal, and other burdens of the said Church, Notwithstanding any letters of the Apostolic See obtained through the foresight of any persons whatsoever, or reservations, or inhibitions made or to be made by them, or any other letters of the Apostolic See, by which a grace of this kind could in any way be hindered or delayed.

"Given at Viterbo xij Kal. Sept. in the third year" [21st August, 1257].

The last document, which we have, belonging to this reign, is of a totally different nature; as, unlike its predecessors, it relates not to the property of the Abbey, but to its internal discipline, and is a letter[g] from the Bishop of Lincoln to the Archbishop of York respecting some scandal in which the sister of the latter had been implicated. It had better, however, be allowed to tell its own tale, which it does most characteristically:—

"To the venerable father in Christ, W[ALTER][h] by the grace of God, &c., R[ICHARD][i] by the permission of the same, humble minister of the Church of Lincoln, greeting, and continual increase of sincere love in the Lord.

"We are anxious from our inmost heart concerning a misfortune, which has occurred in the Abbey of Elvestowe, and grief of this kind afflicts us the more bitterly from our pious compassion, because that from that house, more frequently than from any other, false reports of disgraceful acts are brought to us. And although on this, by the persuasions of certain people, we were somewhat impressed against the Abbess and your sister[k], who, through connivance or remissness, were said to be in fault; yet since, in consideration of yourself, and the venerable father your brother[l], we are through affection specially jealous of the honour of your family, we will take care, so far as we can in accordance with the laws of God and the usages of propriety, and without secular scandal, to correct the fault

---

[g] Rayne's Historical Papers and Letters from the Northern Registers, No. 23. Register of Archbishop Giffard, 75 a.

[h] Walter Giffard, Archbishop of York, 1266-79.

[i] Richard Gravesend, Bishop of Lincoln, 1258-80.

[k] No doubt Agatha Giffard, who will be found holding the office of Prioress a few years later.

[l] Probably Godfrey Giffard, Bishop of Worcester, 1268—1303.

which has been committed with all secrecy, and to visible sores to apply a hidden medicine. Wherefore, if it so please you, let not the occurrence of the aforenamed misfortune further greatly disturb your mind; since your wishes in the matter have been clearly made known to us, through your Clerk and ours, Master G. de Sancto Leophardo; and what we have gathered from your own letters, we will with the favour of the Lord fulfil, as we shall see will best conduce to the well pleasing of God and the honour of your family. May your reverend Paternity prosper in the Lord through all eternity. Given at Bicheswad [Biggleswade] vij Kal. July [26 June], 1270."

From the tone of this letter it is very clear that the Bishop did not at all relish the task of telling his Metropolitan that his sister had been guilty of some impropriety; and with all his evasions, for they can be called by no other name, it is equally evident that he was convinced in his own mind that she was to blame.

Reign of Edward I., 1272—1307.

At the very commencement of this reign we come upon the *Hundred Rolls*, and considering the minute details into which they so frequently enter, the only source of regret is that, owing probably to the returns from many counties being incomplete, we find in them so few records relating to the Abbey property.

Before, however, giving these, it will be as well to mention the causes which led to these Rolls being compiled, especially as we shall be able to trace to them sundry difficulties in which the Nuns were involved in after years; and as these causes are admirably described in the preface to the Rolls, as printed in 1812, the best plan will be to transcribe from that :—

"During the turbulent reign of Henry III., the Revenues of the Crown had been considerably diminished by Tenants in Chief alienating without License; and by Ecclesiastics as well as Laymen witholding from the Crown, under various pretexts, its just Rights, and usurping the Right of holding Courts, and other Jura Regalia. Numerous Exactions and Oppressions of the People had also been committed in this Reign, by the Nobility and Gentry claiming the rights of free Chace, free Warren and Fishery, and demanding unreasonable Tolls in Fairs and Markets; and again, by Sheriffs, Escheators, and other Officers and Ministers of the Crown under colour of Law."

Hence it was that Edward I., immediately on his return from the Holy Land, issued a Commission under the great seal, 11th October, 1274, for an inquiry to be made into all these abuses, the result of which is known as the *Hundred Rolls*, owing to the various counties having been for its purposes taken by the ancient division into *Hundreds*. The inquiry extended in all over five years, and the labours of the Commissioners have filled two folio volumes.

The entries relating to Elstow are, as has been observed, but few in number, but the following, which are all that can be found, are valuable :—

"County of Leicester. Hundred of Guthlaston.
"The Abbess of Alnestowe holds ten and a half virgates of land in Hernedesby [m]. [Arnesby, § 8.]
"County of Buckingham. Hundred of Stodfold.

[m] Rot. Hundr. i. 239.

"Great Leckamsted[n] [§ 18]. The Abbess of Elmstouwe holds one virgate in perpetual elemosiny.

"Morthone[o] [Maid's Moreton, § 18]. William Page and his private tenants hold one virgate of land, which was that of Robert de Foxkote, and pay to the Abbess of Elmstouwe xij*d.* in perpetual elemosiny.

"The Abbess of Elmstouwe has, in the vill of Morton, a rent of twenty shillings per annum, from five virgates of land, in perpetual elemosiny, of the gift of William Basset, and had ingress in the time of King Henry, son of the Empress. [Henry II.]

"Westbury, [§ 51]. The Abbess of Elmstouwe holds the Church for her own uses, with two virgates of land, whence the Church is endowed, and she has one cottage appertaining to the Church, and pays twenty pence.

"County of Oxon. Hundred of Banbury.

"Schutteford[p] [Shutford, § 29]. The Abbess of Elnestowe holds one virgate of land, of the same fee, of the aforesaid lady [Matilda of Gatecumbe], in perpetual elemosiny, and gives as scutage ij*s.* when the scutage amounts to xl*s.*

"County of Oxon. Hundred of Ploughly.

"Godigdon[q] [Goddington, § 52]. The Abbess of Elnestowe holds in the same vill two virgates of land, with the advowson of the Church, in pure and perpetual elemosiny, of the said earl [of Lincoln]."

The result of this inquiry was that, the Commissioners having in many instances reported that they could not ascertain by what warrant property was held, an act was passed, 7th Nov. 1280, known as the statute *de quo Warranto*, under which any person holding property could be compelled to prove his title thereto, and it will be seen hereafter that the Abbess came in for

[n] Rot. Hundr. ii. 339. [o] Ibid. ii. 342.
[p] Ibid. ii. 707. [q] Ibid. ii. 834.

her full share of such attention, as provided thereby.

Previous, however, to the passing of this act, it seems that she had to appear before the Justices at Hertford [1], 3rd Nov. 1278, to support her claim to the Hitchin property (§ 4). The record of this case is very brief, and as others, of a similar nature, but of more importance, will be more fully described in the course of these Chronicles, it will suffice in the present instance to state that the rights disputed in this suit are identical, almost to a word, with those granted by Henry I. (pp. 15—17), and that on evidence being produced that the Abbess had enjoyed them from the time of his grant, without encroaching on the privileges of the Crown, judgment was given in her favour.

From the law-courts we now return once more to the internal affairs of the Abbey, only however to find that, as will be seen from the second of the two following letters [2], the Nuns could not always manage their own affairs without disputes.

1. "To their most excellent Prince and Lord, above all others to be revered, the Lord E[DWARD] illustrious King of England, A[GATHA] Prioress of the Church of St. Helen of Elnestowe, and the Nuns of the same place, everlasting greeting in the Lord.

"Be it known to your Excellency that by the death of the lady Anora, our late Abbess, our Church of Elenestowe, in your patronage, is left destitute of the solace of an Abbess. Hence it is that we send to your Excellency our beloved sisters Clementia of Balliol and Helena de Ripa, bearers of the presents, to seek

[1] Placita forinseca de Assisis. 6 Edw. I. Hertford. Rot. 35.
[2] Royal Letters, Nos. 1244 and 1245.

from you leave to elect another Abbess, with devout prayers beseeching that, taking compassion upon us in our desolation, you will be pleased to grant us permission to act as above requested. May your Excellency prosper for many years to come. In testimony to this we have affixed to the presents our common seal.

"Given at Elenestowe in our Chapter, iiij Ides [10th] June, A.D. MCCLXXXJ."

2. "To his most excellent Lord, the Lord E[DWARD] by the grace of God King of England, illustrious Lord of Ireland, and Duke of Aquitaine, his ever devoted OLIVER[t], by permission of the same humble minister of the Church of Lincoln, greeting in Him through whom Kings reign, and the governments of all kingdoms are upheld.

"Be it known to your magnificent Highness that when recently, on the vacancy of the Monastery of Elenestowe in our diocese, through the death of the lady Anora, formerly Abbess of that place, leave of election was, as is customary, sought and obtained from your most serene Majesty, the Prioress and Convent of that place did afterwards, on the appointed day of election, divide their votes between different persons, some [members] of the Convent, the more in number, electing the lady Beatrice of Scoteny, others, the fewer in number, discordantly electing the lady Agatha Giffard, Prioress of the same house, to the office of Abbess. And when each of the persons elected as aforesaid had afterwards presented herself to your Lordship, for the purpose of obtaining, as was fitting, the royal assent, we received letters from your Majesty, containing instructions that, with regard to the said elections we should discharge the duties of our office, in deciding which was to be preferred to the other. Since therefore, after hearing and more fully understanding the arguments on either side, we have, by the pontifical authority, and in accordance with the claims of justice, promoted the said lady Beatrice (against whom, so far as we can

[t] Oliver Sutton, Bishop of Lincoln, 1280—1300.

learn, no objection can be maintained according to Canonical ordinances) to the Abbacy of that house, we do the more earnestly beseech your royal clemency that you will be pleased to grant to her that which in this behalf appertains to your dignity with grace and favour. May your most serene Majesty prosper in the Lord, for many years to come.

"Given at Edelesberwe [Ellesborough] Non. [5th] November, in the year of the Lord MCCLXXXJ, and of our episcopate the second."

This affair, together with the Bishop's decision thereon, is also recorded in the Lincoln Diocesan Registers; and the Prioress, Agatha Giffard, here mentioned, will be at once recognised as the lady who was the subject of Bishop Gravesend's letter to the Archbishop of York eleven years earlier.

Four years later, in 1285, we are introduced to another piece of property, the advowson of the Rectory of Inworth, Essex (§ 54), eight miles west of Colchester, of which nothing has been heard before, although it had probably been some few years in the possession of the Abbey; the introduction being effected, as in the case of Tingrith, through a law-suit[a] brought for its recovery, but with the difference that in this instance the rights of the Abbess were upheld by the Court. The action was instituted by one William Samuel, whose plea was that the advowson in question had descended to him in the direct line from his great-grandfather, who lived in the reign of John. On the other hand the Abbess brought overwhelming evidence to prove that the great-grandfather had given it to one William Fylol, who in

---

[a] Placita de Assisis. Essex. 13 Edward I. Rot. 34 d.

his turn had bestowed it upon the Abbey of Elstow; hence judgment was given in her favour, and Samuel was mulcted in the costs of the suit. In addition to the advowson, the Abbey appears to have held other property at this place, as Morant[x], giving as reference "Inquis. 6 Edw. III.," states that Sir John Fylol, who died in 1332, held, among other things, seventy acres of arable land, six of meadow, and two of wood, in Inworth and Great Braxted, of the Abbess of Elstow, by service of 18*d.* per ann. This rent reappears only in the *Taxatio Papæ Nicholai*, whereas the Advowson is found mentioned in the two latest records[y], and seems to have continued in the Abbey until the dissolution, after which it was granted, 24 July, 1557 [4 Mary], to William Riggs and others. The first record of a presentation to Inworth by the Abbess and Convent of Elstow is in 1322[z].

In 1287 we have the record[a] of one of the most important cases affecting the Abbey up to this time, the Abbess having to appear by counsel at Westminster, to support her claim, as against the Crown, to all the privileges attaching to the Bedfordshire property. It will be at once surmised, and in all probability correctly, that this suit owed its origin to the report of the Commissioners appointed to compile the Hundred Rolls; and as it is extremely interesting, alike from the value, and the novelty to us, of

[x] History of Essex. ii. 174.
[y] Valor Eccl. and Comp. Ministr.
[z] Newcourt. Repertorium Parochiale. Dioc. Lond. ii. 349.
[a] Placita de quo Warranto. 15 Edward I. Rot. 8. d.

many of the rights involved, it will be as well to give it in full:—

"The Abbess of Elnestowe came by her attorney before the justices by writ [*bilettum*], and claimed view of frank pledge [b] of her men in her vills of Elnestowe, Wilshamstude, Kemeston and Maldone, and claimed weyf [e], and to be exempt from sheriffs' aids [d], gelds, hidages [e], danegelds, assizes, murders, scutages, and claimed infangenethef, and a fair in the vill of Elnestowe once in the year, and warren in her lands in Elnestowe, Wilshamstude and Maldone, and desires to reply without brief [f].

"And she says that the whole vill of Elnestowe is of her fee, and that she has there gallows [*furcas*], and other means of executing justice; and she says that the whole vill of Wilshamstude is of her fee, and in like manner that the whole vill of Maldone is of her fee, and that she has in Kemeston five virgates of land and a mill. And she says that she holds her court [*visum*] over all who dwell in her fee of Elnestowe, Wilshamstude and Kemeston, and that she holds another court at Maldone twice in the year, and [that] without [the presence of] a King's officer. She says

---

[b] View of frank pledge. The right of holding a court leet, which was a court of record, belonging to a hundred or manor, instituted for the punishment of encroachments, nuisances, fraudulent weights and measures, and also some offences against the Crown.

[e] Weyf. Felons' goods, or stolen articles left by the thief, were forfeited to the king, or to the lord of the manor, should the right be granted to him by the Crown.

[d] Sheriffs' aids. The customary dues paid to the Sheriff for the better support of his office.

[e] A hidage was a tax levied on every hide of land in the kingdom. When the lord paid hidage to the king, the tenants paid a proportion to him.

[f] Brief. The writ or licence to plead in the king's courts, for which a fee was charged.

that she has seven tithe payers at Elnestowe, Wilshamstude, and Kemeston, and that she has four tithe payers at Maldone. And she says that no one of her fee comes to the sheriff's court, and that she inquires concerning the articles about which the sheriff inquires in his court, and takes fines of assize of malt [*fractæ cervisiæ*], and proves measures, and takes fines, and holds the standard of the Marshal of the Lord King, and has a cucking-stool [*tumberellum*] at Maldone.

"And those liberties she claims under a Charter of the Lord King Henry I., which testifies that that King granted to the Nuns of the Church of S. Mary of Elnestowe the vill of Elnestowe [§ 3], and the vill of Wilshamstude [§ 2], and two hides and a-half of land in Maldone [§ 1], exempt from all aids, and gelds, and hidages, and danegelds, and assizes, murders, and pleas, and all occasions, and complaints, and scutages, and warpeny, and all customs, and all land service, and [that she] should have sac and soc, and toll and team, and infangenethef, and all liberties which the free Churches of my land have, as well and as peaceably as possible. Witnesses, &c.[g]

"And in like manner she produces a Charter of King Henry II., which testifies that he granted to the aforesaid Nuns land [§ 13] which was that of William Medicus in Kemeston, which yields 20s. per annum, and a mill of the same vill, and five virgates of land, and twelve acres in the same vill, with sac and soc, &c.[h]

"And, as regards the fair, she produces a Charter of the Lord King Henry II., which testifies that he granted to the same Nuns one fair in Elnestowe for four days, namely on the Vigil of the Invention of the Holy Cross, the day of the Festival, and two days after[i].

---

[g] See p. 15. The *five* hides there mentioned have here evidently been miscopied *two*. The names of the witnesses to these Charters, and the full privileges conferred by them, will be found at the pages to which the reader is referred.

[h] See p. 43.   [i] See p. 42.

"And, as regards warren, she produces a Charter of King Henry I. in these words:—'HENRY, King of England, &c. I grant that the Abbess of Elnestowe have warren in her whole land of Bedfordscir, and that on this no one hunt thereon without her license, under penalty of £10.'[k] And those liberties she claims under the aforesaid charters, and by long continued seisin.

"And, as regards view of frank pledge and weyf, she claims those liberties on the ground that herself and her predecessors have been in continued seisin [of them] from time immemorial, and by the general words contained in the Charters; and because twelve [men] of Redburnstoke say upon their oath that the lands have been [in possession] of the Abbess aforesaid up to the present time, exempt from sheriffs' aids, &c. Likewise, as regards acquittances, fair and warren, concerning which she shews charters to the present time, thence *sine die*, saving the right of the Lord King and his heirs.

"And Gilbert de Thornton, who follows for the Lord King, says that the aforesaid Abbess ought not to enjoy the aforesaid liberties, on the ground that the same liberties are not expressly named in the aforesaid royal Charters, which she alleges for warrant, whence he seeks judgment for the Lord King."

"And upon this a day was given her to have her cause heard, before the Lord Treasurer and the Barons of the Exchequer at Westminster, the fifteenth day after Easter, &c. Afterwards, on the fifteenth day after the day of S. Michael in the fifteenth year, came one Ingelran Sporoun, as attorney for the aforesaid Abbess, and because judgment had not yet been given, a day was given him, the fifteenth day after Easter, &c. On which day the aforesaid Abbess came by her attorney, And a day was given her, the fifteenth day after the day of S. Michael, &c. On which day the aforesaid Abbess came by her attorney, And a day was given her, the fifteenth day after Easter, &c. Afterwards

[k] See p. 24.

a day was given her through her attorney in the Octave of S. Michael, &c."

As will be seen from this long string of adjournments, the case was kept dragging on over several years, and probably it eventually lapsed, as the very same privileges are found included in a similar, but more comprehensive, suit in 1331, which will be treated of in its place.

Following close upon the foregoing suit, in fact in the same year, we come upon a little local matter of dispute. It would appear that one Alexander Spirech, and Juliana his daughter, held certain tenements [§ 55] in Bedford of the Abbey, at an annual rent of 3*s.*, and that William Basset was also a tenant at 1*s.* rental. Each of these parties being three years in arrear with their rent, the Abbess brought an action against them[1], laying her damages at 20*s.*, but upon the defendants giving up their holdings, she was content to forego her claim to both damages and arrears of rent.

In 1289, the Abbess is again found appearing in court as a plaintiff[m], the defendant in this instance being one Richard, Parson of Moulsoe, and the point in dispute the right to certain tithes in that place [§ 56]; and on evidence being produced that they had been given to the Abbess by a certain Walter de Cordel, and that she had held them for a long time, judgment was given in her favour, and the sum of £3 was assigned to the Parson as indemnification. Very probably this was a friendly suit, of a similar character to that

[1] Assize Roll. Bedford. 15 Edward I. Rot. 13. d.
[m] Abbrev. Placit. Pasche. 17 Edward I. Rot. 33.

mentioned at p. 55, and instituted for the purpose of determining the ownership of the tithe. This benefaction was of course entirely distinct from, and independent of, the two hides and three virgates of land given by the Langetotes [§§ 6, 7], the one belonging to the head of "Spiritualities," the other to that of "Temporalities;" and it will be observed that they are thus separated in the Ecclesiastical Taxation of Pope Nicholas, which is the next of the public records demanding our attention.

To this frequent reference has been made in the preceding pages, and a brief account of it may therefore be interesting :—

"In the year 1288 Pope Nicholas IV. [1288—94] granted the tenths to King Edward I., for six years, towards defraying the expense of an expedition to the Holy Land; and in order that they might be collected to their full value, a Taxation, by the King's precept, was begun in that year, and finished, as to the Province of Canterbury, in 1291, and, as to that of York, in the following year; the whole being done under the direction of John [de Pontissara], Bishop of Winchester, and Oliver [Sutton], Bishop of Lincoln [a]."

In this valuation the property of the Abbey of Elstow is assessed as under; and as it gives the Archdeaconry[o] and Deanery in which each place is situated, it affords great help in the work of identification.

[a] Taxatio Ecclesiastica Papæ Nicholai. Govt. Ed. Preface.
[o] The names of the Archdeaconries are here printed in small capitals, those of the Deaneries in italics; the figures at the end of each entry give the reference to the folio in which it will be found.

COLCHESTER. *Lexden.*   £ s. d.
§ 54. At Inneworth, from pasture   0 1 6, 27.
  BEDFORD. *Clopham.*
§ 20. At Middleton, in Spiritualities . 0 10 0, 34 b.
§ 33. At Wyrmington, in rent . . 0 5 0, 48 b.
   Eton [Eaton Socon].
§ 57. At Gynelden [Yelden], in rent . 0 3 0, 48.
§ 42. At Bereford, in rent . . . 0 1 0, *ib.*
§ 58. At Rokesden [Roxton], in rent . 1 0 0, *ib.*
§ 59. At Ronhale [Renhold], from a mill 0 13 4, *ib.*
    Flitton.
§ 1. At Maldon, in lands, rent and court 5 0 4, 48 b.
    Bedford.
§§ 3, 13, 17. At Elnestowe, and Kem-
 beston, in land, rent and mills . 11 4 0, 49 b.
At the same places, in crops, flocks and
 animals . . . . . . 1 16 2, *ib.*
§ 2. At Willamste, in lands, rent and
 meadows . . . . . 5 1 4, *ib.*
At the same place, in crops, flocks and
 animals . . . . . . 2 7 6, *ib.*
§§ 15, 16. At Bedford, in rent and lands 7 16 8, *ib.*
  OXON. *Dadyington* [Deddington].
§ 29. At Swaleclive [Swalcliffe] in Spiritualities . . . . . 2 13 4, 31 b.
    Witney.
§ 53. The Church of Clanfield, less a
 portion . . . . . . 6 13 4, 32.
  BUCKINGHAM. *Wycumbe.*
§ 22. At Wouborn, in Spiritualities . 2 10 0, 33.
    Burnham.
§ 23. At Uptone, in Spiritualities . 1 0 0, *ib.*
   Newport Pagnel.
§ 56. Portion in the Church of Molesho 1 10 0, 33 b.
§§ 6, 7. At Molesho, in rent and heriott 1 9 6, 47 b.

88 CHRONICLES OF THE ABBEY OF ELSTOW.

Mursley.

£ s. d.

§ 60. At Soppewell and Weng, in rent   0   8   0, 46.

Buckingham.

§§ 51, 18. At Westbury, Morton and Lechamstede, in lands and rent .   1 12   8, 47.

HUNTYNGDON. *Hichen.*

§§ 37, 38. Portion in the Vicarage of Dynesle 1   6   8, 36 b.
§ 61. At Walden Regis, in Spiritualities   1   0   0, 37.
§ 4. At Hicche, Dynesle and Great Wymundele, in lands and rent . . 2   2   4, 51.

Huntyngdon.

§ 62. At Huntyngdon, in rent . . 0 13   4, 51 b.

St. Neots.

§ 40. At Bokeden, in rent . . . 0 10   0, 52.

NORTHAMPTON. *Daventry.*

§ 63. At Helyden [Helidon] in rent of one mill . . . . . 0 12   0, 54.

Rotel [Rutland].

§ 64. In Temporalities 2   3   0, 67 b.

LINCOLN. *Jordeburgh.*

§ 28. At Halton, in Spiritualities . 2 15   4, 57 b.

STOWE. *Candleshow.*

§ 26. In Temporalities . . . 1   1   8, 74 b.

LEYCESTER. *Gudlakston.*

§ 8. In Temporalities . . . 2   3   0, *ib.*

NORFOLK. *Kernewyz.*

§ 65. At Hokewold [Hockwold], the *Prioress* of Elstow has in rent . 0 15   0, 100 b.

Many of the places mentioned in this list will be at once recognised as old friends, but some require a word or two of comment.

§§ 57, 42, 58, 59. Of these places Yelden is mentioned again in Inquis. 11 Henry IV., and Renhold in a suit in 1333. Roxton is not found elsewhere. Their locality is sufficiently identified by the Deanery in which they lie.

§ 29. Swalcliffe reappears only in a valuation [Linc. Dioc. Reg.] commenced by Bp. Lexington [1254-8], but apparently never completed. In it the Spiritualities of the Abbess in the Archdeaconry of Oxford are thus assessed:—" The Church of Clanfield, less the portions of the Prior of Mynster and the Rector of Alnestok, x marks [£6 13s. 4d.] Portion in Swalcliffe, liijs. iiijd." It is almost certain that the property at the latter place is the same as that described in the *Valor Ecclesiasticus* and *Computus Ministrorum* as at Shutford, § 29, the distance between the two places being only a mile and a-half, and the valuation being the same in each case.

§ 60. Soppewell must be Sopwell Priory, a cell of St. Albans, adjoining that city, and Weng, Wing, seven miles north-east of Aylesbury. Neither name is found elsewhere.

§ 61. King's Walden, three and a-half miles south-west of Hitchin, reappears in the *Valor Ecclesiasticus* and *Computus Ministrorum*.

§ 62. This appears to be the only mention of this property.

§ 63. Helidon lies four and a-half miles south-west of Daventry. It also is only named here.

§ 64. There is nothing to enable us to form even a conjecture whence this rent was derived.

§ 28. Here the valuation, £2 15s. 4d., might be deemed an error for £2 13s. 4d., the four marks originally assigned to the Abbey [see p. 49], but a receipt in 1418 shews other property at Halton of the value of 2s. per annum.

§§ 26, 8. Here again the particulars given are so meagre, that it is only possible to guess at the localities, which were the sources of income. Probably the former relates to the Croft property, § 26, the latter to that at Arnesby, § 8.

§ 65. Hockwold is situated four miles west of Brandon. The name is not found in any other record.

While we are treating of the Abbey property at this period, it may be of interest to add that we have evidence, from the Lincoln Diocesan Registers, and other sources, of the advowson of several Churches having formed part of it; and a list of the same is here annexed, with the date, in brackets, of the first recorded presentation by the Abbey and Convent to each.

§ 54. The Church of Inworth. [1322]
§ 52. The Church of Goddington. [1240]
§ 51. The Church of Westbury. [1225]
§ 3. The Church of Elstow. [1235]
§ 2. The Church of Willshamstead. [1275]
§ 66. The Church of Kempston. [1220]
§ 67. The Church of Flitton. [1261]
§ 4. The Church of Hitchin, with the Chapelries of Dynesley and Wymondley. [1220]
§ 49. The Church of Harringworth. [1228]
§ 68. The Church of Wilbarston. [1281]

With the exception of Flitton and Wilbarston, all these are found mentioned, as belonging to the Abbey, in the earlier records. Goddington alone reappears no more. Flitton lies eight miles south of Bedford; Wilbarston, in Northamptonshire, four miles east of Market Harborough. There is nothing to shew how possession of either of them was obtained.

From this long array of statistics, which, however useful for reference as giving the first recorded valuation of the property with which we have to do, cannot fail to be somewhat dry reading, we pass on once more to trace the course of the Abbey history; and, in doing so, find ourselves at once dealing with another important series of legal documents. These are known as the *Inquisitiones, ad quod damnum*, or *post mortem*, the terms being applied so indifferently, that it is often difficult to trace the ground of their selection; and a few words will be necessary to describe their origin and scope.

In 7 Edward I., 15th November, 1279, an act was passed, known as the *Statute of Mortmain*[p], under which all lands given in the future, without the royal licence, to religious houses were to be forfeited. Hence, when a benefaction was proposed, instead of a Charter or Patent being immediately granted in confirmation thereof, a Commission was issued to the Sheriff of the County, directing him forthwith to summon a jury, and, after due inquiry, report to the King whether it could be made without prejudice to the royal revenue,

---

[p] Mortmain, lit. dead hand, see p. 13, note o.

i.e. whether the benefactor would have sufficient property left afterwards to pay the services due by him to the Crown.

The first of these Inquisitions[q] relating to Elstow occurs in 1304, when the question raised was whether one Roger Jory and Alice his wife might be permitted to give to the Abbey certain property [§ 69] at Moulsoe, consisting of fifty acres of land, three acres of meadow, and one acre and half a rood of wood; the land being valued at 4*d*. per acre per ann., the meadow at 20*d*. per acre, and the wood at 6*d*., total 22*s*. 2*d*. This was decided in the affirmative, and in the same year follows the royal licence[r] for the benefaction, the Abbess paying a fine, the amount of which is not stated. Three years later the transaction was concluded by an agreement[s], entered at Westminster, between the parties thereto, the Abbess Clementia paying £20 to Roger and Alice Jory; so that after all, that which might have been supposed to be an act of beneficence assumed a very ordinary, if not mercantile, character.

It is worthy of remark that in the third of these documents the lady Clementia is designated as Abbess of the Church of "S. Elene" of Elnestowe.

In 1306 and following years we have the record of a matter of great interest, not only as affecting the Abbey, but as shewing the course of procedure adopted in the middle ages in a case of frequent occurrence at the present day, namely

[q] Inquis. post mortem. 32 Edward I. No. 175.
[r] Patent Roll. 32 Edward I. m. 17.
[s] Pedes Finium, Bucks. 35 Edward I.—1 Edward II. No. 5.

stopping or diverting a footpath. It would seem that the brethren of the recently founded[t] Hospital of S. Leonard, Bedford, had erected their buildings on either side of the path leading thence to Elstow, but speedily finding that they suffered from depredations by the passers by, they made application to the King to be allowed to stop this road, and make another, passing round the Hospital; and in accordance with their request a precept[u] was issued in the following terms :—

"EDWARD, by the grace of God, King of England, Lord of Ireland, and Duke of Aquitaine, to the Sheriff of Bedford greeting.

"We order you that you make diligent inquiry, on the oath of just and qualified men of your county, through whom the truth of the matter can be better ascertained, whether it be to our loss or prejudice, or to the injury of our town of Bedford or of any other place, if we grant to the Master and brethren of the Hospital of S. Leonard, Bedford, that they may inclose, for the enlargement of their place there, and when inclosed hold for themselves and their successors for ever, a certain lane in Bedford, of the estimated length of sixty perches, and breadth of one perch, which is called *Pathweye*, and which leads through the middle of the aforesaid Hospital towards Elstow; On condition that they make upon their own land there, in place of the same lane, a certain other lane, equally convenient and of the same length and breadth; And further, if it be to our loss or prejudice, or to the injury of our town aforesaid or of any other place, then to what loss or prejudice of us, and to what injury, and to whom, and how, and in what manner; And what are the contents of that lane in length and breadth; And that you send to us

[t] Before 1302. Dugd. Mon. vii. 753.
[u] Chancery Inquisitions. 34 Edward I. No. 226.

without delay the inquisition thence regularly and openly made, under your own seal, and the seals of those through whom it was made, with this brief. Witness. Myself, at Shene, the vj. day of October, in the thirty-third year of our reign." [1306].

In compliance with this mandate the Sheriff, Walter de Molesworth, summoned as jurors John of Bray, Nicholas Abbot, John Conquest, Gilbert of Stepingle, Richard of Merstone, Gilbert of Scharpenhoo, Philip of the Bourne, Guy of Wroxhull, Philip Appelyn, John of Northwood, John of Maydenebury, and John, clerk, of Herdewik. The Inquiry was held at Bedford on the Sunday next before the Festival of S. Lucy the Virgin [13th December], 34 Edward I. [1306], and the report was to the effect that, 1. The portion of the road included within the bounds of the Hospital was only *thirty* perches in length. 2. The proposed alteration, so far from involving injury to any one, would be a great improvement to the neighbourhood, especially as the Master and Brethren proposed to make the new road double the width of the old one.

In accordance with this report the alteration would no doubt have been speedily made, but on the 1st February following, [1307] the King issued two precepts from Lyndhurst, the one addressed to Roger of Hegham [prob. Higham Ferrers, Northamptonshire] and Henry Spigurnel, ordering them to hold a fresh inquiry before other and impartial jurors; the other to the Sheriff of Bedford, directing him to provide such jurors, at such time and place as the Commissioners named should instruct him. The ground of this fresh inquiry is stated in the same terms in both documents as follows, the report of the former one being first recited at length :—

"Since, however, it has been shewn to us, on the part of our beloved in Christ, the Abbess of Elnestowe, and the Nuns of the same house, the advowson of which is in our hands, and of other different men of those parts, that it would be very greatly to the prejudice, injury, loss, and trouble, as well of ourselves in the time of the vacancy of the said house, as of the Abbess and Nuns aforesaid, and of all others who wished to travel by that lane, if that lane was inclosed; inasmuch as that place, which is called a lane, is our royal highway, and leads in a direct line from the Abbey aforesaid to the town of Bedford, and the said Abbess and Nuns, and other men of those parts, can pass by that highway, with their victuals and other necessaries, more conveniently and securely than by any other way which the aforesaid Master and brethren could make upon their own ground; we have therefore appointed you," &c.

From an indorsement on the former of these documents we gather that the case was carried to Westminster, and there argued before the King's Council; with the result that, after the option of going to Carlisle, and there pleading their cause before Parliament, had been offered to, and refused by, the appellants, the finding of the earlier Inquisition was allowed, and the appeal of the Abbess dismissed.

All the same, however, the Commissioners held their inquiry at Bedford, on the Feast of the Nativity of the Blessed Virgin [8th September], 1307, when the jurors—Edmund of Wedon,

Laurence of Herdewyk, William of Brutteville, William Beynyn, John Percevoyl, Simon of Bayouse, Thomas atte Hache, Richard, clerk, of Ametulle, Ralph, son of Robert of Clopham, and William of Poutone—decided that the only objection that could be taken to the proposed new road was that it was longer than the old one by ten perches, adding that the measurement of a perch was *sixteen and a-half feet of a man*. This again, appears to have been disputed, as, from a nearly illegible endorsement on their report, a petition against it seems to have been presented. From this we conclude that the Abbess fought the battle out to the bitter end, but evidently without success, as in the second year of the

Reign of Edward II., 1307-27,

a Charter[*] was granted in these terms :—

"In the matter of the Master and Brethren of the Hospital of S. Leonard, Bedford.

"The King to all to whom, &c., greeting.

"We have inspected letters patent, which the Lord Edward, of celebrated memory, formerly King of England, our father, granted to the Master and brethren of the Hospital of S. Leonard, Bedford, in these words.

"Edward, by the grace of God, King of England, Lord of Ireland, and Duke of Aquitaine, to all to whom the present letters shall come, greeting.

"Inasmuch as from inquisitions which we have caused to be made, as well by our beloved and faithful [servants] Roger of Hegham and Henry Spygurnel, as by our Sheriff of Bedford, we have ascertained that it would cause no injury to any one, if we should grant

[*] Patent Roll. 2 Edward II. part ii. m. 15.

to our beloved in Christ, the Master and brethren of the Hospital of S. Leonard, Bedford, that they may stop, and inclose, for the enlargement of their place there, that royal way, which is called *Pathweye*, and which runs through the middle of the aforesaid Hospital towards Elnestowe, between the two walls of the same Hospital, and to hold the same thus stopped and inclosed to themselves and their successors for ever; On condition that, in place of the same way, they make another way there, of the same width, on their own ground; The only difference being that the way, thus to be stopped and inclosed, runs directly from the aforesaid town of Bedford towards Elnestowe, and that the way, which the said Master and brethren will make, in place of the same way on their own ground there, will be longer than the aforesaid royal way by ten perches; We nevertheless, in consideration of the very many losses, which, as we have been informed, have hitherto occurred to them frequently in their Church, as much by the theft of the ornaments of the same, as by other means, under pretext of the said royal way; Willing, for the security and well-being of the same Master and brethren, that through the said stoppage and inclosure they may be able to serve God more quietly and decently, Have of our special grace granted, and given leave to the same Master and brethren, for ourselves and our heirs, as far as in us lies, that they may stop and inclose, for the enlargement of their place aforesaid, the aforesaid royal way, and hold the same thus stopped and inclosed to themselves and their successors for ever, without hindrance or impediment, of us, or our heirs, our Justices, Escheators, Sheriffs, or others our Bailiffs or Ministers whatsoever; On condition, however, that the aforesaid Master and brethren make upon their own ground there, in place of the same way, a certain other way, of the same width, on the south side of their Church aforesaid, as has been decreed. In testimony of which we have caused these our letters patent to be issued. Witness. Myself, at Carlisle, the twenty-first day of June, in the thirty-fifth year of our reign.

"And We, holding the aforesaid grant and gift of leave ratified and confirmed, do grant and confirm the same, for ourselves and our heirs, as far as in us lies, as the said letters patent of our father aforesaid duly testify.

"In witness whereof, &c. Witness. The King, at Langley, v day of December [1308]."

From the above, which, it will be observed, is a Charter confirming one granted by the late King but a few days before his death, it may reasonably be inferred that the Abbess took advantage of the accession of a new sovereign, to press her suit afresh, so that every credit must be given her for her persistence in her endeavours.

Who this persevering lady was cannot be ascertained exactly. Probably it was Clementia of Balliol, who was instituted 1294[y]; but as on the occasion of the next institution recorded[z], that of Joanna of Wauton in 1315, it is not stated how the Abbey became vacant, we cannot be certain that we have an unbroken succession.

A few years later the Abbess, probably Joanna of Wauton, found herself in trouble, through neglecting to pay sufficient respect to the royal supremacy over her Abbey. Our knowledge of this matter, however, is limited to that given in the following brief epitome[a] of a MS. in the

[y] Linc. Dioc. Reg. Bp. Sutton's Institutions.
[z] Ibid. Bp. Dalderby's Institutions.
[a] Fourth Report, Royal Commission, Hist. MSS. p. 329. fol. 112.

possession of Lord Harlech, at Brogyntyn, Co. Salop:—

"EDWARD to the Sheriff of Bedford. Tells him to distrain the Abbess of Elverstowe by all her lands and chattels in his bailiwick, and to answer to the King for the issues, and to have her body before the King at the Octaves of Hilary next, to answer why, Whereas she and the Convent, by reason of the new creation of an Abbess, were bound to a pension to a Clerk to be named by the King, and he had transferred the option to his sister Elizabeth, Countess of Hereford, and had asked the Abbess to give it to her nominee, they had neglected to do so. Summons to her."

Our reason for supposing that the lady Joanna was the Abbess implicated in this matter, is that her institution is the only one of which we have the record, in the period which elapsed between the accession of Edward II. and the death of his sister, which took place in May, 1316. How the case ended we have no means of ascertaining.

In 1318 occurs the Charter of Confirmation, mentioned under Henry I. [p. 17]. It is in the usual form of such documents, containing first the preamble, then the recitation of the Charter to be confirmed, and finally the confirmation thereof attested by witnesses. Thus the only question of interest, attaching to this, is how and why it came to be issued, a question which it is much easier to ask than to answer. If, however, it were the case, that some feeling of irritation against the Abbess, for her previous contumacy, was still rankling in the mind of the King, it is easy to understand some one or more of his courtiers suggesting that the tenure by which some of the property was held was open to doubt; and for this purpose the earliest grants would naturally be selected, as the title-deeds of these would be the most likely to have been lost. On such a hint as this being thrown out, an inquiry would have been eagerly instituted; but on the production and proof of the ancient Charters, nothing profitable could be done, but confirm them, and take as heavy a fine as could be exacted for doing so, which in this instance was five marks. The witnesses to this deed were J[ohn Sendale], Bishop of Winchester, and Chancellor; Thomas, Earl of Norfolk, and Marshal of England; Humphrey de Bohun, Earl of Hereford and Essex; Hugh le Despenser, senior; Hugh le Despenser, junior; John Giffard, of Brymmefeld; and William Montacute, Seneschal of the royal hospice [b]. It was issued at Leicester, 11th July.

In 1325, one John Moriz applied [c] for leave to divert a footpath adjoining his house at Elstow, but as it apparently did not touch the Abbey property, and we have had quite enough of such matters, his case may be dismissed as tending to shew us nothing, but that R. of Tyryngham had succeeded to the office of Sheriff of Bedford.

Before closing our account of this reign, it only remains to notice the *Testa de Nevill*, from which two extracts are subjoined. This record has been already briefly noticed [p. 64], as a register of Knights' Fees in England, compiled about 1272, but it was something more than this, as

[b] Hospice. The guest-house, where strangers of distinction were entertained.

[c] Inquis. ad quod damnum. 18 Edward II. No. 10.

"It contains an account of the holdings of the King's chief tenants, with the amount of scutage and aids payable by each; lists of widows and heiresses whose marriage belonged to the Crown; of Churches in the King's hands, forfeited estates, &c. The origin of the name is quite uncertain [d]."

The materials for it appear to have been collected in the reigns of Henry III. and Edward I., but it was probably not published until some time in that of Edward II.

"County of Leicester [e]. Hundred of Barlechsweye.

"They say that Erndesby [Arnesby, § 8] is of the fee of Peverel, and escheat of the Lord King, ancestor of King Henry [III.] which now is, who enfeoffed the same to Hugo de Bello Campo [Beauchamp] by service of one Knight's Fee. . . . . Also the same Hugo gave to the Abbess of Elnestowe ten and a-half virgates of land in free elemosiny [§ 70].

"County of Bedford [f].

"Elnestowe. The Abbess of Elnestowe holds that vill [§ 3], Wilhamstede [§ 2], Maudon [§ 1], in elemosiny of the honor of Huntedon."

With regard to the former of these entries there is this difficulty, that the Arnesby property is described in the Charter of Henry I. [p. 15] as the gift of Nigell of Staford, a discrepancy which can only be explained on the supposition that Hugo's benefaction consisted in discharging it of all dues, with which it was burdened. The latter is confirmatory of the foundation of the Abbey by Judith, Countess of Huntingdon.

[d] Annals of England, Alphabetical list of writers, p. 555.
[e] Testa de Nevill. fol. 88.   [f] Ibid. fol. 243.

Reign of Edward III., 1327—77.

Early in this reign, in 1330, we have the record[g] of the case, to which attention has already been directed [p. 85], and in which the Abbess[h] was once more called into the field to prove her title to the rights appertaining to the Abbey property; and it will be seen, from the account which will be given, that this was not altogether a vexatious prosecution, her administration having been, in several points, characterised by considerable slackness.

The case, which was tried at Bedford before Robert of Arderne, and other justices itinerant, on the Monday next after the Feast of S. John the Baptist, deals with two separate issues, the first having reference to very much the same points as the suit of 1287 [p. 81], while in the second we are introduced to entirely new matter.

Thus, in the former, the rights called in question are those of the view of frankpledge in Elstow and Maulden, weyf and stray, exemption from aids, gelds, &c., free Warren and the fair at Elstow; with the addition of the following, which are not named in the earlier case, namely, view of frankpledge over the tenants at Aldermannesbury[i], assize of bread and beer[k], and

---

[g] Placita de quo Warranto. 4 Edward III. Rot 13.

[h] Elizabeth Beauchamp, instituted 1318. Linc. Dioc. Reg. Bp. Dalderby's Institutions.

[i] See p. 66, note u.

[k] Assize of bread and beer. The power of examining the weight and measure of the same.

exemption from shire and hundred dues. In support of her cause the Abbess, by her attorney, Robert of Ipre, produces her Charters as before, together with one of Henry II., not exhibited on the previous occasion,

"in which it is contained that the same King ordered that the lands and men of the Abbess of Elnestowe should be exempt from all shire and hundred dues, as they were in the time of King Henry his grandfather."

She further pleads that all these privileges, which she claims, were allowed to her in the last circuit of the justices itinerant; and here was the blot, which the Counsel for the Crown, Richard of Aldeburgh, was not slow to hit, as he at once stated that none of these liberties, with the exception of assize of bread and beer, had been then claimed; and prayed that the said liberties should be taken into the King's hands, and that the Abbess should then and there give account of the profits of them since the time of the last circuit. To this the Abbess had no answer to make, but to sue humbly for their restoration, offering a mark in replevin; which being accepted, she was once more confirmed in her rights.

This concludes the first part of the case. The second is so interesting, as shewing the tremendous judicial powers with which the Abbess was invested in right of her position, that part of it at all events must be transcribed in full :—

"The same Abbess, being asked in what manors she claims to hold pleas of the Crown, by reason of the aforesaid liberty of Infangenethef, and if she have gallows for doing execution of the judgments of the same pleas, and if she have a pillory, and a cucking-stool, in all places where she claims to hold her aforesaid courts, says that she has gallows, a pillory and a cucking-stool in her manor of Elnestowe, and there holds pleas of the Crown, and that in other places she has not any means of executing justice.

"And Richard of Aldeburgh says that, since assize of bread and beer is one of the articles to be presented in view of frankpledge, and that the aforesaid Abbess is aware that she has not in her manor of Maldon aforesaid, nor at Aldermannesbury, the means of executing justice which are necessary for holding assize of bread and beer, for the just punishment of transgressors against the same assize, he seeks judgment, and that the courts aforesaid be taken into the hands of the Lord King, &c."

Then follows an inquiry as to whether the Abbess and her predecessors had made due use of the rights claimed, in reply to which she produces witnesses, who take oath that she had done so, this only excepted, "that she has not a pillory in her courts aforesaid; and, although the same Abbess has a cucking-stool in those courts, she has not punished offenders against the assize of bread and beer by sentence of the cucking-stool, but has taken fines to the amount of four shillings and sixpence from offenders against the assize of bread and beer, in a case in which they deserved to be punished by the aforesaid means of executing justice."

This laxity again was held to be fatal to the Abbess' case, judgment was given for the Crown, and she was condemned in costs. She was, however, once more successful on petition, and was reinstated in her privileges, on payment of a fine of 10s.

In 1333 the Abbess recovered seisin [1], in the King's Court at Bedford, against Robert Flamavill and others, of a rent of 13s. 4d., with appurtenances in Ronhale [§ 59]. It will be seen that this sum tallies exactly with the valuation of a mill at that place in *Tax. Pap. Nic.* [p. 87].

A few years later, 1337, we come upon a document [m], remarkable alike as being the first we have met with in the French language, which was then coming into court use, and for its substance, with respect to which it must be left to tell its own tale :—

"PETITION IN PARLIAMENT.

"The Burgesses of Bedford and the Abbess of Elnestow.

"TO OUR LORD THE KING and his council the prayer of the Burgesses of the town of Bedford sheweth :—

"That as they hold of him the said town of Bedford at fee-farm, rendering per annum to his Exchequer xlij pounds, there comes the Abbess of Elnestowe, and sues by petition in parliament holden at Westminster, deposing that she had, by grant of Manklum [n], formerly King of Scotland, [made] long before the time when the said town came into the hands of the ancestors of our said Lord the King, the third penny of the rent of the said town of Bedford, and that the ancestors of our Lord the King granted and confirmed the said rent to the Abbess aforesaid.

[1] Rot. Orig. Abbrev. ii. 72. Rot. 33.
[m] Rot. Parl. 11 Edward III. tom. ii. p. 96.
[n] Prob. Malcolm IV., confirmed in the Earldom of Huntingdon, by Henry II. 1157.

"Whereupon our Lord the King, understanding that this allegation was not devoid of foundation, issued his writ to the treasurer and barons of the Exchequer, that they should summon before them the mayor and bailiffs of the said town, and do justice; when the Abbess exhibited no deed of confirmation by the ancestors of our Lord the King, nor was it found in the records of the Exchequer that this Manklum had ever been lord of the town of Bedford.

"And if under the writ the Abbess recover, she would be seised of inheritance in that rent of him and of his successors for ever, which thing, [namely] that freehold property, or whatever gives inheritance, should be recovered in the Exchequer, is contrary to common law; unless it be a matter which is found in the records of the Exchequer, or otherwise one of which allowance has been there made, or one which consists in acres of Estate of our Lord the King; whereas this suit lies in decrees of the [fee] farm [rent] due to our Lord the King.

"Wherefore the mayor, bailiffs and commonalty of the said town pray our Lord the King, and his Council, that, if it please him, he will issue his writ to the said treasurer and barons that they surcease from this plea entirely; And that she sue at common law, if she so choose, where the suit is maintainable by law; on the ground that this demand belongs to the decrees of the estate of our Lord the King, since allowance of this rent has not been found in the records of the Exchequer."

Response.

"The Council is not advised to grant surcease in this plea, because cognisance of the plea was given to the treasurer and barons of the Exchequer on petition to parliament. But let a writ be issued to the said treasurer and barons, that they do justice and reason to the parties to the process commenced before them."

Where the Abbess got hold of the plea urged above it is more than difficult to say. Of course it is possible that Malcolm may have inherited some of Countess Judith's property at Bedford through his grandfather David, but of this we have no record, historical evidence being rather against than in favour of it. Hence the plea of the burgesses that he had never been lord of Bedford was most likely admitted; and as nothing more is heard of this suit, it was probably very briefly dismissed.

The year 1340 brings us to another valuation, known as the *Nonarum Inquisitiones*, of which the origin was that :—

"Parliament, having regard to the Will, that the King, their liege Lord, hath to them, and to the great Travailes, that he hath made and sustained, as well in his wars of Scotland, as against the Parts of France, and other places, and to the good Will, which he hath to travail to keep his Realm, and maintain his Wars, and to purchase his rights . . . . . granted to him the Ninth Lamb, the Ninth Fleece, and the Ninth Sheaf, to be taken by Two Years then next to come. And of Cities and Boroughs, the very Ninth Part of all their Goods and Chattels, to be taken and levied by lawful and reasonable Tax, by the same Two years, in Aid of the good keeping of this Realm, as well by Land as by Sea, and of his Wars, as well against the Parts of Scotland, the Parts of France, Gascoyne and elsewhere º."

Under the provisions of this, and certain supplementary acts, commissioners were appointed to ascertain the value of these "Ninths," or "Nones," in every parish, and collect them for

º Non. Inquis. Govt. Ed. Preface.

the royal use. They were, however, directed to compare the result of their inquiries with the Taxation of Pope Nicholas, and to levy the ninths by it in the event of its being less than their own computation.

From this valuation we obtain the following :—

"Elnestowe [p] [§ 3]. Eight marks and no more, according to the oath of Simon, Vicar [q], Richard West, Henry le Spencer, Richard le Wrygth, William Belu and Simon Nore, parishioners; less than the Taxation by six marks [r]. And that because the tithes of the sheaves arising from the demesne lands of the religious women of Elnestowe belong to the aforesaid Church, and are contained in its valuation. There are also many other commodities, appertaining to the same Church, videlicet oblations, mortuaries, hay, and other small tithes and commodities, which are worth per annum six marks, and are contained in the valuation of the said Church. They say also that there are no goods of citizens, burgesses, merchants, or others in the said parish not living by agriculture, [none dwelling there] save poor cottagers, gaining their living by their own labour.

"Maldone [§ 1]. Five marks and no more [s]. And that because the Abbess of Elnestowe holds land in the said parish, of which the tithes arising from sheaves belong to the aforesaid Church [of Elstow], and are contained in its valuation, and the ninth thence is worth one mark.

[p] Non. Inquis. fol. 15.

[q] The name of the Rector of Elstow at this date was not Simon. Probably it is an error for Simon *Viker*, which name we meet with a few years later.

[r] Tax. Pap. Nic. fol. 34. b.

[s] According to Tax. Pap. Nic. fol. 35. £4 13s. 4d.

"Middleton Erneys [§ 20]. One hundred and ten shillings, with the portion of the Abbess of Elnestowe in the same. Equal to the Taxation and no more[u], because many other commodities belong to the said Church [of Elstow], videlicet the lands which form part of the endowment of the said Church, hay, with certain other small tithes, all which commodities are worth per annum six marks, and are contained in the valuation of the said Church."

From this time forward to the end of the reign, the documents that have come to hand, with hardly an exception, all relate to acquisitions of property by the Abbey.

In 1344, 4th August the royal licence[x] was issued, permitting the Priory of Kyme, Lincolnshire, to give, and the Abbey of Elstow to receive, a sum of ten marks annually, arising from the rents of the Manor of Thorp next Timberland and other Manors belonging to that Priory [§ 71], which sum of £6 13s. 4d. duly appears in the *Valor Ecclesiasticus*.

In the following year, 5th April, the Abbess obtained letters patent[y] from the Crown, authorising herself and the Convent to "appropriate and convert to their own use, in aid of their sustentation," the second moiety of the Church of Elstow [§ 72]. This, it should be added, had been granted to them[z] 19th April, 1343, by the Bishop [Beck] of Lincoln, with consent of the Cathedral Chapter; and through this we are able

---

[t] Non. Inquis. fol. 18. [u] Tax. Pap. Nic. fol. 34.
[x] Patent Roll, 18 Edward III. pt. ii. m. 26.
[y] Patent Roll, 19 Edward III. pt. i. m. 25.
[z] Linc. Dioc. Reg. Bp. Beck's Institutions.

to explain how it was that the living of Elstow was left so miserably endowed at the dissolution. According to the valuations just cited, the benefice was at this time worth fourteen marks, or £9 6s. 8d., which would represent a goodly sum at the present day. Of this, however, only one half had ever been paid to the Rector, the other having been from time immemorial appropriated to the use of the Abbey. Now they obtained the whole; no appointment was thenceforth made to the Church, the cure of souls being intrusted to the Chantry Priests; and in consequence, after the suppression, the entire revenue of the Rectory passed into lay hands.

In 1347, on the Sunday next after the feast of S. Bartholomew, an inquiry[a] was held at Elstow, for the purpose of deciding whether Thomas atte Brugge, of Elstow, Parson of Camelton [probably Cameston, i.e. Kempston], might be allowed to give four messuages, sixty-four acres of land, six acres of meadow, and a rent of 12d., with appurtenances, in Elstow, Kempston, and Willshamstead, [§ 73] for the purpose of maintaining a Chaplain, to say mass daily for ever in the parish Church of Elstow, for the soul of the said Thomas, and for the souls of his father, his mother, his ancestors, and all the faithful departed. The property thus offered was valued in gross at £1 5s. 6d. per annum; and, though it formed the entire possessions of the donor, leave was given for the benefaction, the land being held, not of the Crown but of the Abbess, by service

---

[a] Inquisitio post mortem. 21 Edward III. No. 72.

of 5s. 6d. per annum. Accordingly, in the following year, 16th June, the first Chaplain, John Message, was instituted to this Chantry [b] by the Bishop of Lincoln.

In 1366, after a similar inquiry [c], at Bedford, on the Monday next after Feast of All Saints, return was made that it would not be to the loss or prejudice of the King, if John Morteyn and others were allowed to demise to the Abbey two messuages, one toft, forty-four acres of land, nine acres of meadow, six acres of pasture, and a rent of 3s. 9d., with appurtenances, in Elstow, Willshamstead, and Maulden [§ 74], for the purpose of keeping two wax candles burning before the high altar of the Abbey Church of Elstow, for a certain time on every Sunday, for ever; and two years later the Royal licence [d] for the gift was forthcoming. The land thus presented was valued in all at £2 1s. 1d., and had previously been held of the Abbess by the donors.

In connection with this benefaction it may be noticed that Elizabeth Morteyn was instituted [e] Abbess of Elstow, 1333; and though no record of the date of her death has been found, it is at least possible that the principal donor, being of the same name, may have been a relative, and so designed to do honour to her memory.

In the year 1370 we come upon a document of a different nature from the foregoing, namely

[b] Linc. Dioc. Reg. Bp. Gynwell's Institutions.
[c] Inquisitio ad quod damnum. 40 Edward III. No. 26.
[d] Patent Roll. 42 Edward III. pt. 1. m. 26.
[e] Linc. Dioc. Reg. Bp. Burghershe's Institutions.

a receipt[f], under the hand of the Abbess Anastasia[g], for certain rents at Moulsoe. In itself it is of little moment, but it is invested with some importance from the fact that a seal is appended to it. This seal, which must not be confounded with the great seal of the Abbey, is in form oval, measuring about 2 in. by 1 in. The impression, which in this instance is in dark green wax, represents, according to Dugdale[h], a female figure, probably S. Helen, crowned and holding a cross, with the letters ELE apparent at the foot; and his description, which is fuller than any that could be safely given in its present state, may be accepted as substantially correct.

In 1377[i], leave was given, 10th March, to Hugh Viker and John Horneshend, Chaplains, to give, and to the Abbey of Elstow to receive, two messuages, fifty acres of land, and five acres of meadow, with appurtenances, in Elstow and Willshamstead, valued at £1 18s. 4d. [§ 75].

These two last acquisitions of property seem both to have been made under a licence[k] granted 19th July, 1352, and preserved in the Confirmation Roll of 2 Henry VIII.; whereby permission was given to the Abbess and Convent to receive either land, provided it were not held of the king in chief, or rents, to the value of

---

[f] Cart. L. F. C. Brit. Mus. x. 9.

[g] We have no record of the institution of this Abbess, but she is mentioned as resigning office 1392. Linc. Dioc. Reg. Bp. Buckingham's Institutions.

[h] Dugdale Mon. iii. 412.

[i] Patent Roll. 51 Edward III. pt. 1. m. 20.

[k] Patent Roll. 26 Edward III.

£10 per annum; and it is specially mentioned in both deeds that the property conveyed was in part satisfaction of that sum.

Reign of Richard II., 1377—99.

With this reign we enter upon a period when our historical materials become extremely scanty. It is not merely that the documents which have come to light are few and far between, but even the Diocesan Registers fail us, only one entry of any interest being found during the Episcopate of four Bishops, extending from 1420 to 1456. After that date they appear to have been somewhat more carefully kept, but it is not until we enter the reign of Henry VIII. that we find them again furnishing anything like a complete record. Probably the cause of this all-pervading laxity may be found in the fact that the fifteenth century witnessed the gradual decay in the Spiritual life of the religious orders in England; and as their members grew more worldly, so were they more careless in the discharge of their proper duties; nor did they manifest any real diligence, until they were roused by the fear of impending retribution.

Be the cause, however, what it may, the effect has been, as above stated, to give us very little to work upon; and in the reign of which we are treating, we have but a single Charter on record, and that only incidentally, as we are indebted for its preservation to the Confirmation Roll of 2 Henry VIII. Its scope is to confirm the Charter of Henry II., which has been given

114   CHRONICLES OF THE ABBEY OF ELSTOW.

at length [pp. 26—29], and it was granted, at the request of the Abbess Margaret[1], 20th November, 1395, the witness thereto being the King himself, at Westminster.

REIGN OF HENRY IV., 1399—1413.

Here we come upon ground slightly more prolific. It is true that only two documents have been preserved to us, but they are both of considerable interest and value.

Of these the first is a petition[m], addressed to the King by the Prioress and Convent, respecting the election of an Abbess; and although other letters relating to the same subject have been already given, we deem this to be worthy of insertion, as well for the terms in which it is written, as for the insight which it gives us, in a few lines, into the various steps by which the election of an Abbess was conducted.

"To their most excellent Prince and Lord in Christ, the Lord HENRY, by the grace of God, illustrious King of England and France, and Lord of Ireland, his humble and devoted suppliants, the Prioress and Convent of his Monastery of Elnestowe, of the order of S. Benedict, Diocese of Lincoln, [send] all kind of reverence and honour due to so great a Prince.

"We intimate by the presents to your Sublimity that, the lady Margaret Pygot, of good memory, having gone the way of all flesh, and leave to elect another to the office of Abbess having been granted to us

---

[1] Margaret Pygot, instituted 1392. Linc. Dioc. Reg. Bp. Buckingham's Institutions.

[m] Record Commission. Transcripts of Petitions, vol. xxxii. No. 27.

by your Majesty, we, the aforesaid Prioress and Convent, have duly and canonically elected as Abbess and *Pastrix* the lady Johanna Trayley, a Nun of our said Monastery, a woman, alike devoted to God, necessary to the discipline of our Monastery aforesaid, and faithful and useful to your reign.

"Hence we present the same to your royal Highness, with devout prayers supplicating that, bestowing your royal assent on our election aforesaid, you will be graciously pleased to direct your letters in this matter to the venerable Father, the Lord Philip[n], by the grace of God, Bishop of Lincoln. In testimony whereof we have affixed our common seal of the said Monastery to the presents.

"May your royal Magnificence prosper in Him who giveth health to kings for many years to come.

"Given in our Monastery of Elnestowe, the fourth day of the month of December, in the year of the Lord MCCCCIX."

From the above, in conjunction with other letters on the subject already quoted, we gather that the course of procedure, on the decease of an Abbess, was that:—

1. The Prioress and Convent sent intimation of her death to the King, with a petition for leave to elect a successor.
2. The King granted the *congé d'élire*.
3. The Prioress and Convent proceeded to elect.
4. They informed the King on whom their choice had fallen, requesting him to issue his mandate of Institution to the Bishop.
5. The Bishop instituted the lady elected, and

[n] Philip Repington, Bp. of Lincoln, 1405-20.

6. The temporalities were, as we shall learn from a later Charter, formally assigned to her.

It may here be mentioned that in the case before us, Joanna Trayley was instituted 14th December, 1409 °.

The second document belonging to this reign is the report of an inquiry ᵖ, held at Bedford on the Sunday next after the Feast of the Epiphany, 1410, into the value of some of the Bedfordshire property of the Abbey. The occasion of this was the death of the Abbess Margaret, which, as we are told therein, had taken place on the Feast of S. Edmund the Archbishop [16th November] in the preceding year. The various items, which are described as having been held by her of the King in chief, in pure and perpetual elemosiny, are thus assessed :—

	£	s.	d.
§§ 3. 2. 1. The Vills, Manors and Demesnes of Elnestowe, Wylshamsted, and Maldon, with appurtenances, valued at per annum	38	19	4
§§ 15. 16. At Bedford.			
A Rent, payable quarterly at the four usual terms	5	0	0
An Annuity, payable half-yearly, by the bailiffs of the town, at Lady Day and Michaelmas	4	0	0
At Kempston.			
§ 17. A rent, payable at the same terms	7	0	0

° Linc. Dioc. Reg. Bp. Repington's Institutions.
ᵖ Inquis. ad quod damnum. 11 Henry IV. No. 13.

		£	s.	d.
§ 13.	A rent, from land in the Bourn, payable at Midsummer and Michaelmas	1	0	0
§ 17.	A rent, from three water-mills in the "Box End," payable at Midsummer	0	13	4
§ 76.	At Felmersham, a rent, payable at Midsummer	0	10	0
§ 33.	At Wemyngton, a rent, payable at Michaelmas	0	5	0
§ 77.	At Bromham, a rent, payable at the Feast of the Assumption of Blessed Virgin Mary [15th August]	0	1	0
§ 78.	At Wotton, a rent, payable at Easter and Michaelmas . . .	0	6	0
§ 57.	At Yevelden [Yelden], a rent, payable at the same terms .	0	6	0
	Total	£58	0	8

In this valuation, it will be observed that we find several places named, in which we had not before heard of the Abbey holding property, and of which we hear nothing in any of the later records. It may, however, be remarked that Bromham is found, coupled with Wymington, in the *Computus Ministrorum*, where the rent derived from the two is given, as here, at 6s.; and we further learn, from the *Valor Ecclesiasticus*[q], that the Hospital of S. John, Northampton, paid 6s. 8d. tithe to the Abbey from Wotton. The rents from the remaining places are probably included

[q] Valor Eccl. iv. 317.

in the same in the item, "Extraneous receipts in sundry townships." On the other hand the Kempston rents come out very clearly [see p. 27].

REIGN OF HENRY V., 1413—22.

The only documents, belonging to this reign, which have been discovered, are three receipts in similar terms, which are preserved among the Harleian Charters. They are dated 1414-18, and one[r] of them is here given in full, because they confirm exactly certain information which we had obtained from other sources.

"KNOW ALL MEN, by the presents, that we, JOHANNA TRAYLIE, by divine permission Abbess of the Monastery of Elnestowe, and the Convent of the same place, have received from the religious [men], the Abbot and Convent of Nusum [Newhouse], the sum of fifty-three shillings and fourpence, for a certain annual payment [due] from the Church of Halton-super-Humber [§ 28], at the terms of the Nativity of the Lord, and [the Feast] of S. Botulph; And a sum of two shillings, for a certain annual rent of tenements, which they hold of us in Halton aforesaid, due to us year by year from the day of S. Martin [11th November] last past before the date of the presents. In testimony whereof our seal is appended to the presents.

"Given at Elnestowe, on the twentieth day of the month of June, in the year of the reign of King HENRY the fifth, after his accession, the sixth, [1418]."

The points confirmed by this receipt are the amount of the annual payment due from Halton, with the terms at which it was payable, [p. 49], and the source of the extra 2s. noticed under the account of *Taxatio Papæ Nicholai*, [p. 90]. The

[r] Harleian Charters. Brit. Mus. 44. D. 35.

seal is the same as that described under the year 1370, the only difference being that in this instance the impression of the figure is in brown wax, that of the ground in red. Unfortunately the whole is so mutilated, imperfect, or both, that it adds nothing to our knowledge of its details.

REIGN OF HENRY VI., 1422—61.

Of this period but two brief records have come to hand, and that only incidentally. Of these the first is that of the death of the Abbess Trayley[s], which occurred about the Feast of the Purification [2nd February], 1430, and the institution of the Prioress, whose name is unfortunately not given, in her place.

The second is an intimation that the advowson of Westoning [§ 79], Beds, about six miles north of Dunstable, had somehow come into the possession of the Abbey. Of this all that can be ascertained is, that the Abbess and Convent are found presenting to it[t], for the first time, 26th November, 1436, and that it is named, as forming part of their property, in both the later valuations[u].

Meagre, however, as is the history of the Abbey in this reign, it yet contrasts favourably with that of the three following ones, for not a single document belonging to the

REIGNS OF EDWARD IV., 1461—83, EDWARD V., 1483, AND RICHARD III., 1483—85,

has been found to shew how its affairs were progressing.

[s] Ann. Monast. Sci. Albani. i. 47.
[t] Linc. Dioc. Reg. Bp. Alnewick's Institutions.
[u] Valor Eccl. and Comp. Ministr.

Reign of Henry VII., 1485—1509.

Here, once more, we find a little material, but very little, confined, in fact, to the notice of the accession of two Abbesses; with respect to which we learn, from Bp. Kennett's collection of rolls relating to the restitution of Temporalities, that Margaret Godfrey[x] received them 2 Henry VII., 23rd March [1487], and Elizabeth Hervy[y] 17 Henry VII., 5th November, [1501].

The Charter granting the Temporalities in the last named case is still extant[z]; it tells us that the Abbey became vacant through the death of Margaret Godfrey; and is of considerable interest, as shewing that, on the death of the head of a religious house, the Temporalities, during the vacancy, went to the Crown. On this occasion, the King appears to have acted liberally, as he not only put the incoming Abbess in possession of the emoluments of her office, but was pleased to allow her all the profits that had accrued, since the death of her predecessor.

Reign of Henry VIII., 1509—1547.

If, in the recent reigns, we suffered from scarcity of material, such a complaint can certainly not be made with regard to this, for the difficulty will be so to arrange the multifarious documents, which have been found, as to keep the continuity of our narrative unbroken.

[x] Lansdowne MSS. Brit. Mus. No. 963. p. 52.
[y] Ibid. p. 55.
[z] Exchequer, L. T. R., Memoranda Roll. 17 Henry VII. Michaelmas Roll 21.

The first of these that we come to is our old friend, to whom we owe so much, the Confirmation Roll of 1510[a], which is of the nature of an *Inspeximus*, each successive Charter being introduced by that word ["we have inspected"]. Every one of these has been in turn given in full or noticed, but for convenience of reference it will be advisable to set out here a brief recapitulation of them, with the page at which each will be found: —

1. 26 Edward III. Confirming licence granted to the Abbey by Edward I., to acquire property to a certain amount, p. 112.

2. 42 Edward III. Benefactions of Morteyn and others, p. 111.

3. 51 Edward III. Benefactions of Viker and Horneshend, p. 112.

4. Henry II. Grant of the Fair, p. 42.

5. Prince Henry. Securing safety for visitors thereto, p. 43.

6. Henry I. Grant of Church of Hitchin, &c., p. 15.

7. 19 Richard II., p. 113. Quoting and confirming long Charter of Henry II., p. 26.

8. Henry I. Grant of Free Warren, p. 24.

9. Henry II. Confirmation of the same, p. 42.

These are all recited at length, and appended to them is the deed of Confirmation in the following words :—

"Now we, holding the aforesaid charters and letters ratified and secured, do, for ourselves and our heirs, as far as in us lies, accept, approve, and now grant and confirm them, to the Abbess and Nuns of the place

[a] Confirmation Roll. 2 Henry VIII. Part 5. No. 8.

aforesaid, as the Charters and letters aforesaid duly testify. In witness whereof, &c. Witness the King at Westminster, 20th day of May."

Thirty years afterwards he appropriated everything to himself.

After this the records yield nothing for the space of about twenty years, but then we come to the *Valor Ecclesiasticus,* a document more familiar to modern ears as "the King's Books," and which is most interesting, as furnishing by far the most minute account, which has been found, of the Abbey property, and as being in itself a link connecting the days of the Reformation with our own times.

This valuation owes its origin to the rupture between Henry VIII. and the Pope. In 1533 an act was passed, 25th July, empowering the King to suspend the payment by the clergy of first-fruits, or *annates,* to Rome. This was supplemented by a further act, 15th January, 1534; and a third, dated 3rd November in the same year, assigned the first-fruits and tenths of all benefices to the Crown. Included in the last-named act was also a provision for a new valuation of these charges, and under it Commissioners were appointed for every diocese, who did their work so rapidly, that their returns were completed between January and June, 1535 [b].

The assessment of the Abbey as given therein [c] is as follows, and it will at once be seen from the figures prefixed what properties appear for the

[b] Extracted from "Introduction to Valor Ecclesiasticus." Rev. J. Hunter.

[c] Valor Eccl. iv. 188.

first time, [i.e. all those numbered 80 and upwards] while the numbers which are wanting will indicate what had been lost or sold prior to this date.

	£	s.	d.
§ 4. Rectory of Hitchin	66	13	4
§ 53. Rectory of Clanfield	5	6	8
§ 68. Rectory of Wilbarston	6	0	0
§ 79. Rectory of Westoning	10	0	0
§ 67. Rectory of Flitton and Silshoe	13	6	8
§ 3. Rectory of Elstow	10	0	0
§ 66. Rectory of Kempston	20	0	0
§ 2. Rectory of Willshamstead	6	13	4
§ 28. Of the Abbot of Newhouse, for land in Halton-super-Humber	2	13	4
§ 42. Of the Prior of Newenham, for a portion in Barford	1	0	0
§ 40. Tithes of mills in Buckden	0	10	0
§ 80. Of the Prior of Dunstable, for portion of tithes in Pulloxhill	0	10	0
§ 81. Portion of tithes of S. Machuts	0	3	9
§ 82. Portion of tithes issuing from the Rectory of Gravenhurst Parva	0	6	8
§ 83. Of the Monastery of S. John, Northampton, for portion of tithes in Irkhamstede	0	6	8
§ 20. Of the Vicar of Milton for portion of tithes there	0	5	0
§ 21. Rectory of Braunston, for portion of tithes there	1	0	0
§ 29. Portion of tithe in Shutford	2	13	4
§ 23. Portion of tithe in Upton	0	13	4
§ 84. Payment of the Vicar of Stonehouse	6	0	0
§ 4. Payment of the Vicar of Hitchin	2	13	4
§ 54. Payment of the Rector of Inworth	1	6	8
§ 49. Rectory of Harringworth	13	6	8
§ 71. Of the Prior of Kyme, for the manor of Thorp	6	13	4
§ 51. Rectory of Westbury	5	0	0

	£	s.	d.
§ 61. Portion in King's Walden	1	0	0
§ 3. In oblations at Elstow	1	2	3
Total	**£185**	**4**	**5**

In Temporalities.

	£	s.	d.
§§ 3. 73. 74. 75. Elstow	30	17	3½
§§ 2. 73. 74. 75. Willshamstead	19	0	5¾
§§ 15. 16. 55. Bedford	4	3	2
§§ 13. 17. 73. Kempston	2	15	8¾
§§ 36. 85. Harrowden and Fenlake	1	1	0½
§ 86. Houghton	0	7	7
§ 1. Maulden	18	18	0
Extraneous receipts in sundry townships, as shewn by particulars	12	2	8
Sundry rents pertaining to the office of chief cook	3	0	0
Sundry rents pertaining to the office of Sacristan	5	3	3½
§ 87. Tolls of Elstow Fair	7	12	0
§ 88. Farm close of Wyldole	2	6	8
§§ 6. 7. 69. Certain lands in Moulsoe	0	18	0
§ 26. Certain lands in Croft	0	15	0
Demesne land to the said monastery pertaining	18	16	10
Total	**£127**	**17**	**8**

Woods.

	£	s.	d.
Woods and underwood within the parish of Willshamstead, containing eighty acres @ 12*l.* per acre	4	0	0
Maulden Wood, containing one hundred and twenty acres	6	0	0
Total	**£10**	**0**	**0**

Perquisites of the Court.

	£	s.	d.
Fines, amercements, and other profits of the Court average by the year	2	0	0

Total   £325   2*s.*   1¾*d.*

Outgoings thence, namely,

	£	s.	d.	£	s.	d.
In rents paid.						
To the Abbot of Wardon, for land in Clapham	0	2	6			
To the Prioress of Sopwell, for land in Madebury . . .	0	2	6			
To the Monastery of S. Leonard, Bedford, from free rent of two tenements in Elstow . .	0	7	6			
Total					12	6

Expenses and Deductions.

In annual payments and portions.

	£	s.	d.
To the Prior of Wymondley, for rent of mills in Hitchin . .	1	10	0
To the Monastery of S. Julian next S. Albans, for portion of tithes in Silshoe	2	6	8
To the Prior of S. Andrew in Northampton, for portion of tithes in Harringworth . . .	0	15	0
To Eton College, for payment issuing from the Rectory of Clanfield	1	3	0
To the Archdeacon of Oxford, for procurations and synodals of the church of Clanfield . .	0	12	$6\frac{3}{4}$
To the Vicar of Clanfield, for three quarters of wheat and three quarters of barley a nominal payment	1	10	0
To the Vicar of Westbury, for two quarters of wheat and two quarters of barley, a nominal payment	1	0	0
To the Archdeacon of Bucks, for procurations and synodals of the church of Westbury . .	0	10	6
To the Vicar of Westoning, for stipend	2	6	8
To the Vicar of Flitton, for stipend .	2	0	0

	£	s.	d.	£	s.	d.
To the Vicar of Wymondley		4	0	0		
To the Vicar of S. Ippolyts		2	6	8		
To the Archdeacon of Northampton, for procurations and synodals of the churches of Wilbarston and Harringworth		0	15	$1\frac{1}{4}$		
To the Archdeacon of Bedford, for procurations and synodals of the churches of Elstow, Kempston, Willshamstead, Flitton, and Westoning		2	0	6		
Total				£22	16	8

Fees.

	£	s.	d.
In the fee of Henry Grey, Kt., Chief Steward	2	13	4
In the fee of Henry Combes, Auditor	2	13	4
In the fee of Edward Wanton, Receiver	5	0	0
In the fee of Henry Whithed, Bailiff of Elstow	2	13	4
In the fee of George Hynton, Bailiff of Maulden	2	0	0
In the fee of William Pulter, Bailiff of Hitchin	2	0	0
Total	£17	0	0

Total, £40 9s. 2d.
And there remains clear . . £284 12 $11\frac{3}{4}$
Tithe thence . . . £28 9 $3\frac{3}{4}$

But few of the entries in this account call for any special comment. Those of which we have heard before have been as fully described as was possible elsewhere; while of the places which are new to us, it has generally to be confessed that we know not how the property came into the possession of the Abbey, and in some cases that we cannot satisfactorily ascertain their locality; so all that remains to be done is to make the most of what little information we have.

§ 80. Pulloxhill appears for the first time, and all that there is to be said of it is that it lies three miles south-east of Ampthill.

§ 81. S. Machuts defies identification. All that has been discovered is that the Abbey of S. Albans held a manor of that name, and that Abbot Whethamstede spent £10 in building a barn there [d]. It is presumed that this is the place whence these tithes were derived, but where it was has not been ascertained.

§ 82. Gravenhurst is much in the same category with Pulloxhill. It lies about four and a-half miles east south-east of Ampthill.

§ 83. Irkhamstede has not been identified. In the later record it will be found described as in Northamptonshire; but, on the other hand, in the valuation of the Hospital of S. John, Northampton, these tithes are said to be derived from Wotton [e].

§ 84. Stonehouse lies nine miles south of Gloucester. The county historians tell us that the Abbey held the advowson, together with a rent charge of £6 per ann., which agrees with the sum at which it is here assessed; but as they give no reference to authorities, we have no means of testing their statement. Probably this property was one of the latest acquisitions of the Abbey. The patronage of the living is now vested in the Crown.

§§ 36. 85. With Harrowden [see p. 33] we now find coupled the name Fenlake, which is that of

---

[d] Ann. Mon. Sci. Alb. ii. 263.   [e] Valor Eccl. iv. 317.

a manor in the same parish. It is now known as Fenlake "Barns," or "Berners."

§ 86. Houghton is no doubt Houghton Conquest, five miles south of Bedford. We have heard nothing of property there before, but it will be found reappearing in the *Computus Ministrorum*, together with the four places last treated.

§ 87. In this we have, for the first time, a valuation of the profits of the fair. These, it should be mentioned, recur in a later document, belonging to this reign, assessed at a somewhat lower figure.

§ 88. Wyldole is also new to us, but Blomefield states [f] that the Abbey held certain lands known by this name in the parish of Walpole, [about seven miles west of Lynn]; and as in the *Computus Ministrorum* we find the latter only, but assessed at the same valuation, it seems safe to conclude that we have, at all events, fixed the locality of the property.

The outgoings may be dismissed in very few words; in fact almost the only points calling for notice are, that the Prioress of Sopwell here appears on the opposite side of the ledger from that on which we found her under *Taxatio Papæ Nicholai;* and that the amount of many of the payments herein named will be confirmed later on, from other and independent sources.

In addition to the valuation of the Abbey, we find also [g] in this record that of a Chantry, which is given as follows :—

[f] History of Norfolk. iv. 716.
[g] Valor Eccl. iv. 191.

ELNESTOWE.

	£	s.	d.
John Mayott, Chaplain of the Chantry there, has in rent and farms	6	0	0
Thence he pays in rent to the Abbess of Elnestowe, one year with another	1	1	2
And there remains over	4	18	10
Tithe thence	0	9	10½

In connexion with this it may be observed, that there arises a difficulty from the fact that, as far as can be judged from the Lincoln Diocesan Registers, there were originally *two* Chantries attached to the Church of Elstow, whereas here only one is mentioned; and as everything tends to prove that the Commissioners were most exact in the discharge of the duties assigned to them, we can only conclude, and, as we shall see hereafter, with good reason, that the two had been merged at some time prior to the Reformation. Other documents will appear later, shewing more particularly the value of this Chantry, and the sources whence its income was derived.

In 1530 a last insight into the internal discipline of the Abbey is afforded by certain injunctions of Bishop Longland[h], which are preserved in the Lincoln Diocesan Registers, and have been published[i] by the Society of Antiquaries. In these, four religious houses in the diocese are selected as calling for special censure, and, sad to say, that of Elstow is among the number. From the language of the letter addressed thereto we are compelled to conclude that reform was

[h] John Longland, Bp. of Lincoln, 1521—47.
[i] The Archæologia. vol. xlvii.

urgently needed, as it will be observed that its admonitions embrace every department, from the condition of the conventual buildings to the dress of the Nuns. Slackness of discipline evidently reigned throughout, and the rebuke doubtless came home most forcibly to the Abbess and Sisters, who must have been conscious that they had, by their own fault, drawn it down upon themselves. Subjoined is a copy of the

Injunctions to Vlnestowe.

"John Longlond by the sufferaunce of god bishope of Lincoln to our wel-beloued susters in charite the abbess and covent of Vlnestowe of our dioces of lincoln sendeth greting grace and our blessing, and forasmoche as in our ordynarye visitation of late exercised within that monasterye diuerse thinges appered and were detected worthy refcrmacon we therefore, for the honour of god, and redresse off the same and mayntenaunce of good religion ther, send to you thies Inunctons folowing whiche we will and commande you to kepe under the paynes ensewing. ffirste forasmoche as the very ordre of sainct benedicte his rules ar nott ther obserued in keping the ffratrye [k] att meale tymes, where the susters should be aswell fedde spiritually with holy scripture as bodyly with meate, butt customably they resorte to certayn places within the monasterye called the householdes[l], where moche insolncy is use contrarye to the good rules of the said religion by reason of resorte of seculars both men women and

---

[k] Fratry. The Conventual Refectory, to which no secular person was admitted.

[l] The "Households," equivalent to the French "Parloirs," were rooms in which the Sisters could converse with their lay friends, and which in time came to be used for more festive purposes than mere conversation.

children, and many other inconvenyents hath thereby ensewed, In consideracon whereof and for that we will the said religion to prospere according unto the foundacon of the house, and the rules of the same, we inioyne and straytely commaunde undre the payne of disobedyence that ye lady abbesse and your successours see that noo suche householdes be then kepte frome hensforth butt oonly oon place which shalbe called the mysericorde where shalbe oon sadde lady of the eldest sorte ouersear and maistres to all the residue that thidre shall resorte, whiche in nombre shall nott passe fyve att the uttermoost, besides ther said ladye ouersear or maistres and those fyve wekely to chaunge and soo . . . . all the covent have kepte the same, and they agen to begynne and the said gouernour and ouersear of them contynally to contynue in thatt roome by the space of oon quarter of a yere, and soo quarterly to chaunge att the nominacon and plesure of the ladye abbesse for the tyme being.

"Ouer this itt is ordered undre the said payne and Iniunction that the ladye abbesse haue no moo susters from hensforth in hir householde butt oonly foure with hir chapleyn and likewise wekely to chaunge till they haue goon by course thrugh the hole nomber off susters, and soo agen to begynne and contynue.

"And we will and chardge undre lik payne that all the sayd ladyes bothe off the abbesse side and of the misericorde doo obserue and kepe the quere att matens, masse, and all other dyvyne seruice, as those that be called the cloystrers without ther be any lawfull impedyment, and that noo ladye of the said twoo places remayne longer in eny of the same, than halff houre after seven of the clock att night and that noo man, preeste ne other, come into the said place called the misericorde without speciall lycence of the lady abbesse for the tyme being, and yett thes to make noo long aboode nether ther to be without honest testymonye of his or ther honeste conuersacon, and this the lydye abbesse to see obserued and kepte undre the payne off contemte, and all the residue of the ladyes daily to sitt in the ffratrye according unto ther rules att ther meales.

"And forasmoche as the more secrete religious persones be kepte from the sight and visage of the world and straungers the more close and entyer ther mynd and deuocon shalbe unto god, we ordeyn and Inioyne to the lady abbesse that before the natiuyte of our lorde next ensewing she cause a doore with twoo leves to be made and sett upp att the lower ende off the quere, and that doore to be fyve foote in hight att the leaste, and contynually to stand shitt the tymes off dyvyne seruice excepte itt be att comming in or out off eny off the ladyes and mynystres off the said churche.

"And under lik payne as is afore we chardge the said ladye abbesse that she cause the doore betwene the covent and the parishe churche contynually to be shitt unles itt be oonly the tymes of dyvyne seruice, and likewise she cause the cloistre door towardes the outtward court to be contynually shitt unles itt be att suche tymes as eny necessaryes for the covent shalbe brought in or borne out att the same, and that she suffre noo other back doures to be opened butt upon necessarye grett and urgent causes by her approved.

"Also we Injoyne to the said ladye abbesse that suche reparacons as be necessarye in and upon the buildinges within the said monasterye, and other houses, tenements and fearmes thereto belonging, be suffycyently doon and made within the space of oon yere immedyately after the date of thies iniuncons.

"Moreover forasmoche as the ladye abbesse and covent of that house be all oon religious bodye unite by the profession and rules of holy sainct benedicte, and [it] is nott conuenyent ne religious to be disseuerd or separate, we will and Inioyne that frome hensforth noon of the said abbesse seruauntes nor no other seculer person or persones what soeuer he or they be, goo in eny procession before the said abbesse betwene hir and hir said covent undre payne of excommunycacon, and that the ladye abbesse ne noon of hir successours hereafter be ladde by the arme or otherwise in eny procession ther as in tymes paste hath been used undre the same payne.

"Also we will command and inioyne to dame Katheryne Wingate the said ladye abbesse her chapleyn undre payne of contempte that nightly she rise and be att matens within the said mon. with her other religious susters ther and that from hensforth she do nott suppe ne breke her faste in the buttry of the said abbesse, nether with the stuard nor eny other seculer person or persones undre the said payne and likeuise we Inioyne to all them that hereafter shalbe in the said office or roome of the ladye abbesse her chapellyn undre the payne aboue expressed.

"Ouer this we ordeyne and by way of Iniuncon commande undre payne off disobedyence from hensforth that noo ladye ne eny religious suster within the said monasterye presume to were ther apparells upon ther hedes undre suche lay fashion as they haue now off late doon with cornered crests nether undre such manour of hight shewing ther forehedes moore like lay people than religious, butt that they use them without suche crestes or secular fashions, and off a lower sorte and that ther vayle come as lowe as ther yye ledes, and soo contynually to use the same unles itt be at suche tymes as they shalbe occupied in eny handy crafte labour, att whiche tymes itt shalbe lefull for them to turne upp the said vayle for the tyme of suche occupacon. And undre like payne inioyne that noon of the said religious susters doo use or were here after eny such voyded shoys, nether crested as they have of late ther used butt that they be of suche honeste fashion as other religious places both use, and that ther gownes and kyrtells be closse afore and nott soo depe voyded att the breste and noo more to use rede stomachers but other sadder colers in the same. In witenes whereof hereunto we haue putte our scale.

"Geven att our manor off Wooborn the first daye off October in the yere of our lord god a thousand fyve hundrede and thirty, and undre payne of contemptc chardge you ladye abbesse and your successours that ye and euerye of them oones in euery moneth doo rede or cause to be redde this our iniuncons openly in the chaptour house before all the ladyes, that ye and they may the better remembere the obseruances of your holy religion."

The only point in the above, which calls for special remark, is the mention of the *Parish Church*, as distinct from the Conventual buildings; and even this would be of little moment, were it not that certain notes to Cole's MSS., by Browne Willis, seem to indicate that at an earlier period there had been another Church for the parishioners. With regard to this he says [m] :—

"Elstow Church is cut off, like Dunstable, at the east end, and the fine choir of the Nunnery pulled down. There was an old parish Church for the use of the Town, which was demolished about 1500, and a Tower built on the north side of the Church, at some small distance, for the use of the parish. The Clerk told me there was a book in Mr. Dennis Farrer's hands, that gave an account of the contracting of this Nunnery Church, and fitting it up for the use of the Town's people."

Could the book here mentioned only be found, it would be simply invaluable; for, as things are, everything, even to the site of the old parish Church, is lost even to tradition; and question

[m] Add. MSS. Brit. Mus. 5830. fol. 141 d.

after question arises to the mind, which it is difficult, if not impossible, to answer. Has the "Gravestone Close," towards the south end of the village, anything to do with the site of the old parish Church? Does the division of the Rectory indicate the existence in earlier days of the two Churches? and if so, why are not presentations to both found in the Diocesan Registers? All these questions may be asked, but whence can a reply come? All that can be done is to give such information as has come to light, and let those who can solve the problem.

With regard, however, to the tower, which Browne Willis says was *built* about 1500, it will be observed that Mr. Buckley, in his "notes on the architectural features of the Church," considers that the upper story only was added at that date, and that the lower part was a portion of the old Conventual buildings.

The name of Katheryne Wingate, mentioned in the injunctions as Chaplain, will be found recurring, in the list of Nuns, pensioned at the dissolution, in the same capacity.

At this point it becomes a little difficult to decide what part of our history can be most advantageously taken up. The documents that come next in order of date are certain leases, granted by the Abbess and Convent, shortly before the dissolution, but these, it is thought, can be best treated when dealing with the dispersion of their property after that event; and that, although the deed of surrender seems to come upon us somewhat suddenly, priority should be accorded to it.

This deed[n], which is preserved in the Public Record Office, runs as follows:—

"TO ALL FAITHFUL [SERVANTS] OF CHRIST, to whom the present writing may come, the Lady ELIZABETH[o], Abbess of the Monastery, or Abbey, of the Blessed Mary[p], of Elnestowe, in the county of Bedford, of the order of St. Benedict, and the Convent of the same place, everlasting greeting in the Lord.

"Know ye that we, the aforesaid Abbess and Convent, with our unanimous assent and consent, with deliberate minds, of our certain knowledge, and mere motion, from certain just and reasonable causes, specially moving us our minds and consciences, have freely and willingly given and granted, and by the presents do give, grant, restore, deliver and confirm, to our most illustrious and victorious Prince and Lord, HENRY VIII., by the grace of God, King of England and France, Defender of the Faith, Lord of Ireland, and upon earth supreme Head, under Christ, of the Church of England, ALL our said Monastery, or Abbey, of Elnestowe aforesaid, and all the Site, Estate, Circuit and Precinct of the same Monastery of Elnestowe aforesaid, ALSO all and singular the Manors, Houses, Messuages, Gardens, Curtilages, Tofts, Lands and Tenements, Meadows, Grazing Grounds, Pastures, Woods, Underwoods, Rents, Reversions, Services, Mills, Ferries, Knights' Fees, Wards, Marriages, Born Serfs and Villanes, with the issues of the same, Commons, Liberties, Franchises, Jurisdictions, Courts, Court Leets, Hundreds, Views of Frankpledge, Fairs, Markets, Parks, Warren, Fishponds, Waters, Fisheries, Ways, Roads, Waste Lands,

---

[n] Exchequer. Augmentation. Surrender of Elnestowe Monastery.

[o] Elizabeth Boyfeld [or Boyvill], instituted 1530. Linc. Dioc. Reg. Bp. Longland's Institutions.

[p] Here note that the dedication of the Abbey is given as *St. Mary* only.

Advowsons, Nominations, Presentations and Donations of Churches, Vicarages, Chapelries, Chantries, Hospitals, and other Ecclesiastical Benefices whatsoever, Rectories, Vicarages, Chantries, Portions, Pensions, Annuities, Tithes, Oblations, and all and singular our Emoluments, Profits, Possessions, Hereditaments and Rights whatsoever, as well within the said county of Bedford, as within the counties of Northampton, Lincoln, Leicester, Buckingham, Hertford, Essex, Norfolk, Gloucester, Huntingdon, and Oxford, and elsewhere, within the kingdom of England and Wales, and the Marches of the same, to the said Monastery, or Abbey, of Elnestowe in any manner pertaining, belonging, appending or attaching; AND our Charters, Evidences, Writings and Muniments of all kinds, to the said Monastery, or Abbey, and to the Manors, Lands, Tenements, and the other premisses, with appurtenances, or to any parcel thereof, in any manner belonging or concerning.

"TO HAVE, HOLD AND ENJOY the said Monastery, or Abbey, Site, Estate, Circuit and Precinct of Elnestowe aforesaid, Lands, Tenements and the other premisses, with all and singular their appurtenances, to our most victorious Prince and Lord King, his heirs and assigns for ever, TO WHOM in this respect, for every effect in law, which thence could or can follow, we, as is fitting, subject and submit ourselves, and the said Monastery, or Abbey, of Elnestowe aforesaid, and all Rights in any way acquired by us, giving and granting to the said King's Majesty, his heirs and assigns, all, and all kind of, full and free faculty, authority and power of disposing of us, and the said Monastery of Elnestowe aforesaid, together with all and every the Manors, Lands, Tenements, Rents, Reversions, Services, and all the premisses, with their rights and appurtenances whatsoever; AND, at his free royal will and discretion, of alienating, giving, converting, and transferring to any uses pleasing to his Majesty, which kind of disposition, alienation, grant, conversion and transference, in whatever way to be made and ratified by his Majesty, we promise by the presents to hold ratified, secured, and established for ever.

"AND that all and singular the premisses may be able to obtain their due effect, we openly, publicly, and expressly, of our certain knowledge and free wills, have renounced and given up, as by the presents we renounce and give up, and from them recede in these writings, elections hereafter for us or our successors, also all complaints, challenges, appeals, actions, suits and instances, or any other remedies or benefits of law whatsoever, which may possibly be now or hereafter competent for us, or our successors, in this respect, by reason of the disposition, alienation, transference, and conversion aforesaid, all exceptions, objections, and allegations, of fraud, error, fear, ignorance, or other matter being altogether removed and laid aside.

"AND we, the aforesaid Abbess and Convent, and our successors, will, by the presents, warrant the said Monastery, Precinct, Site, Mansion and Church of Elnestowe aforesaid, and all and singular, the Manors, Houses, Messuages, Gardens, Curtilages, Tofts, Meadows, Grazing Grounds, Pastures, Woods, Underwoods, Lands and Tenements, and all and singular the other premises, with their entire appurtenances, to our aforesaid Lord the King, his heirs and assigns, against all people for ever.

"IN TESTIMONY WHEREOF, we, the aforesaid Abbess and Convent, have caused our common seal to be affixed to this writing.

"GIVEN in our Chapter House of the Monastery aforesaid the twenty-sixth day of the month of August, in the year of the reign of HENRY VIII., by the grace of God, King of England and France, Defender of the Faith, Lord of Ireland, and upon earth supreme Head of the Church of England, the thirty-first. [1539]."

Anything more abject and unconditional than this deed it would be difficult to imagine, but while we may venture to express a doubt whether the words "freely and willingly" truly represented the feelings of the Abbess and Nuns, there can be little question but that the "just and reasonable causes" implied that they had no choice in the matter.

The seal appended to the surrender is the "common," or "great," seal of the Abbey [q]. It is large, and of oval form; the impression, on dark wax, apparently green, representing, under tabernacle-work, two female figures, one the blessed Virgin, crowned, with the infant Saviour on her lap, the other S. Helen, holding a cross. Beneath are three figures in the attitude of prayer, the centre one that of an Abbess with her pastoral staff.

The legend surrounding it runs thus :—SIGILLV ..... SCE MARIE DE ELENNSTOWE, and the whole is in fairly good preservation, except the inscription, which wants one word, probably, according to Dugdale [r], 'monasterii;' and we might add 'abbathie,' or 'conventus;' but there remains the fact that the edge is so mutilated that all, apparently, who have tried their skill in deciphering it have come to different conclusions respecting it. Thus Archdeacon Rose, in a paper on seals, read before the Beds. Architectural Society, 1848, gives it :—S . COMMVNE .... SC . AR .. DE . ELEWNESTOWE; and of late it has been read :—S . COMMVNE ..... EI . STE . ARIE DE ELEYNSTOWE, of which it may be said that the concluding letters of the incomplete word following COMMVNE certainly look like EI, but here presents itself the difficulty that these

---

[q] See Title-page. [r] Dugd. Mon. iii. 412.

letters do not supply the termination of any of the words we should have expected to find. Setting aside this open question, our engraving, which is taken from that given by Dugdale, may be accepted as faithful in every detail.

From the above it will be observed that, although in the deed and legend the Abbey is designated as that of S. Mary, the body of the seal affords evidence of the double dedication. How long this had existed we have no means of determining, but the two names are, as will have been observed, used apparently so indifferently, that it might have had its origin in very early times.

What rule governed the use of the two seals of the Abbey it is difficult for us to decide. Doubtless the line was drawn somewhere, but the question is, where? We have, however, found the smaller one attached to two receipts, so we conclude that its use was restricted to documents of that nature; and as the "common" seal is named [p. 115] as appended to a petition to the King, we infer that it was employed on all more important occasions. Had the Nuns guessed how these seals would be scrutinised in after ages, they would, we think, have been careful to hand us down more perfect impressions.

At the time of the surrender the inmates of the Abbey were twenty-four in number, and the following is an abridged list* of the—

"Penc'ons graunted unto the late Abbesse and her sisters of the surrendred Monastery of Elnestowe in the Countie of Bedf. as ensueth; in the month of August, in the year of King Harry VIII. xxxj."

* Augmentation Office. See Dugd. Mon. iii. 415.

	£	s.	d.
Dame Elizabeth Boyvill, Abbess	50	0	0
Dame Elen Snow, Prioress	4	0	0
Dame Anne Wake, formerly Prioress	3	6	8
Dame Cecillie Sterky, Sexten	3	6	8
16 Nuns at £2 13s. 4d.	42	13	4
4 Nuns at £2	8	0	0
Total	111	6	8

The names[1] of the nuns were Mawde Sheldon [sub-prioress], Alis Boyvill, Anne Preston, Katheryne Wyngate [Chaplain], Dorothe Comberford, Elizabeth Napton, Alis Blakwall, Elizabeth Steynesmore, Margery Preston, Margarete Nicholson, Barbara Grey, Alys Bolles, Alys fforster, Elizabeth Synklere, Alis Croft, Anne Ardys, Elizabeth Waltam, Elizabeth ffox, Elizabeth Hewis, and Cecillie Hillis.

Appended to the list of pensions thus granted 31 Henry VIII., are the following words :—

"All whiche penc'ons assigned to be paide at two usuall termes in the yere by even porc'ons, viz. at the feest of Saint Mighell the Archaungell next comyng, and at the feest of the Añunciac'on of our Lady, in considerac'on that the King's majestie shall fully receyve the half yere's rent due at Mighelmas now next folowing the day of their surrendre."

This is signed by John Gostwyk and Edmund Harvey, commissioners for receiving the surrender, of whom the former was no doubt Sir John Gostwick, of Willington, master of the horse to Henry VIII., the latter Edmund Harvey of

[1] These names are copied from Dugdale, whose list corresponds exactly, except in some details of spelling, with that given by Cole.

Elstow, fourth son of William Harvey of Ickworth, and Joan, daughter of John Coket of Ampton.

As, however, many members of this family are connected with the history of the Abbey, a copy of the pedigree thereof is appended on the opposite page.

From the foregoing it may be fairly deduced that the Abbey of Elstow was one of some importance, though its place among the greater[a] monasteries could not have been a very high one. In the first place the number of inmates was considerable; in the second it maintained both an Abbess and a Prioress, the former to manage the estates and dispense hospitality, the latter to superintend the internal discipline of the house; but the pensions granted seem rather low. On this point Lingard[x] tells us :—

"The pensions to the superiors of the dissolved greater monasteries appear to have varied from £266 to £60 per annum. The Priors of cells received generally £13. A few, whose services had merited the distinction, obtained £20. To the other monks were allotted pensions of six, four, or two pounds, with a small sum at his departure to provide for his immediate wants. The pensions to nuns averaged about £4. It should, however, be observed that these sums were not in reality so small as they appear, as money was probably, at that period, of six or seven times greater value than it is now."

[a] The lesser monasteries, i.e. those with a revenue of less than £200 per annum, were suppressed, 1536; the greater, three or four years later, 1539-40.

[x] History of England. 4th Ed. vi. 263, note.

PEDIGREE OF THE HERVEY FAMILY.

Sir John Hervey, Kt. [of Co. Beds.] = ... dau. of D'Engayne.

John [of Thurleigh and Riseley, Co. Beds], died = 1396, Margery, dau. of Ralph Parles, by Joanna, dau. of
before 1419; buried at Thurleigh.   Sir John Talbot, of Richard's Castle. She married [2]
    Sir William Argentine; died 1427; buried at Elstow.

John [of Thurleigh], Master of the King's Ordnance, = Joan, dau. and co-heiress of Sir John Niemuyt, of Burnham,
1461; died after 1475; buried at Thurleigh.   Co. Bucks, Kt.

John, Usher of the = Agnes, dau. of Ni-	Sir Nicholas, slain at	Elizabeth, Ab-	Anne, a	Thomas, died = Jane, dau. and heir-	Other
King's Chamber cholas Morley, of	battle of Tewkesbury,	bess of Elstow,	Nun at	about 1467. ess of Henry Drury,	children.
to Edward IV., Glynde, Co. Sus-	May 4, 1471, on the	1501—1524.	Campsey.	of Ickworth.	
died 1474. sex.	Lancastrian side.				

Sir George [of Thur- = Margaret, dau. of
leigh], Kt. Sheriff of   John Stanford.
Beds, &c.; died 1521.

William [of Ickworth], died = Joan, dau. of John Coket,
Aug. 1, 1538; buried at   of Ampton, marriage set-
Bury St. Edmunds.   tlement 2 Rich.II. 1484, 5.

Sir John [of Ick- = Elizabeth,	Francis	Sir Nicholas, Gentleman	Edmund = Mary, dau. of	Anthony = Lucy, dau. of	3 daughters,
worth], died July dau. of H.	[of Witham,	of the Privy Chamber	[of Elstow]. Sir Giles Went-	Humphrey	all married.
11, 1556. Pope.	Essex].	to Henry VIII.	worth.	Lisley.	

Isabel = Sir Humphrey Radcliffe, Kt.

| Thomas, died young. | Edward. | Mary. | Frances = Henry Cheek. | Elizabeth = Henry Owen. | Martha = William Gostwick. |

Sir Thomas = Essex, dau. of Richard, Earl of Warwick.

After the suppression, four of the nuns were buried in the Churchyard of the united parishes of S. Mary and S. Peter, Dunstaple, at Bedford, namely, Alis Boyvill, 16th September, 1540; Ann Preston, 7th December, 1556; Elizabeth ffox, 20th August, 1558; and Elizabeth Napton but one week later, 27th August following.

Having now witnessed the surrender of the Abbey, and the dispersion of its inmates, all that remains to be done to complete its history, *as an Abbey*, is to give as complete a list as can be compiled of the various ladies, who were from time to time called upon to preside over it. Many of these have indeed been mentioned in the course of these pages, but some have probably been omitted; and it is thought that it will be a convenience to the reader to have them here set out in a tabular form.

Before, however, proceeding to this task, it will be well to give some little further insight into the position occupied by an Abbess. The judicial powers, with which she was invested in virtue of her territorial rights, were, as we have seen [p. 103], enormous; but a mere reference to them is unsatisfactory; we want something softer, we want to know what Christian, womanly influence she was enabled to exercise over her neighbours; and if we turn to the writings of Mr. Hugo, we find there[y] an ideal sketched, which shews us what that was, so long as the religious spirit prevailed. He tells us that :—

"A Sisterhood in the mediæval ages was not so much a community rigidly excluded from the world, as

[y] Mediæval Nunneries of Somersetshire. pp. 61, 62.

one living in and leavening the world that lay around. It was a home of peace, of purity, and of refinement, where Woman could best carry out the instincts of her holier nature, and elevate the general character of her sex. Among the Sisters themselves were constantly members of the highest and noblest families; and their society, even apart from its religious elevation, was such as to command unfeigned and universal respect. Nor was there in the cloister that dreary life of forced asceticism, with which modern days have ever loved to associate it. The frequent presence of well-born guests, and the kindly intercourse maintained with the neighbourhood, combined with the hearty free-will, and in most cases deliberate choice of the life itself, united not only to endear the existence to those who took its vows upon them, but constantly to attract strangers to its fellowship. In the neighbourhood of such a Sisterhood the Nuns were well and affectionately known. They were the teachers of the female part of the population, and their presence in the houses of their pupils was by no means uncommon."

He further informs us that confinement to the Convent was one of the commonest forms of punishment for breaches of the Monastic rule; that pupils were occasionally taken to reside in the house; and that the education and training thus afforded were the best that were to be had in those days.

And when to this we add the following duties specially enjoined by the rule of the Order of S. Benedict[1]:—"to relieve the poor, to clothe the naked, to visit the sick, to bury the dead, to help those that are in tribulation, and to comfort the sad," there is enough to shew that the life of an Abbess presiding over such a community must

[1] Rule of St. Benedict. cap. iv.

have been one of very considerable dignity and utility; we are enabled to draw a very pleasing picture of Conventual life in its most perfect form, and we feel an additional interest in the names of those who held such an influential post.

Abbesses of Elstow.

1222. Mabilia.

* * * * * *

1241. Agnes of Westbury, *vice* the Lady Wymar..., deceased.
1250. Albreda de Silcampo, *vice* Agnes, resigned.

* * * * * *

1281. Beatrice of Scoteny, *vice* Anora, deceased.
1294, 26th September. Clementia of Balliol, *vice* Beatrice, deceased.

* * * * *

1315, 15th May. Joanna of Wauton.
1318, 18th November. Elizabeth Beauchamp, *vice* Joanna, deceased.
1331, 12th October. Juliana Basset, *vice* Elizabeth, deceased.
1333, 2nd October. Elizabeth Morteyn, *vice* Juliana, deceased.

* * * * * *

1392, 4th January. Margaret Pygot, *vice* Anastasia, resigned.
1409, 14th December. Joanna Trayley, *vice* Margaret, deceased.

* * * * *

1487, 23rd March. Margaret Godfrey.
1501, 5th November. Elizabeth Hervey, *vice* Margaret, deceased.
1524, 11th July. Agnes Gascoigne, a Nun of the Monastery of S. Mary de pratis, Northampton, *vice* Elizabeth, deceased.
1530, 20th July. Elizabeth Boyfeld, *vice* Agnes, deceased.

PLATE I.

TOMB OF ABBESS HERVEY.

CHRONICLES OF THE ABBEY OF ELSTOW. 147

Few of these names call for any special remark, as what we know about most of them has been already recorded, and only one will demand more than a very moderate space, but a few notes are necessary.

The name of the Abbess deceased in 1241 is uncertain. It is very indistinct in the Register, being written apparently over an erasure, and the terminal letters are so blotted as to be illegible.

Joanna of Wauton, 1315, was instituted by the Archbishop [Reynolds] of Canterbury; but why by him instead of by the Bishop of Lincoln does not appear; nor is it stated how the office became vacant. Appended to the record of her institution is her promise of Canonical obedience to the Archbishop and his successors.

Elizabeth Hervey, 1501, is probably the best known of all the Abbesses, from the fact that her tomb, with effigy in metal, is still in existence, and in a very good state of preservation, in the south aisle of Elstow Church. Of this Cole[a] gives such an excellent description that it is better to reproduce it in full than to attempt to improve upon it. It runs as follows:—

"Near the door of the south aisle, which leads into the Abbey court, lies a very large and fine black marble slab[b], having the full and large figure in brass[c], very well preserved, of an Abbess in her Benedictine

---

[a] Additional MSS. Brit. Mus. 5830. fol. 141.
[b] The slab is of Purbeck marble, and measures 8 ft. 1 in. × 3 ft. 8½ in.
[c] The metal used is Latten, or Rose metal, and it bears traces of being of foreign, probably Flemish, manufacture.

Nun's dress, and a crosier[d] in her right hand. Above her head was a religious picture[e], and, between that and her head, was a scroll of brass, with some religious address on it[f], which the squeamish stomachs of former ages would not digest, and so removed the brasses of such Popish stuff away, to sell it in good Protestant method. There were also four coats of arms, one at each corner of the stone, but time has wasted the three first, and that at the last corner by her left foot only remains, and has these arms still remaining, though much defaced:—Party per pale, Baron and Femme. Quarterly, 1st and 4th a lion rampant, 2nd and 3rd a bend, and on it something indistinct[g], impaling a chief dancetté. If the first two quarterings were the arms of the Abbey, as I have a great opinion they were, though I know not what Countess Judith or her husband bore[h], then the impaled coat is the paternal one of the Abbess; as I find by a curious MS. of Heraldry, copied by me from the original, that the arms given by some of the name of Hervey, or Harvey, of Little Bradley in Suffolk, are thus blazoned:—party per fesse, indented or and gules, which is as near the same arms on this tomb as possible, without being the same, especially as the chief and party per fesse are often confused and taken the one for the other. Besides, the famous Dr. William Harvey, of Hempsted in Essex, gave for their arms on a chief indented sable, three crescents argent, which are the very same arms, bating the crescents added on the chief. So that I have no

---

[d] This would be more properly described as a pastoral staff.

[e] Probably the Holy Trinity, an emblem specially hated by the Puritans.

[f] Such as "Domine miserere mei." Lord have mercy on me.

[g] Probably the Hervey trefoils. Bedford and Neighbourhood. Cary Elwes, p. 75.

[h] Cole forgets what he states later, that the arms of Waltheof were argent, a lion rampant, az. a chief gules.

doubt but that they were designed for the Abbey arms, impaling those of the Lady Abbess. The others that are lost were probably, the first the same as those that are left, and the two others the Abbey arms and her own singly.

"On the brass fillet which surrounds the whole is the inscription, quite perfect as it was laid down, except the dates, which were never filled in, and shew that it was provided by the good Abbess before her death, and that her pious executors never troubled themselves to have them put down."

The inscription was as follows, the parts now wanting being distinguished by inclosure within brackets :—

✠ Orate pro Anima domine Elza[beth][i] Hervy quondam Abbatisse Monasterij de Elnestow que obijt ―― die mensis ―― Anno Domini millesimo quingentesimo ―― Cuius Anime et omniu fidelium defunctorum De[us propici]etur. A. M. E. N.

"Pray ye for the Soul of the lady Elizabeth Hervey, formerly Abbess of the Monastery of Elstow, who died the ―― day of the month of ―― A.D. 15—. To whose soul, and to those of all the faithful departed, may God be gracious. Amen."

Some doubt has been entertained as to who this lady was, but it seems pretty certain she was the daughter of John Hervey of Thurleigh, and Joan, daughter and co-heiress of Sir John Niernuyt of Burnham, Co. Bucks[j], although, if

---

[i] It will be observed that a few letters are introduced here which are not to be found on the plate. This is to be accounted for by the fact that the part of the fillet containing them, being loose, is preserved in the vestry, and evidently had not been put into its place when the rubbing was taken.

[j] See Pedigree, p. 143.

so, she must have been of a great age when she died.

Between Agnes Gascoigne, 1524, and Elizabeth Boyfeld, 1530, Cole mentions Elizabeth Starkey, otherwise Cecily Speckey, as having held office for one year, and resigned in favour of the latter, but this cannot be confirmed from any other source. In fact, the only evidence that has been found is against it, as the Lincoln Registers shew that Abbess Boyfeld's election, held *on the death of Agnes Gascoigne*, was not unanimous, some votes being given to "Cecilia Starkey," [who is described as "Sexten" in the list of Nuns pensioned]; and from this it may be concluded the mistake arose.

It is worthy of remark that, in the record of both these last institutions, the King is described as Patron and "Founder" of the Abbey; though on what his claim to the latter title could be based, unless it be the Confirmation Roll of 1510, it is difficult to say; and, appended to that relating to Elizabeth Boyfeld, is an injunction prohibiting the alienation of valuables of the Monastery, the grant under its common seal of fees, annuities or corrodies[k], or of leases of its lands or possessions for a longer term than twenty-eight years, without the special licence of the said King and Father.

Here also it will be well to give a list of the Clerks, who were instituted to benefices in Elstow Church, on the presentation of the Abbess and Convent. It is not indeed likely that the names will in themselves be of any great interest, but

[k] Corrodies. Allowance of food or clothing.

the succession will throw some considerable light on the vexed question respecting the Chantries, to which allusion has been already made.

INSTITUTIONS OF CLERKS TO ELSTOW.

1223. Ralph of Wescham to *Prebend* of Elstow.
1235. Edmund of Wescham to the same, *vice Roger* of Wescham.
  „   Alexander of Elstow to a moiety of the Church, *vice* Simon of Elstow.
1248. John of Elstow to the same, *vice* Alexander.
1259. John of   to the same, *vice* Hamo.
1272, 16th May. Thomas of Hiche to a newly founded Chantry in the Church, through John, Rector of a moiety thereof.
1273, 21st March. Edward Scot to a moiety of the Church, *vice* Richard of Galeford, deceased.
1284. Robert of Oelye to a moiety of the Church, *vice* John of Darton.
1305, 3rd November. John of Keten to the Chantry, *vice* John of Darton, deceased.
1310, 22nd June. Walter of Lubbenham to the same, *vice* John of K., resigned.
1324, 1st August. John of Felmersham to a moiety of the Church.
1335, 24th June. Robert le Spicer, of Farendon, to a moiety of the Church, *vice* William of Tickhill.
1337, 27th March. The aforesaid Robert is permitted to exchange with Hugh of Estmarcham, Rector of Bradested, dioc. Roffen, who is instituted in his place.
1338, 12th October. Adam of Brandon to a moiety of the Church, *vice* Hugh, resigned.
1340, 7th December. Nicholas of Holkham to the same, *vice* Adam, resigned.
1341, 26th December. Robert de la Seche to the same, *vice* John Sacheler.

1348, 15th June. John Message of Elstow to the newly founded Chantry of Thomas atte Brugge.

1349, 10th January. The same John to the Chantry of Elstow *juxta pontem* [by the bridge].

1350, 3rd November. The same John to a Chantry, *vice* Robert [1], deceased.

1382, 28th September. William Broke to the Chantry of Elstow *juxta pontem*.

1390, 6th August. John Wrottyng[m] to the same, *vice* Broke, deceased.

1404, 6th October. John Whyte to a Chantry, *vice* Wrottyng, resigned.

1419, 24th May. William Salkire to the Chantry of Elstow *juxta pontem*, *vice* Whyte, deceased.

1456, 2nd January. Henry Lewy to the same, *vice* Richard Hyndman, resigned.

1460, 20th September. Richard Hyndman to the same, *vice* William Wryth, deceased.

1462, 25th September. William Shore to the same, *vice* Lewy, resigned.

1468, 6th April. James Multra to the same, *vice* William Purdon, resigned.

1477, 20th December. William Stokys to the same, *vice* Multra, deceased.

1480, 18th February. Laurence Crowder[n] to the same, *vice* Stokes, deceased.

1486, 4th November. John ffauler to a Chantry in the *Parish* Church of Elstow, *vice* Crowder, resigned.

---

[1] Probably Robert de la Seche, instituted to a moiety of the Church, 1341, as he most likely received a Chantry in compensation for that, when it was bestowed on the Abbey. [p. 109.]

[m] The Bishop [Buckingham] seems to have been in doubt as to Wrottyng's character and due ordination, as he commissioned the Prior of Caldwell to enquire into these points, and report to him, before proceeding to institution.

[n] In this case the Bishop presented, so that probably the Abbey was vacant, but of this no record has been found.

1501, 20th December. William Kirkby to the same, *vice* Hynde [alias ffowler] deceased.

1503, 2nd November. Thomas Hume to the same, *vice* Kyrkby, deceased.

1504, 2nd August. Alexander Symson to the same, *vice* Hume, *bachelor of laws*, resigned.

1508, 17th May. Robert Watson to the same, *vice* Symson, resigned.

1517, 28th August. Richard White to the same, *vice* Watsley, resigned.

1526, 20th November. Henry Ashton to a Chantry in the *Conventual* Church of Elstow, *vice* White, resigned.

From the foregoing it seems at first well-nigh impossible to produce anything like a satisfactory account of the Chantries, but it is believed that a key to the difficulty is to be found in the institutions of John Message, 1348—50. It will be observed that he was presented, first to the Chantry of T. atte Brugge, then six months later to that of Elstow *juxta pontem*, and finally to the earlier one, vacant by the decease of Robert; the explanation of which seems to be that his second institution was probably rendered necessary through this Chantry having received some additional endowment, and a name, though of this there is no record extant; and that on the other falling vacant, the two were merged, and from that time forward held by the same man. This is, of course, only conjecture, but the subsequent institutions tend to confirm it, as we find no further trace of a second Chantry, and it was evidently that of Elstow *juxta pontem* which survived until the dissolution.

It may be of interest to mention here that the

last act of patronage, recorded as exercised by the Abbess and Convent of Elstow, was a presentation to the Rectory of Kempston, 8th May, 1535.

After this digression we return once more to the history of the Abbey, in which we shall speedily be involved in an entirely new phase of affairs; as, instead of having to deal with the fortunes of the Abbess and Nuns, our task will be to trace out, as far as may be, the fate of the property which they formerly held, and especially that of the Conventual buildings and demesne land at Elstow.

It will be remembered that it has been mentioned that, just prior to the dissolution, leases were granted of certain parts of the Abbey property; and whether with, or without, the royal licence, required by the last clause of the record of Abbess Boyfeld's institution, we have no means of determining. At any rate three were completed, each for a long term of years, and it is a significant fact, or sign of the times, that in every case the term was made to commence either at or after the date at which the Abbey was suppressed. Coming events were evidently casting their shadows before, and though no fine is mentioned as having been taken at the time when the leases were granted, there can be little doubt that they were not given for nothing.

Thus, on 1st October, 1533, a lease° was granted to Sir John and Lady Mordaunt of certain lands, tenements, rents, and tithes at Moulsoe

° Exchequer Q. R. Memoranda Roll. Hilary. 36 Elizabeth. Ro. 192.

for a term of sixty years, commencing at the feast of St. Michael the Archangel, 1539, at an annual rent of £2 13s. 7d.

Another[p], 22nd September, 1537, to Francis Morgan, gentleman, of Maulden, of certain lands belonging to the manor of that place, for a term of forty years, from the feast of St. Michael the Archangel, 1541, at a rent of £2 16s. 8d.

A third[q], 13th January, 1539, to George Carleton, gentleman, of the Parsonage, Rectory, and tithes of Kempston, with appurtenances, for a term of ninety-nine years, from the feast of St. Michael the Archangel then last past, at a rent of £20.

At this point, although in so doing it becomes necessary to encroach somewhat on the records of subsequent years, it seems better to follow out at once the fate of these leases, than to leave them to be dealt with later on, when other matters are calling for attention, and the following particulars are forthcoming :—

The first-mentioned of them was terminated 20th June, 1548, by a composition[r] entered into by the Court of Augmentation of the revenues of the Crown, by which it was decreed that certain rents arising out of the Moulsoe property should be paid to John, Lord Mordaunt, or his heirs, annually, until the expiration of the term of sixty years. The rents thus allotted amount-

[p] Augmentation, Miscellaneous Books, vol. 101. Fol. 104 d. 33 Henry VIII.

[q] Augmentation Office, Conventual Leases. Bedford, No. 12.

[r] Augmentation Office, Decrees, vol. 15, fol. 50 b. 2 Edward VI.

ed in all to 21s. 6d., and as the names of the fields, on which the different sums, of which this was made up, were charged, may be of interest to present inhabitants of the place, it will be as well to give them. On Bolyons was charged 18s., on a close of pasture called Rolls, 8d., on another close or parcel of ground called Paynes, 13d., on one messuage and a close called Cesses, 9d., and on one other messuage and certain lands called Bakers, 12d.

The second, which included various fields at Maulden, known by the names Wheatcroft, Woodmerles, Thorowberd, Halescroft, Buryfield, Combesfield, Mancelfield, and 'Amery, was confirmed* to Francis Morgan, by a decree of the Augmentation Court, 24th February, 1542.

Of the third there is no certain information, but it would seem to have been terminated very speedily, as the property demised thereby forms a part of that leased by the crown to Edmund Hervey of Elstow, 1541.

By the terms of this lease the advowsons of the churches of Elstow, Kempston, and Willshamstead were specially reserved, as also all timber growing upon the estate; and the King further evidently retained all the manorial rights, as the Court Rolls of the manor of Elstow from 33 Henry VIII. to 1 Edward VI. (with the exception of that of 35 Henry VIII., which is missing) are preserved in the Public Record Office, nor was it till 7 Edward VI., 1553, that the manor passed into other hands.

* Augmentation, Miscellaneous Books, vol. 101, fol. 104 d.

In relation to this lease there are two deeds extant, the valuation[t] made prior to granting it, and the lease[u] itself, both of which are most interesting from the particulars which they furnish of the property demised; but, as they are nearly identical in terms, it will suffice to give the former at length :—

THE Demaynes of the late Mon'y of Elnestowe wythin the County of Bedd' :—

The Scyte of the howse there.	FFIRST the scyte of the same howse, with barnes, stabulle, curtilage, Dovehowses, howses of office, Curcheyerd, Orcharde, Gardeyns, and other grounde lyinge wythin the precincte of the same, are estemed to be worthe by the yere . .	xl^s
Arrable grou'd.	ITEM in Bedd'ford' hole xij acr', It'm Nunesgore cont' v acr', It'm A pece next the same content' xij acr', It'm in Romere viij acr', It'm a pece next Potton Bawke content' v acr', It'm a pece next Wests content' xvj acr', It'm A pece next the gravell pytts content v acr', It'm in barne brede xiiij acr', It'm the bake howse croft ix acr', It'm A pece next the same cont' ix acr', It'm an other pece abbuttynge on the clay pytts cont' xxij acr', It'm in the same ffurlonge xij acr', It'm adioynynge to the same xvj acr', It'm an other pece adioynynge to the same x acr', It'm a pece next pep' balke cont' vij acr', It'm in sowthe brede viij acr', It'm a pece called Presswell cont' xxvj acr', It'm in brakdyche xiij acr', It'm an other p'cell called ba^{r}ne brede ix acr', It'm in galow Pece x acr'.	
	IN TOTO—ccxxviij acr' at vj^d the Acre . .	cxiiij^s
Pasture Ground.	IT'M the barne Brede vj acr', It'm the Cony'gre cont' viij acr', It'm a close called Mosseclose cont' viij acr', It'm a close called Kow pasture cont' vj acr' ev'y thyrd yere com̄en.	
	IN TOTO xxviij acr' at xij^d the Acr' . .	xxviij^s

[t] Augmentation Office, Miscellaneous Books, No. 402, fol. 7.
[u] Ibid. vol. 213, fol. 69.

Medow ground.	It'm East Mead cont' xvj acr', It'm the West Mead conteynyng xxiiij acr', It'm in a Mead called P'eswell vj acr'.	
	In toto xlvj acr' at ij^s iiij^d the Acr'	cvij^s iiij^d
The personag' of Willesh^{a}msted'.	It'm the p'sonage of Willesh^{a}mstede, Wyth all maner of tythes, oblac'ons, obvenc'ons, and other commodit' and adv^{a}ntags belonging to the same, ys estemed yerly to be Worth	viij^{li}
Pasture ground in Willesh^{a}msted'.	It'm a Close called Vicares Close cont' xj acr', It'm a Close called Cowe pasture cont' c acr', It'm a Close called Guldyngton feld' cont' xxx acr', Item a feld called Newfeld' cont' xl acr'.	
	In tot' ciiij^{xx}j ac'r at xij^d the Acr'	ix^{li} xij^d
Medowe ground in Willesh^{a}msted'.	It'm a Close called the highfeld cont' iiij^{xx} acr' at viij^d the Ac'r	liij^s iiij^d
Medowe grounde in Willesh^{a}msted'.	It'm a Close called Crosse Meade cont' x acr' at ij^s the Acr'	xx^s
Kempston Mill.	It'm the Watermylles lying & beinge in Kempston, & the howses that they stand & be in, Wyth ther appurt', in the tenur' of Will'm Heyes, by Indentur' Dated vnder the Convent seale of the seyde late Mon'y the iiijth Daye of August, in the xxvij yere of the Reygne of o' soverayne lorde Kyng Henry the viijth, yeldynge therfore yerly	viij^{li}
The p'sonage Elnestow.	It'm the seyd p'sonage of Elnestowe, wyth all [and] sing'ler Tythes, oblac'ons, obvenc', and other commodyts & adv'ags what so ev' they be, to the seyd p'sonag' belongyng, is estemed to be worth	xiij^{li} vj^s viij^d
The pfytte of the fayre.	It'm the pfytte cōmyng, risyng, and growyng of the fayre there yerly holden & kept, ys estemed to be worth co'ibz annis	vj^{li} xiij^s iiij^d
The tythes of the Demay's.	It'm the tythes of the p'miss', wyth the tythes of Demaynes of Wyllysh^{a}msted', are worth yerly	liiij^s ij^d
	Sm^a Tot'lis of the sayde pticul[e]rs ys .	lxv^{li} xvij^s x^d

Ex p' me Gregoriū Richardsone, Deput' Will'mi
Cavendissh, Audit' ib'm.

[Order for demise to Edmund Harvy.]

It will be observed that this document is undated, but as the lease, which was for the term of twenty-one years from the Feast of S. Michael the Archangel last past, bears date 10th March, 32 Henry VIII. [1541], it is easy to place it in either the beginning of that, or the end of the preceding year. The rent reserved by the lease, £77 17s. 10d., exceeds the amount of the valuation by £12, but this is accounted for by the fact that the former includes the Rectory of Kempston, valued at £20, whereas the latter deals with the water-mills of the same place valued at £8.

To print the Court Rolls above mentioned in full would occupy too much space, and it is thought that it will be sufficient to give the first only, and that for the double reason, that in the first place, it is the most interesting of all, as furnishing the date of the death of a Bonyon, probably an ancestor of John Bunyan; and in the second, the others are of an exactly similar character. It may, however, be mentioned that, in almost every one of the later rolls, the wife of Thomas Bonyon is fined for infringement of the assize of either bread or beer. The first roll[1] is as follows:—

Elnestowe. "View of frank pledge before the court of the most excellent Prince the Lord HENRY VIII., by the grace of God, King of England, France, and Ireland, Defender of the Faith, and upon earth supreme Head of the Church of England and Ireland, there held the xiijth day of the month of April, in the year of his reign, after his accession, the thirty-third [1541].

[1] Exchequer. Court of Augmentations. Court Rolls. Portfolio 11, No. 21. Bedfordshire.

160 CHRONICLES OF THE ABBEY OF ELSTOW.

Essoiners[1]. "Thomas Whytebred, by Master Ard, Stephen Estwyk, by [his] bailiff.

Homagers. William Jurden, Gent. ⎫
William Corteys. ⎬ Jurors.
William Ballard. ⎭

William Yonge. ⎫
Thomas Colsell. ⎬ Jurors.
William Wolmer, sen. ⎭

William Tyte. ⎫
Robert Thorpe. ⎬ Jurors.
Thomas Bonyon. ⎭

John Goughge. ⎫
William Denott. ⎬ Jurors.
John Ry. ⎭

Suitors. "The Jurors present that Lord Mordaunt; John $iiij^d$ appeared Gascoign, Knight; Thomas Spencer, Gent.; George sick appeared Mayotte, Clerk; Thomas Harward, Clerk; Thomas appeared Blakysley, Clerk, owe suit to the court, and have made default, thereby incurring a fine.

Constables there. "William Heyes and John Goughge. Jurors present all well.

Bakers and Brewers. "They also present that Robert $iiij^d$ Thorpe, Robert $iiij^d$ Leed, and Nicholas $iiij^d$ Cowper, are common bakers of bread, and have infringed the assize, thereby incurring a fine. And that the wife of William ij^d Corteys, the wife of Robert j^d Thorpe, the wife of Thomas ij^d Sharpe, the wife of William j^d Dale, and Robert ij^d Wyllyamson, are common brewers of beer, and have infringed the assize, thereby incurring a fine.

Recognizances. "To this court came Henry Ballard and Elizabeth his wife, and did fealty, and were admitted tenants in fee of the lord King, by fealty, suit of court, and at the yearly rent of fourpence, of one tenement with appurtenances, situated in Elnestow, bounded by the tenement of William Roberd on the north side, and the tenement of Richard Gatys on the south side, and abutting towards the east on the King's highway,

[1] Essoiners. Those who made excuse for non-attendance.

which same tenement the same Henry and Elizabeth held to themselves, their heirs and assigns for ever by gift, grant, and deed of confirmation of William Ecop, the younger, as more fully appears by a certain deed of the same William thereupon executed to them, the date whereof is the xxixth day of November in the aforesaid xxxiij^d year of the present lord King [1540].

Relief. iij^s o½^d.

"At this court it is testified by the homagers that William Bonyon, who held of the lord King, as of his manor of Elnestow, one messuage, and one pightell, with appurtenances, in Elnestow, and nine acres of land lying singly and separately in the fields of Elnestow by fealty, suit of court, and at the yearly rent of three shillings and one halfpenny, has, since the date of the last court, ended his days; And that Thomas Bonyon is the son and next heir of the said William Bonyon, and is of the age of forty years and more, whence there accrues to the lord King as a relief in soccage iij^s o½^d. And the said Thomas Bonyon is admitted as tenant in fee of the aforesaid messuage, pightell and nine acres of land at the rent and services aforesaid, and that the aforesaid messuage and pightell are situated and lie in Elnestow aforesaid, bounded by the messuage and close of Thomas Whytebred on the western side, and the King's highway there on the eastern.

"They also present that John Carter keeps ten sheep above the number appointed to him, contrary to the order formerly made in that behalf. Whereby, &c., viij^d.

"And that John Gatys keeps xvj sheep above the number limited and appointed to him, contrary to the order in that behalf made and provided. Whereby, &c., xij^d.

Fines.

"And further they present that Thomas ^{ij^d} Lovell, Thomas ^{iiij^d} Kent, Agnes ^{iiij^d} Vanne, William ^{ij^d} Dale, and John ^{iiij^d} Carter have incurred fines for keeping more animals than they ought to keep according to their tenures, contrary to the order from olden time established. Whereby, &c.

Constables.

"Thomas Clowley and John May were elected to the office of Constables and Jurors.

{ Amercements ij^s iij^d. attested William Corteys. } Jurors.
{ Relief   iij^s o$\frac{1}{2}^d$. by Thomas Colsell. }

"Total of amercements and other perquisites viij^s iiij$\frac{1}{2}^d$.

"Whence the fines were iij^s.

In addition to the pensions allotted to the nuns, certain other annuities, chargeable on the estates of the Abbey, were about this time granted by the Court of Augmentation [1] to various persons, in lieu of the emoluments of the offices which they had held, or of pensions for the services which they had rendered.

Thus, to Sir Francis Bryan, chief steward of the Abbey manors, was granted [a], 11th February, 1540, the pay of four marks per annum, assigned to him by the Abbey when he was appointed to office, vice Sir Henry Grey, deceased.

On 5th June, in the same year, Thomas Buckland received a grant [b] of £1 13s. 4d. per annum, in compensation for £1 6s. 8d. pay, 6s. 8d. for a gown or livery, with lodging, meat and drink, secured to him by deed under the Abbey seal, dated 11th April, 1538, for true and faithful service rendered.

---

[1] A court established 1535, mainly for the purpose of dealing with the property of the dissolved monasteries, annexed to the Exchequer, 1554.

[a] Augmentation Office. Miscellaneous Books. No. 94. fol. 213 b.

[b] Augmentation Decrees. v. 225.

On 6th July following a decree[c] passed the Court, allowing an annuity of 40s. out of the manor of Harringworth, co. Northampton, to John Harnyngton and John Markham, a pension of that amount having been assigned to them by the Abbess and Convent 1st October, 1537, though in consideration of what services it is not stated.

On the 10th of the same month an order[d] was issued for the annual payment of £2 0s. 6d. to the Archdeacon of Bedford, for procurations and synodals for the parishes of Elstow, Kempston, Willshamstead, Flitton, and Westoning, with arrears from the date of the dissolution.

On 26th January, 1542, an annuity of £2, chargeable on the manors of Elstow, Kempston, Willshamstead, and Maulden, which had been granted by the Abbess to Edmund Harvey, "for his good and faithful counsel to us given," 21st December, 1538, was confirmed[e] to him by the Court; and shortly afterwards sundry decrees were issued, restoring to certain Vicars the stipends, with arrears, which they had formerly received from the Abbey, in the following amounts :—

	£	s.	d.
To the Vicar of Wymondley, 20th June, 1542[f]	4	0	0
To the Vicar of Flitton, 4th November, 1542[g]	2	0	0

[c] Augmentation Office. Miscellaneous Books. No. 95. fol. 226.

[d] Augmentation Decrees. v. 152 b.

[e] Augmentation Office. Miscellaneous Books. No. 101. fol. 42 d.

[f] Augmentation Decrees. xii. 178 b.

[g] Ibid. xiii. 72.

	£	s.	d.
To the Vicar of Westoning, 23rd January, 1543[a]	2	6	8

these sums, as well as the amount of the fee of the chief Steward, agreeing exactly with those given in the *Valor Ecclesiasticus*.

We now come to the last of the great valuations, namely the *Computus Ministrorum*, which contains the Ministers' accounts of the Rents, Profits, and Revenues arising from the Honors, Manors, Rectories, &c., which came to the Crown on the dissolution of Religious houses. These accounts were compiled 34 Henry VIII., and the property of the Abbey was assessed as under:—

ABBEY OF ELNESTOWE.

Co. Bedf. § 3, &c. Elstow; § 2, &c. Willshamstead; § 13, &c. Kempston; § 36, Harrowden, and § 85, Fenlake; § 89, Wilden; § 90, Cotton; § 86, Houghton, and § 6, Moulsoe. } Land and Tenements. { Not reckoned, because annexed to the Honor of Ampthill.

£ s. d.

Co. Hertf. § 4. Hitchin. Rectory . . . .
§ 91. Welbury in the Parish of Offley. Rectory and Tithe . . . .
§ 4. Hitchin, Wymondley, and S. Ippolyts. Land, &c. . . . .
§ 4. Hitchin. Payment from Church ,
§ 61. King's Walden. Payment from Church . . . . .
§ 4. Hitchin, S. Ippolyts and Wymondley. Advowson of Churches . . .
} 66 16 8

[a] Augmentation Decrees. xiii. 129 b.

		£	s.	d.
Co. Oxon.	§ 53. Clanfield. Rectory	5	6	8
Co. Northt.	§ 68. Wilbarston. Rectory	6	13	4
Co. Bedf.	§ 79. Westoning. Rectory	11	0	0
	§ 67. Flitton and Silshoe. Rectory	15	6	8
	§ 42. Barford. Rent of Assize	0	1	0
Co. Hunt.	§ 40. Buckden. Tithe of Mills	0	10	0
Co. Bedf.	§ 82. Gravenhurst. Portion of Tithe	0	6	8
Co. Northt.	§ 83. Irkhamstede. Rent	0	6	8
	§ 21. Braunston. Portion of Tithe	1	0	0
Co. Oxon.	§§ 29, 30. Shutford and Great Barton. Tenements and Tithe	2	13	4
Co. Glouc.	§ 84. Stonehouse. Vicar's payment	6	0	0
Co. Hertf.	§ 4. Hitchin. Payment	2	13	4
Co. Essex.	§ 54. Inworth. Rector's payment	1	6	8
Co. Northt.	§ 49. Harringworth. Rectory	14	0	0
	§ 88. Walpole. Land	2	6	8
Co. Hertf.	§ 61. King's Walden. Portion of Tithe	1	0	0
Co. Bedf.	§ 92. Gravenhurst Magna. Portion of Tithe	1	2	0
	§ 13. Kempston Bourn. Rent of Assize	1	0	0
	§§ 15, 16. Town of Bedford. Land	4	3	0
Co. Leic.	§ 8. Arnesby. Rent of Assize	1	13	4
Co. Linc.	§§ 26, 93. Croft and Friskney. Rent of Assize	0	18	4
Co. Bedf.	§§ 33, 77. Wymington and Bromham. Tenements	0	6	0
	§ 94. King's mead. Meadow	0	10	0
	§ 14. Sibell. Land and Tenements	0	10	9
	§§ 1, 67. Maulden and Flitton. Rent and Farm	not reckoned		
	§ 3. Elstow. Site of Monastery, with demesne land	77	17	10
	§ 17. Kempston. Water-Mills	8	0	0

Few of the properties[1] here mentioned call for

[1] For convenience of reference, the modern spelling of names has been adopted both here and in the *Valor Ecclesiasticus*.

much remark, and unfortunately very little has been ascertained about those that do.

§§ 36, 85, 90. Harrowden and Fenlake. With these we find associated the name Cotton, doubtless Cotton-End, in the same parish, Cardington.

§ 89. Wilden, four miles north-east of Bedford, appears for the first time, unless, as is possible, it be an error for Yelden, § 57.

§ 91. Offley lies three miles south-west of Hitchin. Judging from the position in which it occurs in this record, it was probably appurtenent thereto, and included like Wymondley and Preston in the original gift of that place. S. Ippolyts and Wymondley are united parishes.

§ 92. This is the first mention of property in Gravenhurst Magna.

§§ 26, 93. With Croft we now find coupled the name Friskney, which is that of a neighbouring village, but as this property was much scattered, it is by no means certain that the latter name indicates a new acquisition.

§ 94. The King's Mead is an island, of between fifteen and twenty acres, inclosed by two branches of the river Ouse, which separates just below Cardington Mills, and unites again about half-a-mile lower down. There is a local tradition that it was given to the Abbey by King John. After the dissolution it appears to have passed to the Burgesses of Bedford, from whom it was purchased by Mr. Whitbread.

§ 14. Sibell, see p. 34.

On comparing this valuation generally with the *Valor Ecclesiasticus*, it will be found that many of the properties named are assessed at exactly the same value, and where there is a difference, the later record, in almost every instance, puts on a higher estimate.

The last records belonging to this reign, which come to light, are two Chantry Certificates, the former being apparently an amended valuation thereof, while the latter would seem to indicate that its property had entirely disappeared. This, however, we shall find from a similar document, issued only two years later, was not the case, and we shall further learn in what its property consisted, and upon whom it was bestowed.

CHANTRY CERTIFICATE (BEDFORDSHIRE), NO. 1.

"Commission for cos. Bucks and Beds,
    dated 14 February, 37 Henry VIII. [1546].

"The parishe of Elstowe

"The chauntrie of sayncte Elene in the said p'ishe fownded

"To fynde a prieste for ev^r to synge masse in the chapell of sayncte Elene w^{t}in the same churche

"The said chauntrye is fownded w^{t}in the p'ishe churche of Elstowe aforesaid And thincombente that was laste is deceased. And the Baylyff there is Co'maunded to Receive the Revenneu therof to o^r sov'eigne lorde the kings vse: vntill his ma^{ties} pleasure be further signyfied and knowne in that behalfe. And there is cccxx^{te} houslinge people in the said p'ishe. And there is A Vicare to mynist^r to the said p'ishe

"The said Chauntrye is of the yearlye
    value of . . . . . .   ciiij^s
                                              whereof
Paied to the kings ma^{tie} for quyte Rents⎫
    xxii^s . . . .⎬xxxj^s x$\frac{1}{4}$^{d}
Tenths ix^s x$\frac{1}{4}$^{d} . . . . .⎭

And so Remayneth to thuse of the laste Incombente . . . . . } lxxjˢ j¼ᵈ

Theire app'teynethe to the said chᵃuntrye neither Goods Catalls ornaments ne Juells. As it is c'tefied to the Co'myss. . . . . . . }

"There hathe bene no dissolucyon purchace or obteignynge of anye Possessiones or Goods of the said chᵃuntrie or chapell sithe the fourthe of februarye in the xxvij^th yere of the Kyngs maᵗⁱᵉˢ Reigne aforesaid. And it is to be noted that the said chauntrye was valued to mooche in the booke of Tenthes by xvijˢ."

CHANTRY CERTIFICATE (BEDFORDSHIRE), NO. 2.

"The booke of the pencyons in Bedf'shyre.

"The Countye of Bedforde

"A brevyate p'ticulerly declaring the names of all the late collegis chauntries ffraternities Brotherhedds Guyldes ffrechapells and suche others in the Countye abovesayd wᵗʰ the yerely values of ev'ry of theym and the names of the Maysters Wardens and Incumbents of the sayd Collegs & the others and what ev'ry of theym hath in lyveng out of the same and what scoles preachers & poore folke have ben found kept & relyved of the p'miss

The chantry of Saynt Elen in the p'ishe of Elvestowe above all the deduccons is worth by yere . . . . . }

Prieste is there none resydent
Gramʳ scole kepte
Preacher mayntened } none
Poore people releved

[In another hand] penc'—nⁱ."

REIGN OF EDWARD VI., 1547—53.

The records of this reign open most conveniently with a continuation of the subject last treated in the preceding one, namely the history of the Chantry, the very first document, which has been found, being a detailed valuation[j] thereof, made under a Commission dated 14th February, 2 Edward VI. [1548], and which is hereunder transcribed:—

"The Ch^auntry of Elnestowe

"The landes and tent' to the said Chauntry belongyng valued in

The ferme of a mesuage one pightell[k] iiij acres of medowe ij closses of pasture and lxx acr' of arable land wth thap'ten'nc' in Elvestowe in the tenure of John Walton by yere at the feast' of the anuncyacyon of o^r lady and saynt Mighell tharch^aungell by even porcyons . . . . . . lxxiij^s iiij^d

The ferme of one cotage there in the tenure of Nicholas Diccons by yere as is abovesaid   iiij^s

The ferme of a Pightell there in the tenure of Will^am Ballard by yere as is abovesaid   v^s iiij^d   } cj^s iiij^d

The ferme of certen land' there in the tenure of John Page by yere as is abovesaid   iij^s iiij^d

The ferme of certen other land' there in the tenure of John Wyld by yere as is abovesaid . . . . . . xv^d

The ferme of one toft & a Garden wth ij lyttle closses of pasture in the tenure of Will^am Swymowe by yere as is abovesaid . . xiiij^s

Repris'

In rente resolute to o^r sov'eyn lord the Kyng as to the late monastery of Elvestowe by yere   } x^s xij^s

And so remayneth clere by the yere . lxxix^s iij^d

Plate good' & ornament' belongyng to the sayd Chauntry . . . . n^l

M^d that the said Chauntry is ffounded wthin the p'ishe

---

[j] Chantry Certificate [Bedfordshire].   2 Edward VI.
[k] Pightell. Any small enclosure of land.

churche of Elvestowe for a prest to syng w^{thin} a chapell of S. Elen' in the sayd [church] as it is said THE ffoundacyon whereof can not be ffound or sene because the same remayned amongest the record' of the late Monastery of Elvestowe IT'M there is in the said p'ishe of Elvestowe iij°xx^{ti} houselyng people IT'M there hath no Gram' scole nor preacher ben kept there syns the ffeast of saynt Mighell tharch-aungel last past IT'M there hath no money nor other p'fett ben payd to any poore p'son out of the sayd Chauntry at any tyme w^{thin} theise vj yeres entended to have contynuaunce for ev' ALSO there is no Incumbent there."

In the month of December in the same year occurs another valuation[1] of the property of the Chantry, apparently taken on the occasion of its being leased to one Thomas Robinson, one of the ministers of the King's bedchamber. The first part of it is identical in terms with that just recited, but the last item, the garden, &c., is omitted, whereby the value is reduced to £4 7s. 3d. At the foot is appended :—

"In rent resolute to the Lord King as of his manor of Elvestowe for ten years . . . nothing
And there remains clear by the year . £4 7 3
My Lord protector's grace's pleasure is that Thomas Robinson shall have in ferme the premisses and therefore commandeth that a leas be made to hym of the same under the seale of the Augmentation Courte for terme of xxj yeres yelding to the Kinge's Majestie the saide yerely rent according to such order as other leases use to passe in the same Courte."

This is dated 5th December, 2 Edward VI. Included in the same document with the first

[1] Harleian MSS. Brit. Mus. No. 605, 79 b.

named of these valuations of the Chantry is the record of certain other property [§ 94], which had been given to the Abbey for another purpose, namely for the sustentation of an *obit*ᵐ and lamp. Nothing has been found to shew what became of this endowment, which, as will be seen, was of comparatively little value :—

OBYTE and LAMPE in Elvestowe valued in

THE FERME of one closse and iij acr' of land wᵗʰ the app'tenᵃnc' in the tenure of Thomas Monke gyven for the sustentacon of an obyte by yere at the fest' of the anuncyacon of oʳ lady and Saynt Mighell tharchᵃungell by even porcyons . . viijˢ iiijᵈ

THE FERME of xj acr' and iij rod' of land in the tenure of the Churchwardens there gyven for an obyte by yere as is abovesaid . . . . . . vijˢ ixᵈ

} xxiijˢ iijᵈ

THE FERME of one rode of Medowe in the tenure of the said Wardens gyven to the sustentacyon of a lampe by yere as is abovesaid . . . . . . vjᵈ

THE FERME of Dyv's others p'cells of land in the tenure of the said Churchwardens gyven for an obyte by yere as is abovesaid . . . . . . vjˢ viijᵈ

REPRISES.

IN RENTE RESOLUTE to oʳ sov'ein lord the Kyng as to his man' of Elvestowe by yere . . . . . . xviijᵈ

} iijˢ v½ᵈ

RENT RESOLUTE to Sʳ John Gascoyn Knyght by yere . . . . . xxiijᵈ ob

AND SO REMAYNETH clere by the yere . xixˢ ix½ᵈ

Following upon these documents, at an interval of five years, we come upon a grant, by the Crown,

---

ᵐ Obit. A funeral service held on the anniversary of a death.

of the demesne land of the Abbey, and adjacent property to a large extent, to Sir Humphrey Radcliffe. What the property consisted of, and by what tenure it was to be held is fully set forth in the Patent[a] granting it, which is hereunto annexed :—

"Grant to Sir HUMFRY RADCLYFF, Knight.

"THE KING, &c. to all to whom, &c. greeting. Know ye that we, as much in consideration of good true and faithful service, by our beloved and faithful servant HUMFRY RADCLYFF, Knight, to us heretofore done and rendered, as for other reasonable causes and considerations, specially moving us to the presents, of our special grace, and from our certain knowledge, and mere motion, have given and granted, and, by the presents, do give and grant to the aforenamed Humfry Radclyff, Knight;

"THE whole demesne and site of the late Monastery or Abbey of Elnestowe, in our County of Bedford, dissolved, and all houses, edifices, barns, gardens, orchards, pleasure grounds, dovecotes, curtilage, cemetery, land and soil, and other our hereditaments whatsoever, being within the site and precinct of the said late Monastery or Abbey. Likewise all those our lands containing by estimation xij acres, with appurtenances, in the field called Bedforde Hole; And all those our lands, with appurtenances, containing by estimation v acres, called Nonnesgore; And our whole piece of land, containing by estimation xij acres, to the same land called Nonnesgore next adjacent; And all those our lands, containing by estimation viij acres, with appurtenances, in Romere; Likewise our whole piece of land, containing by estimation v acres, next Potton Bawke; And our whole piece of land, containing by estimation xvj acres, next and near Wests; Another our piece of land, containing by estimation v acres, next le gravell pytt; And our whole close of arable land, called Barnebred, containing by estimation xiiij acres; And our whole croft of land, called Bakehouse Croft, containing by estimation ix acres; And one other our piece of land, con-

---

[a] Patent Roll.   7 Edward VI.   Part 11. m. 12.

taining by estimation ix acres, to the same le Bakehouse croft next adjacent; One other our piece of land, abutting upon lez Cleypytts, containing by estimation xxij acres; And also all those our lands, containing by estimation xij acres, with appurtenances, in the same le Furlong; And all those our lands, containing by estimation xvj acres, to the same xij acres of land adjacent; And one other our piece of land, to the same adjacent, containing by estimation x acres; And one other our piece of land, lying next Peper Bawke, containing by estimation vij acres; And also all those our lands, containing by estimation viij acres, with appurtenances, in Southbrede; And our whole piece of land, called Preswell, containing by estimation xxvj acres; And also all those our lands, with appurtenances, containing by estimation xiij acres, in Brakdyche, alias Brokedyche; And one other our parcel of land, called Barnebrede, containing by estimation ix acres; And also all those our lands, containing by estimation x acres, in Galowe pece; And also our whole close of pasture, called Barnebrede, containing by estimation vj acres; And our whole close of pasture, called the Conygre, containing by estimation viij acres; And our whole close of pasture, called Mosse close, containing by estimation viij acres; And our whole close of pasture, called Cowe pasture, containing by estimation vj acres; Likewise our whole meadow, called Eastmeade, with appurtenances, containing by estimation xvj acres; And our whole meadow, called le Westmeade, with appurtenances, containing by estimation xxiiij acres; And also our vj acres of meadow, in a certain meadow called Preswell; And all other our lands, tenements, meadows, pastures and hereditaments, called lez demeanes of the said late Monastery or Abbey, with their entire appurtenances; Which premisses, all and singular, lying and being in Elnestowe and Bedford, or elsewhere in the said County of Bedford, to the said late Monastery or Abbey belonged and pertained, and are commonly called lez demeane lands of the said late Monastery or Abbey; And which were reserved and occupied in the hands, cultivation, and proper occupation of the Abbess of the said late Monastery or Abbey before, and until the time of, the dissolution of the said late Monastery or Abbey.

"AND further, of our more abundant grace, and of our certain knowledge and mere motion, and for the considerations aforesaid, we have given and granted, and, by the presents, do give and grant to the aforenamed Humfry Radclyff, Knight, our whole close of pasture, called Vycar's close, containing by estimation xj acres; And our whole close of pasture called Cowe pasture, containing by estimation c acres; And our whole close of pasture, called Guldyngton felde, alias Goldyngton felde, containing by estimation xxx acres; And our whole close of pasture called Newefelde, containing by estimation xl acres; And also our whole close of meadow, called the hyghe felde, containing by estimation lxxx acres; And our whole close of meadow, called Crossemeade, containing by estimation x acres; With their entire appurtenances, lying and being in Wylleshampsted, in the said County of Bedford, to the said late Monastery or Abbey belonging and pertaining, and being parcel of the possessions thereof.

"We have further given and granted, and for the considerations aforesaid, and of our grace aforesaid, and of our certain knowledge and mere motion, by the presents, do give and grant to the aforenamed Humfry Radclyff, Knight, all those our Rectories and our Churches of Elnestowe, Willeshampsted and Kempston; And the advowsons, donations, liberties, dispositions, and rights of patronage, of the Vicarages of the Churches of Elnestowe, Wylleshampsted and Kempston, with their entire rights and appurtenances, in our said County of Bedford, to the said late Monastery or Abbey belonging and pertaining; And all houses, buildings, lands, glebes, tithes of corn and grain, and of hay, and other tithes whatsoever; Likewise oblations and other rights, profits, obventions, commodities and advantages whatsoever, to the same Rectories and Churches, or to any one of them, in any manner belonging and pertaining; Likewise all those our fairs at Elnestowe, in the said County of Bedford, annually held and to be held; And court of Pie Powder°; And stallage⁾ and piccage ⁽, and liberty, and all other profits and advan-

* Court of pied poudrè, i.e. dusty foot. A court held at fairs and markets by itinerant justices, to do justice between buyer and seller on the spot.
⁾ Stallage. The right of erecting stalls or booths in a fair.
⁽ Piccage. The right of breaking ground for the erection of the same.

tages whatsoever, annually and from time to time forthcoming, arising and happening from the same fairs, at Elnestowe aforesaid to be held or kept, or to the same fairs belonging or pertaining; Likewise all and singular tithes of corn and hay, and other tithes whatsoever, of, in and upon all and singular the aforesaid lands, tenements and other premises above specified, annually and from time to time accruing, renewing and forthcoming; And also all that our water mill in Kempston, in our said County of Bedford, and all our waters, water-courses, streams, pools, and banks, and other commodities, profits, emoluments, and hereditaments whatsoever, with appurtenances, to the same mill belonging or pertaining, or with the same mill heretofore usually demised, let or occupied, lately being in the tenure of William Heyes, and to the said late Monastery or Abbey formerly belonging or pertaining, and being parcel of the possessions thereof.

"AND further, of our more abundant grace, and our certain knowledge and mere motion, we have given and granted, and, by the presents, do give and grant to the aforenamed Humfry Radclyff, Knight, all and all kinds our woods, underwoods, and trees whatsoever, of, in and upon all and singular the premises growing and being; And the whole land, estate and soil of the same woods, underwoods and trees; And the reversion and reversions whatsoever of all and singular the premises, and of any parcel thereof; Likewise the rents and other annual profits whatsoever reserved upon any leases or concessions of the premises whatsoever, or of any parcel thereof, in any manner made.

"FOR we give, and, by the presents, grant to the aforenamed Humfry Radclyff, Knight, all and singular the premisses above expressed and specified, As fully, freely and entirely, and in as ample mode and form, as any Abbess of the said late Monastery or Abbey of Elnestowe, or any other person or persons, heretofore having, possessing, or being seised of the premisses, or any parcel thereof, ever had, held or enjoyed, or ought to have, hold or enjoy the same, or any parcel thereof; And as fully, freely and entirely, and in as ample mode and form, as all and singular those premisses came, or ought to come, into our hands, or into the hands of our very dearest father, HENRY VIII., late King of England, by reason or pretext of the dissolution of the said late Monastery or Abbey, or by reason or pretext of any act or acts of Parliament, or by any other mode, right or title whatsoever, and are now, or ought to be, in our hands; Which premises, however, all and singular, with appurtenances, only extend to the clear annual value of eighty-five pounds, seventeen shillings and ten pence.

"To HAVE, HOLD AND ENJOY the aforesaid site of the said late Monastery or Abbey, and the aforesaid rectories, advowsons, messuages, mill, lands, tenements, meadows, pastures, tithes and, all and singular, the other premises above expressed and specified, with their entire appurtenances to the aforenamed Humfry Radclyff, Knight, his heirs and assigns for ever, to the proper behoof and use of himself Humfry Radclyff, his heirs and assigns for ever; To HOLD of us, our heirs and successors, as of our manor of Estgrenewyche, in our County of Kent, at fee farm, by fealty only, in free soccage, and not in chief; And to render thence annually to us, our heirs and successors, eighty-five pounds, seventeen shillings and ten pence of lawful money of England, at our Court of Augmentations and Revenues of our Crown, to be paid annually at the feast of St. Michael the Archangel only.

"AND further, of our more abundant grace, we have given and granted, and, by the presents, do give and grant to the aforenamed Humfry Radclyff, Knight, all issues, rents, revenues and profits of all and singular the premisses, with appurtenances, from the feast of St. Michael the Archangel last past up to this time forthcoming or accruing, To HAVE to the same Humfry Radclyff, Knight, by our gift, without account, or any other modus, to us, our heirs or successors to be thereupon in any way rendered, paid or done.

"AND further we will, and by the presents grant to the aforenamed Humfry Radclyff, Knight, his heirs and assigns, that we our heirs and successors for ever, annually, and from time to time, will exonerate, acquit and preserve indemnified as well the same Humfry Radclyff, Knight, his heirs and assigns, as the aforesaid site, Rectories, messuages, lands, tenements, and all and singular the other premisses, above expressed and specified, with appurtenances, and any parcel whatever thereof, against us, our heirs and successors, and against other persons whatsoever, of all and all kinds of corrodies, rents, fees, annuities, pensions, portions, sum of money, and charges and incumbrances whatsoever, except from the service above by the presents reserved, and except from demises and grants, for term of life or years, made of the premises, or any parcel thereof, upon which an ancient rent, or more, is reserved; And except from covenants, in the same demises and grants expressed and specified; And except from charges, which are held to exonerate farmers of the premises, or any parcel thereof, by reason of any indentures and demises to them made. WILLING however, and by the presents ordering it to be strictly enjoined, as well upon the Chancellor and general supervisors, and upon the Council of our said court of Augmentations and Revenues of our Crown, as upon all and singular Receivers, Auditors and other officers and ministers, of us, our heirs and successors, whatsoever, for the time being, that they themselves, and any one of them, upon the sole exhibition of these our letters patent, or the inrolment of the same, without any other brief or warrant from us, our heirs and successors, in any manner to be obtained, or before, shall make, and from time to time shall cause to be made, to the aforenamed Humfry Radclyff, Knight, his heirs and assigns, a full, entire and due allowance, and manifest exoneration from all and all kinds of corrodies of this kind, rents, fees, annuities and sums of money, and charges and incumbrances whatsoever, except the above exceptions. AND these our letters patent, or the inrolment of the same, shall be annually, and from time to time, as well to the said Chancellor, and general supervisors, and to the Council of our said Court of Augmentations and Revenues of our Crown, as to all Receivers, Auditors and other officers and ministers, of us our heirs and successors, whatsoever, for the time being, sufficient warrant and exoneration in this behalf. We will also, and, by the presents, grant to the aforenamed Humfry Radclyff that he may have, and shall have, these our letters patent under our great seal of England in due manner done and sealed, without fine or fee, great or small, to us in our Hanaper, or elsewhere, to our use to be thereupon in any manner rendered, paid or done. On the ground that express mention, &c. In testimony whereof, &c. Witness the King at Westminster the third day of July. [1553.]

"By brief of the privy seal granted, &c."

From the date of the above it will be seen that it was granted by the King only three days before his death. What became of Edmund Hervey's interest in the property, through the lease granted to him 1541, does not appear, but there can be no doubt that it was made the subject of a family arrangement between the parties concerned.

Reigns of Mary, 1553-8, and Elizabeth, 1558—1603.

In the former of these reigns we have no record of any event, affecting the demesne lands of the Abbey, but in the latter occurred the death of the grantee, Sir Humphrey Radcliffe, who appears to have been resident at Elstow at the time of his decease, which took place in 1566. He was buried in the Church, though whether in the nave, which is the only portion now standing, or in the choir, or in one of the transepts, is a question which at the present date it is difficult, if not impossible, to decide. One thing only seems to be pretty certain, and that is, that the monument to his memory could not have been originally placed in its present position, against the east wall[1] and immediately over the altar, as it is highly improbable that the eastern portion of the church would have been demolished at so early a date; and, if this conjecture be correct, it would seem to indicate that the remains of the knight were interred somewhere to the east of the present Church.

[1] It will be seen below [p. 200] that Mr. Buckley places the date of this wall at about 1580.

PLATE II.

ELSTOW CHURCH, VIEW OF INTERIOR, LOOKING EAST.

Of this Cole, in his MS. previously quoted, says :—

"The site was granted to Sir Humphrey Radcliffe, who, or one of his family, indecently has a monument, exactly in the middle of the east wall, over the altar, and where an image was formerly placed, as appears by a projecting stone close under it. I had no time to take the inscription; perhaps in the autumn I may pass that way again, and be more particular."

Now it is rather hard to charge poor Sir Humphrey with indecency for placing a monument in such a position, as it is quite certain he did not put it there himself, nor, if the wall were not built at the time of his decease, could he even have proposed to do so; and it is much to be wished, as far as we are concerned, that Cole, instead of spending all his time in taking such minute particulars of other monuments, which are still in good preservation, had devoted a part of it to deciphering the inscription on this, as he might, by so doing, have saved a world of trouble to antiquarians at the present day; for, the letters being only painted on the black marble tablet and not incised, the hundred-and-twenty odd years, which have elapsed since he wrote, must have made a vast difference for the worse in their condition.

The inscription, which is now in parts, especially towards the end, almost illegible, is given by Mr. Cary Elwes[s] as follows; and as far as can be judged from a comparison of his version with the faded characters of the original, it may be taken as substantially correct.

[s] Bedford and Neighbourhood. p. 74.

HERE LYTHE BODIES OF Sr HVMPRE RADCLIF KNIGHT AND DAME
ISABEL HIS WIFE W^{ch} Sr HVMPHREY WAS SECOND SONNE OF ROBERT E OF SVSSEX AND ELIZABETH DAVGHTER OF HENRY DVKE OF BVCKINGHAM AND SAYD ISABEL, DAVGHTER AND
SOLE HEYR OF EDM HARVEY ESQ. AND MARY WENTWORTH HIS WIFE. THEY HAD ISSVE 2 SONNS, THOMAS DECEASED EDWARD YET LIVINGE 4 DAVGHTERS MARY ONE OF THE GENTEL WOMEN OF THE PRIVY CHABYR TO Q. ELIZA FRANCES MARRIED
TO HENRY CHEK ESQ. SOMETIME SECRETRY OF HER LAT MAJESTY'S COVNSEL ESTABLISHD IN Y^e [NORTH] ELIZIBET MARRIED TO HEN. OWEN ESQ.
MARTHA MARIED TO GOSTWICK Y^e S^d Sr HVMPHREY DIED THE 13 DAY OF AVGVST, 1566, BEING OF THE AGE OF 57 AT Y^e TIME OF HIS DEATH AND DAM ISABEL HIS WYFE LIVING AFTER HIM 28 YEARS, DECEASED BEING ABOVT THE AGE OF 76, IN THE Y^r OF OVR LORD 1594, IN MEMORY OF WHOM Y^e AFORSAYD MARY.

From this it appears that the deceased knight was closely connected, through his wife, and the marriage of his daughter Martha to one of the Gostwick family, with the Commissioners appointed to receive the surrender of the Abbey. Allusion has already been made to both of these, but it may here be added that the Gostwicks appear to have been settled at Willington, though not as lords of the manor, as early as, if not earlier than, 1209. The manor, which was conveyed to John Gostwyke and his heirs 21 Henry VIII., remained in the family until Sir William Gostwick, Bart., who had greatly impoverished his estate by frequent Parliamentary contests, sold it in 1731, with others, to Sarah, Duchess of Marlborough. It was afterwards purchased, in 1774, by the then Duke of Bedford, in whose family it still remains[t]. From the time of the sale of these estates the fortunes of the Gostwick family would seem to have taken a downward course, if at least the current report, that the last representative thereof died a pauper in Bedford Union, have any foundation in fact.

Reign of James I., 1603-25.

Belonging to this period are documents relating to three matters, two of which are of considerable interest, and the other, which comes first in order of date, may very probably be of local, if not of general, value.

This is an order[u] of the Court of Exchequer, from which it appears that Edmond Dean, John Clerk, and William Cranfield, had brought an action against William Ballard with respect to certain rights of pasture, which, as they alleged, they held all the year round, on land at Elstow, and had obtained an injunction of the Court in their favour. To this Ballard had demurred, on the ground that their rights only extended from the end of harvest to Candlemas Day [2nd February], and they were therefore called upon to prove their claim on oath within fourteen days, failing which, the Court would proceed to dissolve the injunction.

The next record is that of the gift[v] by the Crown, 27th July, 1611, to Sir Christopher Hatton, Kt., and Francis Nedham, Esq., their heirs

[t] Bedford and Neighbourhood. pp. 102—104.
[u] Exchequer Orders and Decrees, Hil. 4 James I. No. 2. fol. 195.
[v] Patent Roll, 9 James I., Part 32, No. 8.

and assigns for ever, of the fee-farm-rent of £85 17s. 10d., reserved under the grant to Sir Humphrey Radcliffe. What became of this rent in later times does not appear, nor is there anything to shew who Nedham was [probably he was one of the Nedhams of Wymondley], but Hatton was a cousin of his famous namesake, who was Chancellor to Queen Elizabeth, being the grandson of a younger brother of that personage's father. Both alike would appear to have been imbued with a penchant for Church property, probably no uncommon failing among the nobility in those days, the younger one obtaining the grant just mentioned, and the elder having built his town house in Holborn, on part of the Bishop of Ely's garden, with respect to which the Queen wrote her memorable letter in reply to the remonstrances of that Prelate :—

"Proud Prelate,—You know what you were, before I made you what you are. If you do not immediately comply with my request, by G— I will unfrock you. Elizabeth."

"The names of Hatton Garden and Ely Place still bear witness to the encroaching Lord Keeper and the elbowed Bishop[w]." It would seem, however, that retribution was before long to overtake the younger Sir Christopher, as, about 1634[w], he was fined £12,000 for an alleged encroachment upon one of the royal forests.

After the death of Sir Humphrey Radcliffe, some of his family would seem to have come into possession of the Elstow property, and to

[w] Hallam's Constitutional History. i. 224 and 429.

PLATE III.

RUINS OF MANSION, ELSTON.

have held it till 1616, when Sir Edward, son of Sir Humphrey, joined with Sir Thomas Cheeke and Essex his wife, daughter of Richard, Earl of Warwick, in a sale[x] of it to Thomas Hillersden. Sir Thomas was son of Sir Henry, husband of Frances Radcliffe, and the property conveyed by the sale consisted of "the site of the lately dissolved Monastery of Elvestowe, alias Elstoe, with appurtenances, one messuage, two cottages, two dovecotes, three gardens, four orchards, two hundred acres of land, one hundred acres of meadow, three hundred acres of pasture, two hundred acres of wood, one hundred acres of moor, free warren, goods and chattels of felons and fugitives, fairs, markets, and profits, piccage, tolls and dues, with appurtenances, in Elvestowe, Willshamstead, Bedford, Kempston, and Cardington; likewise the Rectory of Elvestowe, with appurtenances, and all manner of tithes whatsoever arising, growing, or renewing in Elstow; likewise the advowson of the Vicarage of the Church of Elvestowe;" the price paid for the whole being £700.

There seems to be little, if any, doubt that the house, now in ruins, to the south-west of the church, was built about this time, though whether by Radcliffe or Hillersden is uncertain. Cole, speaking of it, says:—

"The mansion-house, rebuilt with the materials of the Abbey, is large and regularly built, I suppose about the time of James I. It stands on the south-west side of the Church, and has now a large window from it

[x] Feet of Fines, Michaelmas, 14 James I. Bedford.

into the body of the Church, probably the same which was there in the time of the Abbey."

Of these ruins, however, nothing need be said here, as it will be found that Mr. Buckley has in his " Notes" fully described them.

From this time forward, for a considerable period, the records relating to the Elstow property are so few, and far between, that to mention the various reigns, to which the return would be *nil*, would be simply to copy out a certain number of lines from any table of the Kings and Queens of England, nor is it until we come to the

Reign of George II., 1727-60,

that anything at all has come to light; but what has been found then is of some interest from its bearing on earlier history.

It will be remembered that mention has been made [p. 154] of the cruel wrong done to the parish in 1345, by the appropriation to the Abbey of the whole endowment of the Rectory, and now we find the record of, what we may suppose to be, the first effort made towards securing something in the way of a permanent stipend for the incumbent.

This document is a conveyance[y] by John Towersey, of Bedford, gentleman, to the governors of Queen Anne's Bounty, of certain lands in the parish of Keysoe, as an endowment of the Vicarage of Elstow, which was at that time held by the Rev. Robert Phipps. This land would appear to have been very

[y] Close Roll, 15 George II. Part 5, No. 17.

much scattered, as, from a Terrier annexed to the deed, we learn that there were in Fortune's field five acres; in Popwell field two acres; in Ewer's Croft three acres; in a field called Stocking two acres three roods; in another Stocking, near Peacock House, one acre; in the lord's Stocking field one acre; in Millfield two plots of an acre each; in Hogland furlong four plots, containing respectively, one acre, one acre and a-half, half an acre, and one rood; in Church field five plots, of one acre, one acre, one rood, two roods, and three roods; in Chalk field three roods, and in Graving field two plots of one acre and three acres,—in all thirty acres, the price paid for which was £195. In lieu, presumably, of these scattered pieces of land, the Vicar of Elstow now holds in Keysoe, under an award dated 1819, 16 A. 1 R. 16 P., and in Biggleswade about 6 A.[1]

Reign of George III., 1760—1820.

In this reign the Elstow estates once more changed hands, as they were purchased, 1792, by Mr. Whitbread of Southill, great-grandfather of the present proprietor, of the representatives of the Hillersden family, in whose possession they had remained since 1616.

In 1797, 37 George III., an Act of Parliament was passed for inclosing the commons of Elstow, the scope and object of which will be most easily gathered from the preamble, which is as follows :—

[1] Communicated by the present Vicar.

"Whereas there are in the parish of Elstow, in the County of Bedford, certain common and open fields, common meadows, and other commonable lands and waste grounds, containing in the whole, by estimation, one thousand and sixty acres, or thereabouts.

"And whereas Samuel Whitbread is Lord of the manor of Elstow aforesaid, and is also proprietor of the said common and open fields, common meadows, and other commonable lands, and is also Impropriator of the Impropriate Rectory of Elstow aforesaid, and as such is seised of or entitled to all tithes great and small arising and renewing within the said parish.

"And whereas Sir Philip Monoux, Baronet, John Leach, John Rogers, Richard Rogers, and other persons are entitled to the residue of the said commonable lands, and that they and some other persons, owners of ancient cottages in Elstow aforesaid, are respectively entitled to common of pasture for their cattle in, upon, and over the said common and open fields, common meadows and waste lands, or some part thereof, at stated times in the year, and in certain proportions.

"And whereas the said lands and grounds lie intermixed, and are inconveniently situate, and are in their present state incapable of any considerable improvement, and it would be advantageous to the several proprietors thereof if the same were divided and inclosed, and specified shares thereof allotted to them in lieu of, and in proportion to their several and respective estates, rights and interests therein, but as such division and inclosure cannot be effected and carried into execution without the authority of Parliament, may it therefore please your Majesty that it may be enacted, &c."

By this act, under which John Lilburne of Cardington, land surveyor, was appointed first commissioner for carrying out its provisions, not

PLATE IV.

THE NORTH DOORWAY, ELSTOW CHURCH.

only were the common lands divided and inclosed, but boundaries were defined, the course of streams straightened, roads set out and fenced, and an allotment of land made to the Impropriator in lieu of tithes.

In 1810, we have the record of a further benefaction towards the endowment of the Vicarage of Elstow, in a deed[a], dated 13th January, 49 George III., which secures to the Incumbent, who was then the Rev. Thomas Cave, the annual payment, on the part of Mr. Whitbread and his successors, of the sum of £22 11s. 10d. to be paid on the usual quarter-days, "by even and equal portions, at or in the porch or door-place of Elstow aforesaid, between the hours of nine and eleven of the clock in the forenoon."

With this our Chronicles come to an end, and it only remains to notice a few of the monuments in the Church, which, as they incidentally bear a part in the history of the Abbey, belong more properly to this part of the work than to Mr. Buckley's architectural notes.

In addition to those already mentioned, there is another fine and most interesting brass, in almost as good preservation as that to the memory of Abbess Hervey, from which it is but a few feet distant. Of this Cole, at the conclusion of his description of the Abbess' tomb, goes on to say :—

"At the foot of this lady lies a larger old marble[b], with the portraiture in full length of a lady, in brass[c],

[a] Close Roll. 49 George III. Part 25. No. 7.
[b] This slab is of a greenish oolitic stone, measuring 8 ft. 9 in. × 3 ft. 9 in.
[c] The metal is the same as that on the tomb of Abbess Hervey.

pretty large dressed, as I conceive in the habit of a Nun, though she has not the same sort of gown or robe, with large full sleeves, such as the Benedictine Nuns wore, and as the lady Abbess has them: yet she has a veil on her head, and a sort of plaited band, or wimple, under her chin, which, however, does not cover part of it, as it does in the figure of the Abbess. Probably this lady, after the death of her two husbands, might retire to the Monastery, as a Novice, to spend her days in retirement, recollection and devotion, though never professed, and so might not be obliged to wear the whole habit of the Order. Her hands are in a praying posture, and a little lap-dog lies at her right foot."

Here our author is certainly in error as regards the dress, which is no conventual habit, but simply the ordinary mourning garb of a widow, thus described by Viollet le Duc[d]:—

"The wimple [*guimpe*] envelops the head, the chin and the neck...... the wimple passes over the robe, and the veil falls below the eyebrows....... under the wimple appears a sort of chin piece [*mentonnière*], and the veil lies close to the lower part of the face. This chin piece had the name Barbette, and Eleanor de Poitiers, authoress of the 'Honours of the Court,' considers the Barbette an emblem of mourning ..... it is eminently the veil of a widow, advancing over the face like a hood."

The robe which she wears is the ordinary cotte or gown, which dates from the end of the eleventh century, and was worn by all ladies, whether seculars or nuns; and that she was not a nun is proved by the pug-dog represented at her feet, such an appanage being strictly forbidden to inmates of religious houses, though dogs,

[d] Dictionnaire Raisonné du Mobilier. iii. 212-213.

and also hawks, are often shewn on or near the effigies of secular ladies.

To return, however, to Cole's description. He goes on to say that—

"At the four corners of the stone are as many shields of arms. On the first are three covered cups for Argentine, the second is reaved and lost, and the third * is party per pale indented, being the same bearing as that of S. Lis, Earl of Huntingdon and Northampton. The fourth shield has a bend on it. Round the whole marble goes a fillet of brass, which is not perfect, having some part of it reaved off and stolen; but that the lady was an Argentine is plain, not only for the first coat, but from several covered cups between the words on the fillet."

The epitaph on this brass is a curiosity in its way, as it is in Latin Hexameter lines, the termination of each being marked by one of the cups noticed above. Unfortunately a considerable portion of it is lost, but thanks to Cole having, in his MS., preserved a part, which has since disappeared, it is possible, by the insertion of a couple of words, which he suggests, to make sense of what remains to us. Various guesses have been made respecting the missing portions, but as there is nothing in what we have to give any clue to that which we have not, except that we can see that the missing words must have contained some allusion to Sir John Talbot, the lady Margery's grandfather, they are guesses only. The text of the inscription is as follows :—

* This is the only coat of arms now remaining, and the bearings are said [Bedford and Neighbourhood, p. 76] to be identical with those of Parlys.

. . . . . 𝔐argeria bis bidunta
𝔉ilia 𝔅adulphi . . . .
. . . . . . de turre 𝔅icardi
𝔓ac jacet in fossa data [sunt ubi bermibus] [ossa]
[Cujus] ut alta petat loca florida pace p'henni
Spiritus ista bidens trini pulses pietatem. Amen.
Obiit autem Anno d̄n̄i MCCCCXXVII°. . . . in bigil s̄c̄i
    mictris Archangl.

Of the words in the above, which are inclosed in brackets, those in Old English type are those which are now lost, but are mentioned by Cole as having been *in situ* in his day; those which are in ordinary type are his suggestions. Taking the words as they stand, they will read thus :—

Margery, twice widowed, daughter of Ralph ... of Richard's Castle, lies in this tomb, where her bones are given to the worms, and that her spirit may seek the high places, flowery with everlasting peace, do thou [reader] implore the piety of the Trinity. Amen. But she died A.D. 1427, on the Vigil of S. Michael the Archangel.

This lady appears to have been the daughter of Ralph Parlys, by Joanna, daughter of Sir John Talbot, of Richard's Castle. She married, [1] 1396, John Hervey, of Thursleigh and Risely, co. Beds, grandfather of Abbess Hervey, and great great-grandfather of Edmund Hervey, of Elstow—see pedigree, p. 143; [2] Sir William Argentine, who died 1419. She died 1427, and by her will, made at Alston, in the diocese of Norwich, 26th April, and proved at Lambeth, 26th October, in the same year, she directed that her body should be buried at Elstow, and left a sum of twenty marks to be expended in masses for the repose of her soul. Her second husband, Sir William Argentine, was a descendant of Reginald Argentine of Wymondley, who, as we have already seen, brought an action against the Abbess for the recovery of the advowson of that place.

There are also memorials in the Church to several members of the Hillersden family, the earliest, a mural tablet to the memory of Thomas Hillersden, being dated 1656. The inscription on this relates that he was the "son of Thomas Hillersden and Margaret his wife, daughter of Sir William Litton, Kt., grandson to Sir Thomas Hillersden, of Elnestow, in the County of Bedford, Kt., both likewise buried in this Church." This Sir Thomas was no doubt the purchaser of the estates from the Radcliffe family, but though it is thus stated that both he and his son were buried in the church, there is nothing now existing to indicate whereabouts either of them was interred.

Cole tells us that in his time Mr. Dennis Hillersden Farrar, living at Brayfield, Co. Bucks, was lord of the manor and patron of the living, of which Mr. Phipps, Rector of Croxton, Cambridgeshire, was then Incumbent, but there is no monument bearing this name. There is, however, one, dated 1787, to Dennis Farrar Hillersden, and two, bearing date respectively 1769 and 1815, to daughters of Dennis Farrar, of Cold Brayfield.

Of course a place of the antiquity which Elstow boasts would not be complete without a ghost, and Mr. Hurst, in a paper read before the Bedfordshire Architectural Society, between 1854 and 1856, mentions this indispensable appendage, though he is unable to say whether it be the spirit of one of the nuns, who had been unfaithful to her conventual vows, or that of the Foundress, come to lament over the ruin of her charitable intentions. There is, however, no certain information of any one having seen it, and should any one have the good fortune to do so, it is earnestly requested that he or she will immediately communicate the fact to the compiler of these pages, in order that it may be duly chronicled in the second edition, should such ever be called for, which is most improbable.

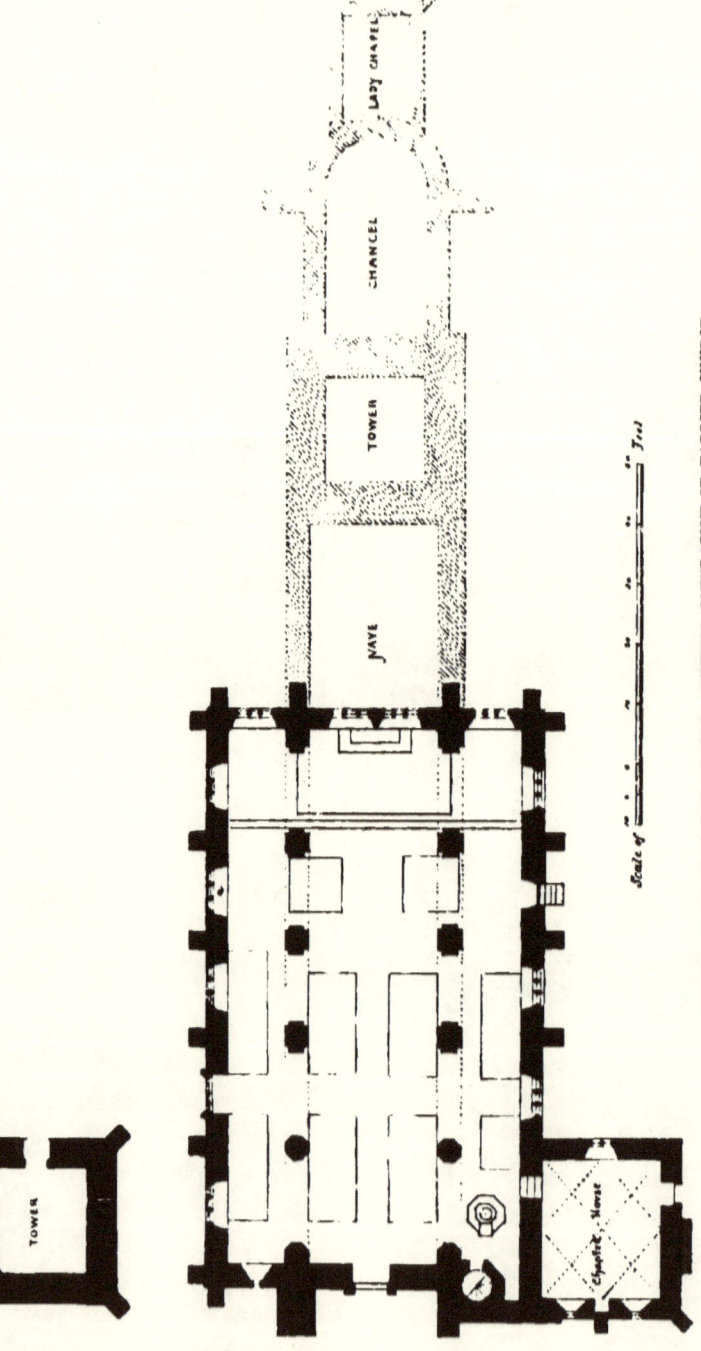

GROUND PLAN OF ELSTOW CHURCH, SHEWING FOUNDATION OF EARLIER CHURCH.

NOTES ON THE ARCHITECTURAL FEATURES OF ELSTOW CHURCH.

FROM the plan, which Mr. Jackson has kindly furnished, of the foundations which were discovered on examining the ground to the eastward of the Abbey Church of Elstow, it is possible to form some idea of the portions of it which have been demolished. In this plan is set out the position of the central tower, as well as that of the apsidal chancel, with the Lady Chapel beyond. The circular termination of the Chancel shews that it belonged to the early Church, whilst the quadrangular form of the Lady Chapel, with buttresses at the angles, proves that it was of later date, added on probably in the fourteenth century. The two remains of walls on the sides of the apse belong most probably to the foundations of the *claustra*, or enclosures, of the inner and outer cloisters. The foundations of the central tower were very solid, in order to enable the superincumbent walls to support the thrust of the domical vaulting, which was frequently used in such construction.

From pieces found in the debris, it seems probable that the Church was originally paved with embossed tiles, the designs of which were relieved in yellow and green glazes upon a red ground. The walls also bear traces of having been decorated with colour, and ornamented with various devices, in brown, black, white, and yellow, executed on the original plastering, which was very thin. Decoration of the same character may still be seen in various churches of the Romanesque, or Norman, period in England and France.

The present remains of the Church consist of the nave, with north and south aisles, the tower, or campanile, standing detached at the S.W. angle of the building, and a vaulted chamber, now used as a vestry, which communicates with the north aisle by a door near its western end.

The nave comprises five bays, or arcades. Of these bays, the three eastern ones are of the early part of the twelfth century, and belong to the first Church, which was built on the foundation of the Countess Judith. Their arches are semi-circular in form, the key-stones irregular in shape, and the filling-in of the walls is composed of rough rubble, embedded in a sort of concrete. They rest on *abaci*, or capitals, of simple character, which, as well as the key-stones, appear to have been dressed with adzes, or hatchets, as was usual in early Norman stone-work. To each arcade are two square *archivolts*, the angles of which are continued down the piers on which they rest. The masonry of this part of the Church is both remarkable and interesting, as it corresponds exactly with the work executed

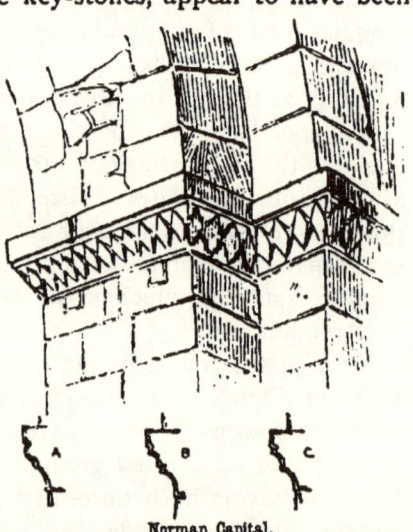

Norman Capital.

throughout Europe during the tenth, eleventh, and twelfth centuries, so that in itself it tells the story of its date. It consists of regular cubes of axed stone, filling in the *intrados* of the arches to the level of their crowns, whilst, above these, the walling is composed of smaller stones, set in thick lines of mortar, which latter style of work is continued up to the cornice, or wall-plate, of the roof. In the wall above these arcades are, on either side, three long, narrow, round-headed clerestory windows, splayed on the interior, but shewing no trace of a string-course having existed beneath them.

Beyond, i.e. to the west of, these three early bays, are two of later date, the pointed arches of which rest on octagonal piers, or columns, the capital of each being enriched with foliage of a fine type, deeply carved. The arches themselves are of graceful and

Early English Capital.

lofty proportions, and elaborately moulded, the north-eastern one alone being further embellished by a dog-tooth ornament introduced on the inner moulding. In the clerestory above these arches are windows of the same style, of graceful form, and having, on the sides of their splays, *colonettes* ornamented with the caps and *annuli*, or rings, common to the architecture of the period.

The west wall is pierced by a doorway, with moulded jambs, having boldly carved foliage over the capitals of its columns, and flanked on the exterior by two widely projecting buttresses, which still shew traces of arcading on their faces, and, in this respect, somewhat resemble similar supports on the west front of the Abbey Church of S. Albans. The outer angles of these western buttresses are hollow chamfered, and in the recesses of these chamfers were formerly pilasters, probably of marble, of which the caps only now remain. The upper part of the west wall is apparently not of earlier date than the end of the fourteenth century, and the present west window, which is of a very debased type, is later still, dating probably from the sixteenth century; but, from the appearance of an off-set in the wall, it seems likely that a large and fine window once existed in it.

In the west wall of the north aisle is a doorway of Early English style, surmounted by a window of the same period, deeply splayed, and still retaining its interior angle *colonettes* divided by rings. The doorway yet possesses its original oak door, with massive iron strap hinges, and in it is cut a postern, through which, if village tradition speak truly, John Bunyan often passed when, as a boy, he was a chorister in the Church.

Near this doorway is another[*], the principal entrance to the Church, which is situated in the wall of the north aisle, and has recently been most carefully restored to its original condition, and fitted with a new oak door with appropriate hinges. This doorway, or porch, consists of a semi-circular arch of five *archivolts*, resting on a curiously moulded *abacus* of Attic type, which is ornamented with a deeply-cut chevron moulding, simple but effective in treatment, and in the angles of the piers are columns with cubical capitals, carved with bossed flutings. Above the arch, resting on a simple, square cornice, is a very quaint, but beautiful, carving, representing our Lord in the attitude of blessing, seated on

[*] See Plate IV., p. 187.

the rainbow, and surrounded by an *aureola*, or glory. The right hand is raised, the fingers being held as in the Latin form of benediction, and the left holds a book; the dress of the figure consists of the *peplum*, or outer robe, plaited with small plaits, as was usual in the eleventh and twelfth centuries, and an inner robe with large sleeves; the head is environed with a cruciform *nimbus*. On the right of the central figure of the Saviour is that of S. Peter, holding the symbolical keys; on the left that of another Apostle, probably S. John. Each of these figures holds a book in the left hand, the right being raised, with the fingers extended in the attitude of admiration, and their heads are inclined towards their Lord, as shewing reverence and deep attention. The whole of this carving is executed in low relief, and it is most probable that, like most other sculptured subjects of the period, it was richly coloured, and the background gilt. This remarkable portal, with its bas-relief, belongs evidently to the same original structure as do the early semi-circular arches of the nave; and it is most likely that, on the extension of the Church in the thirteenth century, it was, as is the case in many other instances, spared by the masons of the period, and re-inserted, on account alike of its interest and its antiquity.

In the interior wall, over this doorway, as well as in the soffit of the door itself, are several fragments of chevron mouldings, evidently belonging to the older portions of the church; whilst immediately over the carved tympanum thereof is one of the small windows of the earlier aisle; and at the left, on entering, may be seen a small ogee arch, surmounting the traces of a broken holy-water stoup, placed in this position, as in all early churches.

Farther on, in the wall of this same north aisle, is another doorway[b], now stopped up, of late type, dating probably from the end of the fourteenth century, which

[b] See Frontispiece.

appears to have served as an entrance for the Chaplains from the outer court of the Abbey. It seems, in fact, to have been a priest's door, affording, from its own

position and that of the cloister-screen, the most convenient access to the nave for the chaplain who said daily mass at the altar provided for the laity therein. In the angle spaces of the archway of this door are two very remarkable carvings; that on the west side representing the Sacred Heart, exactly as that famous symbol is shewn at the present day; that on the right a shield bearing the various instruments of the Passion.

Evident traces still exist of screens, and an altar for the laity in this part of the church: of the former, in the fact that the mouldings of some of the capitals have been cut away to allow of their erection; of the latter, in a *piscina* with *aumbry* in the wall of the south aisle. This *aumbry* has a trefoiled arch, the hood-mould of which rests on two grotesque heads, similar in character to the figure of a man, in a fine corbel, now built into the east wall of the Church, and it unquestionably served for an altar originally placed in this spot against a wooden screen. The semi-circular arch inside this aumbry is a relieving arch over the drain which served to convey the ablutions into the earth.

In all probability, at this spot, i.e. the east end of the south aisle, stood the altar of the combined Chantries, mentioned in the "Chronicles of Elstow" [p. 153], for the Piscina corresponds very nearly in date with the foundation of the earlier one, as do the windows with that of the later; while the south aisle of the Church, being that nearest to the stream running through the village, may have suggested the name of "juxta pontem."

In the S.E. pier of the Norman arcade is a curiously pierced stone, at about four feet from the ground, which, from its position, appears to have served as a support for holding the Pastoral Staff of the Abbess, whose stall most probably stood at this spot, as is usual in Benedictine and other abbeys.

The windows of the aisles are of Early Pointed date, but the tracery is Perpendicular in style. These windows, as well as the walls, have been recently most heedfully restored in a thoroughly conservative spirit, all the old features being retained, and the new work marked by a difference in the masonry wherever it was practicable. The whole of the stonework in the interior has been stripped of the coats of plaster and whitewash, which had quite filled up the delicate members of the mouldings, and carefully repointed. The oaken roof of the Church is new throughout, but of excellent type, harmonising admirably with the architecture of the edifice. The king-posts rest on corbels,

WINDOW IN N. AISLE.

carved in the form of quaint heads, some of which are ancient examples.

The present east wall could not have been erected at the same time as the nave and aisles, as in no place do its courses of masonry correspond with theirs, and from its general style it would appear to date from about 1580. In it, on the interior, are two curious brackets, or corbels, one situated on the north side, just where the spring of the old chancel-arch would have commenced, representing the bust of a man clad in the tight-fitting tunic of the thirteenth century, out of whose ears, like those of a satyr, grow leafy branches, which cover the lower part of the bracket. Unfortunately, the face of this figure has been much mutilated, at some former period, by the insertion in it of a small wooden joist. The other, which is placed in the centre of the wall, immediately over the monument to Sir Humphrey Radcliffe, is a beautiful and elaborate example of the period of the Early English Renaissance. The upper portion of it is carved with a very rich design of dolphins and vases, while on the lower, are two figures of cherubs upholding a lozenge-shaped shield, on which are shewn the various instruments of the Passion. In the centre of this shield is a hole, which evidently held the socket of a metal branch for suspending tapers or a lamp. The type of this bracket is very like that of the work executed by carvers of the school formed in England about the time that Campeggio was erecting the monument to Henry VII. in Westminster; and it is not at all surprising to find work of this character existing at Elstow, for, the Abbey being a rich one, the Abbess could well afford to employ the skilled labour of the best artists of the day. The position occupied by this corbel before the dissolution is difficult to determine, but it is most likely that it supported a statue of the Mater Dolorosa, or a similar subject, in the cloisters of the Abbey, of which no traces now remain save this solitary specimen.

In the east wall are three windows of a very late Perpendicular type, one of them containing a few small remnants of ancient stained glass, evidently fragments from a fifteenth-century window.

The font, which is also Perpendicular, and a good example of that style, stands at the west end of the south aisle. It is octagonal in plan, the sides of the basin being panelled in quatrefoils, while the angles of the base rest on grotesque figures. These figures represent the vices and sins which are cast out by Holy Baptism. Such at least is the interpretation of them, either in this position, or as *gurgoyles*, according to

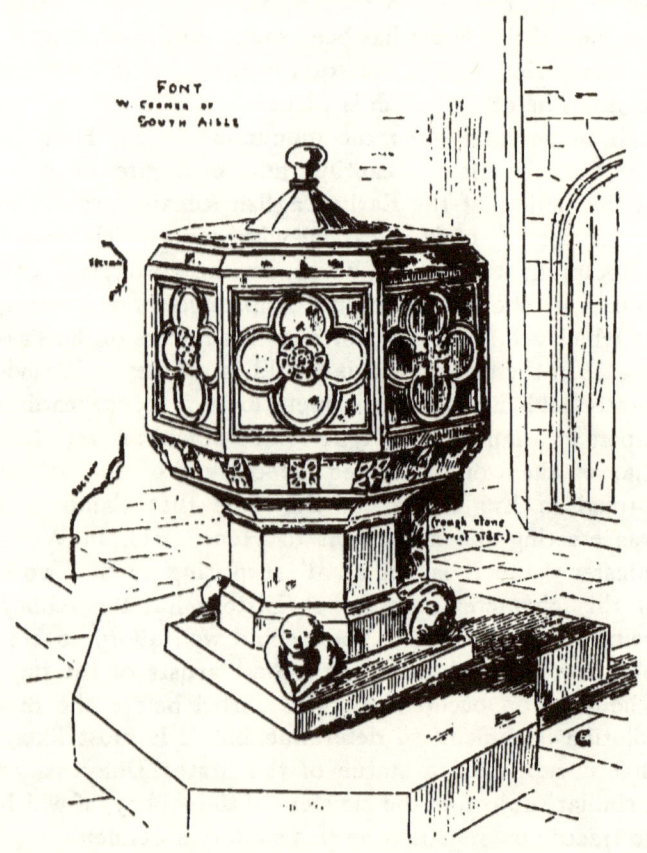

Vincent of Beauvais, and Durandus, Bishop of Mende. Many fonts have similar figures at their bases, e.g. those of Pont-a-Mousson and Vermand [France], and Zedelghem [Belgium]. One side of the Elstow font is rough, shewing that it must have been attached to a wall or pillar before it was removed to its present position. Near the font are laid the fragments of some

PLATE VI.

INTERIOR OF VESTRY, ELSTOW CHURCH.

ancient stone coffins, the lids of which bear raised crosses with floriated heads and stems, evidently of the thirteenth and fourteenth centuries.

In the south wall, immediately opposite the font, is the entrance to a low vaulted chamber, now used as a vestry, and misnamed the Chapter-house. This chamber could not, from its size, have formed the Chapter-house of so important a community as that of Elstow; but beside that reason, there is a more weighty one to be found in its position at the western end of the Church, instead of at the eastern, and within the cloistered bounds of the Abbey. It is difficult now to determine absolutely for what use this room was designed, but most likely it was an adjunct to the western entrance of the inner court, which must formerly have stood near the spot, and was used for the temporary storage of such goods as were received thereat. The vaulting of this room is quadripartite in construction, the plain chamfered ribs all centring on the capital of an octagonal pillar of Purbeck marble, of which the sides are in sunk flutings, and the cap and base still shew their leaden settings. The way in which the ribs of the vaulting are *quirked* before they reach the capital is very curious and quaint in effect, entirely removing the idea of weakness and distortion of lines which the arches would otherwise have presented.

The tower or *campanile* is evidently of earlier date than is commonly supposed, and probably served originally as a sort of flanking-tower to the western entrance of the church, and the approach to the cloisters and the Abbey buildings; like the Abbot's tower at Buckfast Abbey in Devonshire, still existing close by the Church there. As a quasi-domestic edifice, it was not higher than up to a parapet which surmounted the actual buttresses, nor was the present very meagre upper story added until the ancient central tower of the Church had been pulled down, and it became necessary to provide some other place wherein to hang the bells. The existing entrance is much narrower than the former one, as may be seen on the interior, where still remains the early, almost semi-circular, arch, into which the present doorway seems to have been built on one side of it at the same time that the bell-chamber was added. On the west wall of this tower, at the ground level, is a stone, carved with a raised cross, under a triangular heading; this stone is similar in character to some which may be seen outside monasteries abroad at the present day, and it probably served to mark the bounds of sanctuary.

Within the tower there still hang, from pegs in the wall of the ground-floor chamber, two old leathern buckets, inscribed with the initials "D. F. H.," and the name and date "Elvestow, 1782." On the floor is deposited the stone lid of an early coffin, bearing a "staff" cross, of the same form as that of one which is affixed to the south wall of S. Peter's Church, Bedford.

From the remains of plastering in this chamber, as well as from the traces of flooring-joists in the walls, at a lower level than that of the present beams, it seems evident that it must have served, at some time, as a domestic habitation. Perhaps it formed part of the Abbess' lodgings.

On the south side of the Church, and in a line with its western end, are the ivy-covered and dismantled ruins of the mansion[e] built in the reign of James I. out of the materials of the Abbey, as is shewn by the fact that, on examination of the walls, &c., many traces and remnants of early work are to be found in them. Portions of the mediæval walls, *bonded* with oak, are in fact encased in the Jacobean work. These walls probably belonged to the inner cloisters, above which was most likely the dormitory of the lay sisters or novices. The parts of the house now standing are portions of the wall of the east front and of the south wing. Against the former of these stands a very graceful porch, in the best style of the English Renaissance. It consists of

[e] See Plate III., p. 183.

a semi-circular-headed doorway or portico, flanked by pilasters, of which the details and mouldings are Doric in style, and between which are coved niches, once occupied by statues. Probably this portico was surmounted by another story, in which the lower pilasters and niches were repeated. The harmony of its proportions, and the grace of its details, shew this little edifice to have been the work of a master hand; in the masques and arabesques which decorate the *intrados* of the arch, as well as the panels on the pediments of the pilasters, are traces of Italian taste; and from the general style of the work there seems every reason to believe that Inigo Jones planned and added this elegant porch to the old manor-house, to which it is evidently a more recent erection, as it is not even bonded to the walls. It is now fast hastening to utter ruin, and in common with many of our most cherished monuments of antiquity, is miserably defaced by the vulgar and ignorant scratchings of the public; while close to it, and sharing a similar fate, are the mouldering remains of the old oaken church screen, the original site of which has been indicated above.

In a field W.S.W. of the Church are the ancient Abbey fish-ponds, now almost choked up with weeds. On the village green, where the fair is still held, stands the base of the old market-cross, reduced to a shapeless stump, but still bearing traces of leaden setting, similar to that observed on the central column of the vaulted chamber. A short distance eastward of this is a large building of wood and brick, the framing of which shews traces of the workmanship of the fifteenth century; it was probably the *hospitium* for travellers, being situated close to the public highway, but within the *ballium*, or outer court of the Abbey. This curious building, which is a remarkably fine example of Domestic architecture of its period, is shewn in a stained-glass window, lately put up, at the east end of the south aisle of the Church, in memory of John Bunyan. Nearly opposite to it, on the other side of the road, is an ancient hostelry for pilgrims now converted into cottages, which, as well as the last-named edifice, is well worthy of intelligent preservation.

PLATE VII.

VIEW OF ELSTOW CHURCH, AFTER RESTORATION.

INDEX TO THE ABBEY PROPERTY.

		Locality.	Donor.	First mentioned at page
William I.	§ 1.	Maulden.	Countess Judith.	12
	§ 2.	Willshamstead.	do.	13
	§ 3.	Elstow.	do.	14
	§ 4.	Hitchin.	The King.	15
	§ 5.	Weston.	do.	ib.
Henry I.	§ 6.	Moulsoe.	Richard of Langetote.	ib.
	§ 7.	do.	Ralph of Langetote.	ib.
	§ 8.	Arnesby.	Nigell of Staford.	ib.
	§ 9.	Oxford.	Nicholas Basset.	ib.
	§ 10.	Rissington.	do.	ib.
	§ 11.	Avington.	Richard Basset and Jeva.	ib.
	§ 12.	Denton.	do.	ib.
	§ 13.	Kempston.	Countess Judith.	ib.
Stephen.	§ 14.	Siwell.	Matilda of Mundeville.	25
Henry II.	§ 15.	Bedford.	Countess Judith.	26
	§ 16.	do.	do.	ib.
	§ 17.	Kempston.	do.	27
	§ 18.	Maid's Moreton.	William Basset.	ib.
	§ 19.	Desborough.	do.	ib.
	§ 20.	Middleton Ernest.	do.	ib.
	§ 21.	Braunston.	Walter of Einecourt.	ib.
	§ 22.	Woburn.	do.	ib.
	§ 23.	Upton.	Simon Beauchamp.	ib.
	§ 24.	Cotes.	Helgot, son of Diogenes.	ib.
	§ 25.	Torendone.	do.	ib.
	§ 26.	Croft.	{ Ralph, Steward of Gilbert of Gaunt. }	ib.
	§ 27.	Tottenham.	David, King of Scotland.	ib.
	§ 28.	Halton.	Roger Murdac.	28
	§ 29.	Shutford.	Walter of Buisseia.	ib.
	§ 30.	Barton.	do.	ib.
	§ 31.	Maldon [Essex].	William Peverell.	ib.
	§ 32.	Ludgarshall.	Geoffrey of Trailli.	ib.
	§ 33.	Wymington.	Walter of Buisseia.	ib.
	§ 34.	East Mersey.	Aelasia.	ib.
	§ 35.	Radwinter.	do.	ib.
	§ 36.	Harrowden.	Simon Beauchamp.	ib.
	§ 37.	Dynesley.	Oliver of Maleverer.	ib.
	§ 38.	do.	Roger Chandos.	ib.
	§ 39.	Mixbury.	Nicholas Basset.	ib.
	§ 40.	Buckden.	Alexander, Bp. of Lincoln.	ib.
	§ 41.	Fernecumba.	Roger of Frievill.	29
	§ 42.	Barford.	Roasia of Creint.	ib.
	§ 43.	Caldwell.	Countess Judith.	ib.
	§ 44.	Berchesdich.	do.	ib.
	§ 45.	Rungeton.	William Fitz-Richard.	ib.

INDEX TO THE ABBEY PROPERTY.

	Locality.	Donor.	First mentioned at page
	§ 46. Sandy.	Hugh Beauchamp.	29
	§ 47. Westcott.	William of Buckland.	ib.
	§ 48. Bedford.	do.	ib.
	§ 49. Harringworth.	Unknown.	50
John.	§ 50. Tingrith.	do.	56
Henry II.	§ 51. Westbury.	Ralph Hareng.	64
	§ 52. Goddington.	Unknown.	65
	§ 53. Clanfield.	Ralph Hareng [prob.]	72
Edward I.	§ 54. Inworth.	William Fylol.	80
	§ 55. Bedford.	Unknown.	85
	§ 56. Moulsoe.	Walter of Cordel.	ib.
	§ 57. Yelden.	Unknown.	87
	§ 58. Roxton.	do.	ib.
	§ 59. Renhold.	do.	ib.
	§ 60. Sopwell and Weng.	do.	ib.
	§ 61. King's Walden.	do.	88
	§ 62. Huntingdon.	do.	ib.
	§ 63. Helidon.	do.	ib.
	§ 64. Rutland.	do.	ib.
	§ 65. Hockwold.	do.	ib.
	§ 66. Kempston.	do.	90
	§ 67. Flitton.	do.	ib.
	§ 68. Wilbarston.	do.	ib.
	§ 69. Moulsoe.	Roger and Alice Jory.	92
Edward II.	§ 70. Arnesby.	Hugh Beauchamp.	101
Edward III.	§ 71. Thorp.	Priory of Kyme.	109
	§ 72. Elstow.	Bishop of Lincoln.	ib.
	§ 73. Elstow, &c.	Thomas atte Brugge.	110
	§ 74. Elstow, &c.	Morteyn and others.	111
	§ 75. Elstow, &c.	Viker and Hornesbend.	112
Henry IV.	§ 76. Felmersham.	Unknown.	117
	§ 77. Bromham.	do.	ib.
	§ 78. Wotton.	do.	ib.
Henry VI.	§ 79. Westoning.	do.	119
Henry VIII.	§ 80. Pulloxhill.	do.	123
	§ 81. S. Machuts.	do.	ib.
	§ 82. Gravenhurst Parva.	do.	ib.
	§ 83. Irkhamstede.	do.	ib.
	§ 84. Stonehouse.	do.	ib.
	§ 85. Fenlake.	do.	124
	§ 86. Houghton.	do.	ib.
	§ 87. Elstow.	Henry I.	ib.
	§ 88. Wyldole.	Unknown.	ib.
	§ 89. Wilden.	do.	164
	§ 90. Cotton.	do.	ib.
	§ 91. Welbury.	do.	ib.
	§ 92. Gravenhurst Magna.	do.	165
	§ 93. Friskney.	do.	ib.
	§ 94. King's Mead.	do.	ib.

INDEX

TO CHRONICLES OF THE ABBEY OF ELSTOW.

ABRINCIS, Roland [or Ruelland] of, 24, 25; benefaction of, 27.
Aelasia, benefaction of, 28; 37.
Aids, 15, 102.
Aldeburgh, Richard of, Counsel for the Crown v. Abbess, 103, 104.
Aldemanneby, 66.
Aldermannesbury, 67 n., 102, 104.
Alexander III., Pope, Bull of, re Newhouse, 47.
────── IV., Pope, Bull of, granting Clanfield Church, 72, 73.
Alnestou, Alnestoua, Alnestow, Alnestowe: see Elstow.
Altmannus, 9.
Alwold, 13.
Anglo-Saxon Chronicle, 18.
Arderne, Robert of, Justice, 102.
Ardesbia: see Arnesby.
Argentain [orArgentine], Margery, 143; epitaph, 190.
────── Reginald, suit of, v. Abbess, re Wymondley Church, 52—55; 191.
────── Richard, 60.
────── Sir William, 143, 190, 191.
Arnesby, 90, 101, 165.
    Ardesbia, 27, 34.
    Erendesby, gift of land at to Abbey, 15.
    Erndesby, 101.
    Hernedesby, 76.
Assizes, 16, 82, 83.
Augmentation, Court of, 155, 156, 170, 177.
Aumale, Adelaide, Countess of, 1.
Aunestowe: see Elstow.
Avintona [or Avintone], gift of land at to Abbey, 15; 22, 28.

Ballard, Henry, 160.
────── William, 181.
Balliol, Jocelin of, sig. 29; 42.
Banbury, Hundred of, 77.
Barford, 39, 40, 123, 165.
    Beref, gift of tithe at to Abbey, 29; 39.
    Bereford, 87.
Barlechsweye, Hundred of, 101.

Barton, Great, 36, 165.
    Burton, gift of tithe at to Abbey, 28; 36.
Basset, Nicholas, benefaction of, 15; 21, 28, 38.
────── Ralph, 21, 38, 39.
────── Ralph, jun., 38, 39.
────── Richard, sig. 24; 28, 31, 37.
────── William, benefaction of, 27; 31, 32, 77.
────── William [of Bedford], 85.
Bayeux, Bp. of, 32.
Beauchamp [or Bello Campo], Hugh, benefaction of, 29; 32, 40, 101.
────── Hugh, jun., 40.
────── Milo, 32, 40.
────── Oliver, 40.
────── Paganus, 32, 33.
────── Rohasia, benefaction of, 29; 39.
────── Simon, benefaction of, 27; 28, 32.
────── Simon, jun., 33.
Beaumont, Henry of, witness to grant of Countess Judith, 12.
────── Roger of, 12.
Bede, 11.
Bedford, 30, 66, 85, 87, 94, 95, 97, 100, 102, 105, 106, 107, 116, 124, 165, 166, 183, 184.
    Bedfordia, grant of property at to Abbey, 26.
────── Archdeaconry of, 126, 163.
────── Burgesses of, 29, 40; petition of v. Abbess, 105; 166.
────── County of, 101, 165.
────── Castle, 59, 67, 68.
────── Duke of, 180.
Bedefordscire, 12.
Berchesdich, grant of land at to Abbey, 29; 40.
Beref, Bereford: see Barford.
Beverley, 46.
────── Alan of, sig. 46.
────── Philip, Canon of, sig. 46.
Beynyn, William, 96.
Biggleswade, 75, 185.
Biscop, Hugh, sale of land to by Abbess, 70.

P

Biscopelanda, grant of tithe at to Abbey, 27.
Biset, Manasser, sig. 29 ; 41, sig. 43.
Blois, Henry of, papal legate, 55.
Bochelanda : see Buckland.
Bokeden : see Buckden.
Bonyon, Thomas, 160, 161.
────── William, 161.
Borlar, 14.
Borleaux, Council of, 21.
Bosco, William of, Counsel to Reg. of Argentan v. Abbess, 55.
Braibroc, Henry de, 67.
Braunston, 32, 123, 165.
────── Brandeston, 32.
Braxted, 81.
Bray, Milo of, Benefactor of Abbey, 12.
Bread and Beer, Assize of, 102, 104.
Breaute, Falk de, 58, 59, 66, 67, 68.
────── William de, 68.
Bridlington, Gregory, Prior of, papal commissioner re Newhouse, 45, 47.
Brief, 82.
Bromham, 117, 165.
Browne Willis, 64.
────── MSS. extr. from, 134.
Brugge, Thomas atte, benefaction of, 110 ; 152, 153.
Brus, Robert of, sig. 17 ; 23.
Buckden, 39, 123, 165.
────── Bokeden, 88.
────── Bugendena, gift of rent at to Abbey, 28 ; 39.
Buckingham, Archdeaconry of, 87, 125.
────── County of, 76.
────── Deanery of, 88.
────── Henry, Duke of, 180.
Buckland, Hugh of, 40.
────── Thomas, 162.
────── William of, 40.
────── Bochelanda, William de, benefaction of, 29 ; 40.
Bugendena : see Buckden.
Buissela, Walter of, benefaction of, 28 ; 35.
Buniun, William, 55, 56.
Bunyan, John, 55, 159.
Burnham, Deanery of, 87.
Burton : see Barton.
Byzantium, 10.

Cæsar, 10.
Caldwell, 40.
────── Caldwella, gift of land at to Abbey, 29 ; 40.
Camelton, Cameston : see Kempston.
Camuilt, Thomas de, Agreement of Abbess with, re Goddington, 65.

Candleshow, Deanery of, 88.
Canterbury, 29, 42, 43.
────── Abps of :—
Hubert, 57.
Reynolds, 147.
Richard, letters of, re Newhouse, 47, 49.
Theobald, sig. 29 ; 39, 41, 43.
Cardington, 166, 183, 186.
Carleton, George, lease to by Abbey, 155.
Carlisle, 95, 98.
Carucate, 13.
Cave, Rev. T., Vicar of Elstow, 187.
Cavendissh, William, 158.
Chandos, Robert of, 38.
────── Robert of, jun., 28, 38.
────── Roger of, benefaction of, 28.
Chantries, 151, 152, 153.
Chantry Certificates, 167, 169.
────── Valuation of, 128.
Cheeke, Sir Thomas, joins in sale of Abbey to Hillersden, 183.
Chek, Henry, 180, 183.
Chester, Hugh, Earl of, 22.
Chiselhampton, Cecilia of, 71.
Chronicon Paschale, 10.
Clanfield, 64, 72 ; grant of Church to Abbey, 73 ; 87, 89, 123, 125, 165.
Clapham, 125.
Clopham, Deanery of, 87.
Close Rolls, Henry III., extr. from, 66.
Coel, 10.
Colchester, 10, 87.
Cole's MSS., extr. from, 147, 179, 183, 187.
Combes, Henry, Auditor to Abbey, 126.
Complaints, 16.
Computus Ministrorum, 23, 33, 34, 36, 54, 89, 117, 127.
────── extr. from, 164.
Confirmation Charter of Henry II., 22, 23, 26.
────── Roll, 2 Henry VIII., 17, 24, 26, 42, 43, 112, 113, 121, 150.
Constantia, 10.
Constantine, 3, 5, 6, 7, 8, 9, 10, 11.
Constantinople, 9, 10, 11.
Constantius, 7, 10.
Cordel, Walter de, benefaction of, 85.
Cornwall, Reginald, Earl of, sig. 29 ; 41.
────── Richard, Earl of, 64.
Cospatrick, 1.
Cotes, gift of tithe at to Abbey, 27 ; 33.
Coton under Guilsbro', 33.

INDEX.

Cotton, 164, 166.
———— MSS., extr. from, 60, 62, 63.
Court of Pie Powder, 174.
Creint, Roasia de, 29, 39.
Croft, gift of tithe at to Abbey, 27; 34, 90, 124, 165, 166.
Crokerst, William, Abbot of, 46.
Cross, The, 4, 5, 7, 8, 9.
Crowland, 2.
———— Ufketyl, Abbot of, 2.
Cucking stool, 83, 104.
Customs, 16.

Danegeld, 16, 82.
Daventry, 88, 89.
Deddington, Deanery of, 87.
Denton, Dentune : see Dunton.
Derby, Earl of, 12.
Desborough, 31.
    Disburc, gift of tithe at to Abbey, 27; 31.
Dineleshou : see Dynesley.
Doomsday Survey, extr. from, 12; 18, 19, 20, 21, 22, 30, 53.
Drepanum, 3, 10.
Dues, Shire and Hundred, 103.
Dumeslai : see Dynesley.
Dunstaple, 67, 70, 123.
———— Annals of, extr. from, 57.
Dunton, 22, 28.
    Denton, 15.
    Dentune, gift of mill at to Abbey, 15.
Dynesley, 38, 62, 88, 90.
    Dineleshou, gift of land at to Abbey, 28 ; 38.
    Dumeslai, gift of Church to Abbey, 28 ; 38.

East Mersey, 37.
    Estmera, gift of tithe at to Abbey, 28.
Eaton Socon, Deanery of, 87.
Edward the Confessor, 13, 14.
———— I., 76, 78, 79, 86, 101.
———— Reign of, 75—96.
———— II., 17, 99, 101.
———— Reign of, 96—101.
———— III., Charters of, 109, 110, 111, 121.
———— Reign of, 102—113.
———— IV., Reign of, 119.
———— V., Reign of, 119.
———— VI., 156, 169, 170; grant of Abbey to Radcliffe by, 172.
———— Reign of, 168, 178.
Einecourt, Walter of, benefactions of, 27 ; 32.
Einesford, 30.
Elemosiny, 13.
Elizabeth, 180, 182.
———— Reign of, 178—184,

Elstow, 1, 19, 20, 24, 25, 44, 45, 49, 50, 53, 55, 58, 69, 76, 81, 86, 90, 92, 93, 100, 102, 109, 110, 111, 112, 123, 124, 125, 126, 129, 142, 147, 149, 150, 151, 152, 153, 154, 156, 163, 164, 165, 167, 178, 181, 182, 184, 185, 186, 187, 190, 191.
    Alnestou, 57.
    Alnestoua, 51.
    Alnestow, 58.
    Alnestowe, 49, 54, 66, 76.
    Aunestowe, 65, 70.
    Elmstouwe, 77.
    Elnestou, 13 ; granted to Abbey by Countess Judith, 14 ; 26, 42, 43.
    Elnestow, 46, 149, 191.
    Elnestowe, 47, 61, 62, 63, 69, 71, 72, 73, 77, 78, 79, 82, 83, 87, 95, 97, 101, 104, 105, 108, 109, 115, 116, 118, 129, 136, 137, 140, 157, 158, 159.
    Elsloe, 183.
    Elverstowe, 99.
    Elvestowe, 74, 169, 170, 171, 183.
    Helenestowe, 11.
    Helenestue, 58.
    Helenstowe, 15.
    Vlnestowe, 130.
Elstow, Abbesses, Table of, 146.
———— Abbesses of :—
    Anastasia, 112, 146.
    Anora, 78, 79, 146.
    Balliol, Clementia of, 78, 92, 98, 146.
    Basset, Juliana, 146.
    Beauchamp, Elizabeth, 102, 146.
    Boyfeld, Elizabeth, 136, 141, 145, 146, 150, 154.
    Gascoigne, Agnes, 146, 150.
    Godfrey, Margaret, 120, 146.
    Hervey, Elizabeth, 120, 146 ; tomb of, 147 ; 187, 190.
    Mabilia, 60, 61, 62, 65, 146.
    Morteyn, Elizabeth, 111, 146.
    Pygot, Margaret, 114, 116, 146.
    Scoteny, Beatrice of, 79, 146.
    Silcampo, Albreda de, 72, 146.
    Trayley, Joanna, 115, 116, 118, 119, 146.
    Wauton, Joanna of, 98, 146, 147.
    Westbury, Agnes of, 70, 71, 72, 146.
    Wymar . . . Lady, 146.
———— Abbey, grant of to Radcliffe, 172 ; lease of to Hervey, 156 ; sale of to Hillersden, 183 ; sale of to Whitbread, 185 ; surrender of to the Crown, 136.

Elstow Abbey, Seals of:—
　The Common, or Great, 115, 139.
　The lesser, 112, 119.
　—— Clerks instituted to, 151.
　—— Common Rights at, 181.
　—— Court Rolls of, 156.
　—————— Extr. from, 159.
　—— Fair, 82, 84, 102, 174.
　———— Grant of, 42, 43, 83.
　———— Tolls of, 124, 128, 158.
　—— Ghost, 191.
　—— Mansion of, 183.
　—— Nuns buried at Bedford, 144.
　—— Parish, Inclosure of, 186.
　—— Pensions to Nuns of, 141.
　—— Prioresses of:—
　　Giffard, Agatha, 78, 79, 80.
　　Isilia, 71.
　—— Robert, Chaplain of, 65.
　—— Writ to Abbess of, 99.
Ely, Bp. of, 182.
Emifosbia, 26, 38.
Erendesby, Erndeshy: see Arnesby.
Essex, Henry of, 37.
Estgrenwyche, Manor of, 176.
Estmera: see East Mersey.
Eton College, 125.
Eusebius, 6, 7, 11.
Eutropius, 11.

Farrar, Dennis, 134, 191.
　———— Hillersden, 191.
Felmersham, 117.
Fenechelanda, 27.
Fenlake, 124, 127, 166.
Fernecumba, 29, 39.
Ferrers, Henry of, witness to grant of Countess Judith, 12.
　—— Walkelin of, 12.
Fitz Gerold, Warin, sig. 29; 41.
Fitz John, Philip, sig. 17; 23.
Fitz Walter, Eustace, Attorney for Abbess v. Argentan, 53.
Flamavill, Robert, suit v. by Abbess, 105.
Flitton, 70, 87, 90, 91, 123, 125, 126, 163, 165.
　Flitte, 70.
　—— Philip of, 70.
Foxkote, Robert de, 77.
Frank Pledge, View of, 82, 84, 102, 159.
Free Warren, 102.
　—— grant of, 24, 42, 84.
Fridai [or Fridei], Ivo, 15, 28, 37.
Frievill, Roger de, benefaction of, 29; 39.
Friskney, 165, 166.
Fylol, Sir John, 81.
　—— William, benefaction of, 80.

Gallows, 82, 104.
Gascoyn, Sir John, 171.
Gatecumbe, Matilda of, 77.
Gelds, 15, 82, 83, 102.
Geoffrey of Monmouth, 10.
George II., Reign of, 184, 185.
　———— III., Reign of, 185-7.
Gisburne, Abbey of, 23.
Goddington, 65, 77, 90, 91.
　Godendon, 65.
　Godigdon, 77.
Goldelanda, 27.
Golgotha, 8, 9.
Gostwick family, the, 180, 181.
　———— Sir John, commissioner for receiving surrender of Abbey, 141; 180.
　———— Sir William, 180.
Gravenhurst, 165.
　———— Magna, 165, 166.
　———— Parva, 123, 127.
Gregory IX., Pope, Bull of re dispute with Abbey of St. Albans, 69.
Grey, Sir Henry, Chief Steward of Abbey, 126; 162.
Grimbald, Robert, sig. 25.
　———— Warner, sig. 25.
Gudlakston, Deanery of, 88.
Guiz, Simon le, Attorney for Abbess v. Argentan, 52, 54, 56.
Guthlac, 2.
Guthlaston, Hundred of, 76.
Gynelden: see Yelden.

Halton, gift of property at to Abbey, 28; 35, 45, 46, 47, 48, 49, 88, 90, 118, 123.
Hanaper, 177.
Hareng, Ralph de, 64, 72.
Harenkwod: see Harringworth.
Harleian Charters, extr. from, 45, 47, 49, 51, 69, 118.
Harnyngton, John, Pension to, 163.
Harold, 20, 53.
Harringworth, grant of Church at to Abbey, 50, 51; 90, 123, 125, 126, 163, 165.
　Harenkwod, 49, 50.
Harrowden, 33, 124, 127, 164, 166.
　Herghedona, gift of land at to Abbey, 28; 33.
Hatton, Sir Christopher, grant of fee-farm rent to, 181; 182.
Hegham, Roger of, Commissioner re Pathweye, 94; 96.
Helenestowe, Helenestue: see Elstow.
Helenopolis, 3, 10.
Helenstowe: see Elstow.
Helgot, son of Diogenes, benefaction of, 27; 33.

INDEX.

Helidon, 88, 89.
    Helyden, 88.
Henry I., 12, 14, 15, 17, 18, 20, 21, 24, 30, 53, 54, 78, 83, 84, 101.
——— Charters of, 15, 42, 43, 83.
——— II., 20, 24, 53, 54, 77, 113.
——— Charters of, 26, 42, 83, 103.
——— Reign of, 25—52.
——— III., 71, 76, 101.
——— Charter of, 59.
——— Reign of, 59, 75.
——— IV., Reign of, 114—118.
——— V., Reign of, 118, 119.
——— VI., Reign of, 119.
——— VII., Reign of, 120.
——— VIII., 17, 18, 65, 112, 113, 136, 138, 141, 156, 158, 159, 164, 175.
——— Confirmation Roll of : see under Confirmation.
——— Reign of, 120—168.
——— Prince, Charter of, 43, 44.
Hereford, Elizabeth, Countess of, 99.
Hereford and Essex, Earl of, sig. 100.
Herghedona : see Harrowden.
Hernedesby : see Arnesby.
Hertford, 78.
Hervey, Edmund, commissioner for receiving surrender of Abbey, 141; lease of Abbey to, 156; 158; annuity to, 163; 178, 180, 190.
——— Family, Pedigree of, 143.
——— John, 190.
Hiccha, Hiche, Hichen, Hichene : see Hitchin.
Hidage, 82.
Hillersden Family, sale of Abbey by the, 185.
——— Thomas, purchase of Abbey by, 183 ; 191.
Hitchin, Grant of Church to Abbey, 15; 18, 53, 60, 78, 90, 119, 123, 125, 126, 164, 165, 166.
    Hiccha, 28.
    Hiche, 15, 54, 55.
    Hichen, 88.
    Hichene, 60, 61, 63.
    Hiz, 53.
Hockwold, 88, 90.
Holy Land, The, 7.
Holy Trinity, The, 12.
Horneshend, John, benefaction of, 112.
Houghton, 124, 126, 164.
Hugo, Rev. J., extr. from work of, 144.
Humet, Richard of, sig. 29 ; 41, sig. 42 and 43.
Hundred Rolls, The, 31, 65, 81.
——— descr. of, 76.
——— extr. from, 76.

Huntingdon, 88, 101.
Hynton, George, Bailiff of Maulden, 126.

Infangenethef, 17, 82, 83, 104.
Inneworth : see Inworth.
Inquis. "ad quod damnum," or "post mortem," Descr. of, 91.
——— 11 Henry IV., 116.
Inspeximus, 14, 17, 42, 121.
Inworth, suit v. Abbess, re advowson of, 80, 81 ; 87, 90, 123, 165.
    Inneworth, 87.
Ipre, Robert of, Attorney for Abbess v. the Crown, 103.
Irkhamstede, 123, 127, 165.

James I., Reign of, 181—184.
Jerusalem, 4, 5, 7, 8, 9, 11.
Jeva, joint benefaction of with R. Basset, 15 ; 22, 28, 37.
John, 21, 59, 166.
——— Reign of, 52—59.
Jordeburgh, Deanery of, 35, 88.
Jory, Roger, and Alice, benefaction of, 92.
Judith, Countess, 1, 2, 11 ; original grant by, 12 ; 15, 18, 20, 22, 23, 26 ; additional benefaction by, 29 ; 31, 33, 34, 40, 41, 50, 54, 101, 107, 148.

Kempston, 31, 43, 56, 90 ; gift of land at to Abbey, 110 ; 116, 123, 124, 126, 154, 155, 156, 158, 159, 163, 164, 165, 174, 175, 183.
    Camelton, 110.
    Cameston, 14, 23 ; grant of land at by Countess Judith to Abbey, 27 ; 110.
    Kembeston, 87.
    Kemeston, 82, 83.
Kempston Bourn, 23, 165.
——— Box End, 117.
Kennett, Bp., 120.
Kernewyz, Deanery of, 88.
Keysoe, gift of glebe at to Vicarage, 184, 185.
King's Mead, The, 165, 166.
King's Walden, 88, 124, 164, 165.
    Walden Regis, 88.
Kyme, Priory of, grant of rent from to Abbey, 109 ; 123.

Land service, 16.
Langecote [or Langetote], Ralph of, benefaction of, 15 ; 20, 21, 86.
——— Richard of, benefaction of, 15 ; 20, 86.
Langley, 98.
Lansdown MSS., 120.

INDEX.

Leckampstead, gift of land at to Abbey, 31.
    Lechamstede, 88.
    Leckamsted, 77.
le Despenser, Hugh, sen. and jun., sig. 100.
Leicester, 100.
—— Co. of, 15, 27, 76, 101.
—— Robert, Earl of, 12.
—— Robert [Bossu], Earl of, sig. 29; 41.
    Leycester, Archdeaconry of, 88.
Leland, 11, 12.
Lexden, Deanery of, 87.
Licinius, 6.
Lilburne, John, commissioner under Act 37 Geo. III., 186.
Lincoln, Archdeaconry of, 88.
—— Bishops of:—
    Alexander, benefaction of, 28; 39.
    Alnewick, 119 n.
    Beck, 109.
    Buckingham, 152 n.
    Burghershe, 111 n.
    De Chesney, sig. 29.
    Gravesend, 74; letter of, 80.
    Grosseteste, 71 n., 72 n.
    Gynwell, 111 n.
    Lexington, 89.
    Longland, injunctions of, 129.
    Repington, 115 n.
    S. Hugh, 57.
    Sutton, letter of, 79; commissioner for Tax. Pap. Nic., 86.
Litton, Sir William, 191.
London, Bishops of:—
    De Beaumes, sig. 29.
    De Fauconberg, 68.
Ludgarshall, 36, 37.
    Lutegareshala, gift of tithe at to Abbey, 28.
Lyndhurst, 94.

Macarius, Bp. of Jerusalem, 4, 6.
Madebury, 125.
Magnaville, Geoffrey de, 32.
Maid's Moreton, 31.
    Mordona, gift of land at to Abbey, 27; 31.
    Moreton, 88.
    Morthone, 77.
    Morton, 77.
Maldon, Maldona, Maldone: see Maulden.
Maldon [Essex], 36, 56.
    Mealdon, gift of tithe at to Abbey, 28; 36.
Maleverer, Cecilia and Oliver de, benefaction of, 28.
Malherbe, Nigel, 56.
Malt, Assize of, 83.

Markham, John, pension to, 163.
Marlborough, Duchess of, 180.
Mary and Elizabeth, Reigns of, 178—181.
Matilda [or Maud], Countess, benefaction of, 15; 22, 23, 35, 50.
Matthew Paris, 58, 67.
Maulden, 20, 70, 102; gift of land at to Abbey, 111; 124, 126, 155, 156, 163, 165.
    Maldon, 87, 104, 116.
    Maldona, 70.
    Maldone, 82, 83, 108.
    Maudon, 101.
    Meldona, 26.
    Meldone, original gift of land at to Abbey, 12; 15.
Maximian, 11.
Mayott, John, Chaplain, 129.
Mealdon: see Maldon [Essex].
Meldona, Meldone: see Maulden.
Mellent, Robert of, witness to grant of Countess Judith, 12; 41.
Message, John, Chaplain, 111, 152, 153.
Middleton Ernest [or Erneys], 31, 32, 87, 109.
    Middelt, gift of tithe at to Abbey, 27; 31.
    Milton, 123.
Middleton [Oxon], 15.
Mixbury, 38, 65.
    Mixberia, gift of mill at to Abbey, 28.
Molesho: see Moulsoe.
Molesworth, Walter of, Sheriff of Bedford, 94.
Montacute, William, sig. 100.
Mordaunt, Sir John, lease to by Abbess, 154.
—— John, Lord, 155, 156.
Mordona, Moreton: see Maid's Moreton.
Morgan, Francis, lease to by Abbess, 155.
Moriz, John, 100.
Morteyn, John, benefaction of, 111.
Morthone: see Maid's Moreton.
Mortmain, Statute of, 91.
Morton: see Maid's Moreton.
—— William, Earl of, 25.
Moulsoe, 92, 112, 124, 154, 155, 164.
—— Richard, Parson of, 85.
    Molesho, 87.
    Mulesho, gift of land at to Abbey, 15.
    Muleshou, 27.
Mundeville, Maltilda of, benefaction of, 25.
—— Nigel of, 24.

Mundeville, William of, 25.
Murdac, Roger, benefaction of, 28; 35, 45.
Murders, 16, 82, 83.
Mursley, Deanery of, 88.

Nedham, Francis, grant of fee farm rent to, 181; 182.
Nehus: see Newhouse.
Newenham, Priory of, 33, 59, 123.
Newhouse, Abbot of, suit by *v.* Abbey, 45—50; 68, 118, 123.
——— Nehus, 46.
Newport Pagnel, Deanery of, 87.
Nicæa, Council of, 7.
Nonarum Inquisitio, descr. of, 107.
——————— extr. from, 108.
Norfolk, Archdeaconry of, 88.
——— Thomas, Earl of, sig. 100.
Northampton, Archdeaconry of, 88, 126.
——————— Council of, 67.
——————— and Huntingdon, Waltheof, Earl of, 1.
——————— Senlis [or S. Lis], Earl of, 22, 189.
Northumbria, Siward, Earl of, 1, 2.
Nottingham, 59.
Noyon, Robert of, 57.

Obit and Lamp, endowment for, 171.
Occasions, 16.
Offley, 164, 166.
Offruit, gift of tithe at to Abbey, 26.
Orderic Vital, 2, 12, 18, 21.
Oseney, Abbey of, 38.
Oundle, 67.
Owen, Henry, 143, 180.
Oxford, 38.
    Oxenforda, 28.
    Oxineford, gift of property at to Abbey, 15.
Oxon, Archdeaconry of, 87, 89, 125.
Oxon, Co. of, 77.

Page, William, tenant under Abbey, 77.
Palestine, 9, 10.
Panegyrists, 10.
Parliament, petition in *v.* Abbess, *re* rents at Bedford, 105.
Parlys, Ralph, 143, 190.
Pathweye, suit *v.* Abbey, *re,* 92—98.
Peverel, 101.
Peverell, Ralph, 36.
——— William, benefaction of, 28; 36, 56.

Phipps, Rev. Robert, Vicar of Elstow, 184.
Piccage, 174, 183.
Pightell, 169.
Pilate, 4.
Pillory, 104.
Pipe Roll, 18.
Pleas, 16.
Ploughly, Hundred of, 77.
Poictiers [Pict], Richard, Archdeacon of, 44.
Preston, Agreement with Templars at, 60—64; 166.
Pulloxhill, 123, 127.
Pulter, William, Bailiff of Hitchin, 126.

Queen Anne's Bounty, 184.
Quo Warranto, pleas of *v.* Abbess, 81, 102.
——————— Statute of, 77.

Radcliffe, Sir Edward, 143, 180; joins in sale of Abbey, 183.
——— Elizabeth, 143, 180.
——— Frances, 143, 180, 183.
——— Sir Humphrey, 143; grant of Abbey to, 172; 174, 175, 176, 177, 178, 179; epitaph, 180; 182, 183.
——— Isabel, 143, 180.
——— Martha, 143, 180.
——— Mary, 143, 180.
——— Thomas, 143, 180.
Radwinter, 37.
    Redewint, gift of tithe at to Abbey, 28; 37.
Ralph, Steward of G. of Gaunt, benefaction of, 27; 34.
Reate, 69.
Redburnstoke, Hundred of, 12, 84.
Redewint: see Radwinter.
Regesta Pontificum Romanorum, 48, n. 51.
Renhold, 87, 89.
    Ronhale, suit of Abbess, *re* rent at, 105.
Richard I., and John, Reigns of, 52—59.
——— II., Reign of, 113, 114.
——— Charter of, 113, 121.
——— III., Reign of, 119.
Ridel, Geoffrey and Maud, 22.
Rievaulx, Sylvan, Abbot of, papal commissioner *re* Newhouse, 45, 47.
Ripa, Helena de, 78.
Rissington, 22, 38.
    Risendona, 28.
    Risendune, gift of mills at to Abbey, 15.

INDEX.

Rivesby, Hugh, Abbot of, sig. 46.
Robinson, Thomas, lease of Chantry lands to, 170.
Rokele, Sarra de la, 71.
Rokesden : see Roxton.
Rome, 46, 68.
Ronhale : see Renhold.
Rotel : see Rutland.
Roxton, 87, 89.
 Rokesden, 87.
Rufinus, 8.
Rungeton, gift of tithe at to Abbey, 29.
Rutland, 88.
 Rotel, 88.

Sac and Soc, 14 n., 17, 83.
S. Albans, 66, 89, 125.
——— Abbey of, dispute of Abbess with, re tithes, &c., 69 ; 127.
——— Abbot Whethamstede of, 127.
S. Ambrose, 8.
S. Andrew, Northampton, Priory of, 24, 25, 105.
S. Benedict, rule of, 145.
S. Chrysostom, 8.
S. Cyril of Jerusalem, 7.
S. Helen, 3, 5, 7, 8, 9, 11, 12, 78, 112, 139.
 S. Elene, 92, 167, 168, 170.
S. Ippolyts, 126, 164, 166.
S. John, Northampton, Mon. of, 117, 123, 127.
S. Julian, Mon. of, 70, 125.
S. Laurence, J., Cardinal of, 73.
S. Leonard, Bedford, Hosp. of, suit *v*. Abbess, re Pathweye, 92—98, 125.
S. Machuts, 70, 123, 127.
S. Mary, 12, 14, 15, 136, 139, 140.
——— of Citrez, Mon. of, 53.
S. Maur, Almeric de, Master of the Temple, 59, 60.
——————— Covenants of with Abbess re Preston Chapel, 60.
S. Neots, 88.
S. Paul, Bedford, Church of, pulled down by Falk de Breaute, and materials used in fortifying Bedford Castle, 58, 59.
Salisbury, Roger, Bp. of, sig. 17.
Samuel, William, suit of *v*. Abbess, re Inworth, 80, 81.
Sancto Leophardo, G. de, 75.
Sandeia : see Sandy.
Sandon, John of, Attorney for Argentain *v*. Abbess, 55.
Sandy, 40.
 Sandeia, gift of rent at to Abbey, 29.

Schutteford : see Shutford.
Scotland, David, King of, 17 ; sig. 18, 22 ; benefaction of, 27 ; 35, 50, 107.
——— Malcolm IV., King of, 35, 105 n., 107.
——— Manklum, King of, plea of Abbess, re grant by, 105, 106.
Scutage, 16, 82, 83.
Senlis [or S. Lis], Simon of, 22, 189.
Sepulchre, The Holy, 4, 5, 6, 7, 9.
Serfs, 13, 14.
Sheriff's aids, 82.
Shutford, 36, 89, 123, 165.
 Schutteford, 77.
 Stutesforda, gift of tithe at to Abbey, 28 ; 36.
Sibell, 34, 165, 166.
Silshoe, 70, 123, 165.
Simeon of Durham, 18.
Siward, Earl of Northumbria, 1, 2.
Siwell, 24 ; gift of land at to Abbey, 25 ; 27, 34.
Socman, 13.
Socrates, 3, 6, 8, 10.
Sopwell, 89, 125, 127.
 Soppewell, 88, 89.
Sozomen, 5, 6, 10.
Spigurnel, Henry, Commissioner re pathweye, 94 ; 96.
Spirech, Alexander and Juliana, prosecuted by Abbess for arrears of rent, 85.
Sporoun, Ingelran, Attorney to Abbess, 84.
Stabularia, 8.
Staford, Nigell of, benefaction of, 15 ; 20, 21, 27, 33, 101.
Stallage, 174.
Starkey [or Speckey], Cecilia, 141, 150.
Stephen, 41.
——— Reign of, 24, 25.
Stodfold, Hundred of, 76.
Stonehouse, 123, 127, 165.
Stow, 3.
Stowe, Archdeaconry of, 88.
Stutesforda : see Shutford.
Sudbrant, gift of tithe at to Abbey, 27 ; 32.
Sussex, Robert, Earl of, 180.
Sutton in the Marsh, 34.
 Suttona, gift of tithe at to Abbey, 27 ; 34.
Swalcliff, 87, 89.

Talbot, Sir John, 143, 189, 190.
Taxatio Papæ Nicolai, 31, 32, 33, 35, 81, 105, 108, 118, 128.
——————— descr. of, 86.
——————— extr. from, 87.

INDEX. 217

Templars, 60, 61, 62, 63.
Testa de Nevill, 64, 100.
———— descr. of, 101.
———— extr. from, 101.
Theodora, Empress, 11.
Theodoret, 5.
Thornton, Gilbert of, Counsel for the Crown v. Abbess, 84.
Thorp next Timberland, grant of rent from to Abbey, 109.
    Thorp, 123.
Thorpe, S. Peter, 34.
    Torp, 27, 34.
Tindene, 59 and note.
Tingrith, suit re advowson of v. Abbess, 56, 80.
———— Nicholas of, 56, 57.
Toll and Team, 17, 83.
Torendona, 27; gift of tithe and land at to Abbey, 33.
Torp: see Thorpe, S. Peter.
Tottenham, 34.
    Toteham, gift of wine at to Abbey, 27; 34.
Towersey, John, benefaction to Vicarage of Elstow, 184.
Tralli, Geoffrey de, benefaction of, 28; 36, 37.
Traylly, Sir Nicholas, sig. 62, 63.
Treves, 10.
Tutbury, Castle of, 12.
Tyringham, R. of, Sheriff of Bedford, 100.

Ufketyl, Abbot of Crowland, 2.
Upton, 123.
    Upeton, gift of tithe at to Abbey, 27.
    Uptone, 33, 87.
Urban III., Pope, Bull of, granting Church of Harringworth to Abbey, 51.

Valor Ecclesiasticus, 33, 34, 36, 70, 89, 109, 117, 164, 166.
———— descr. of, 122.
———— extr. from, 123, 129.
Vatican Transcripts, 72 n.
Vere, Alberic de, 32, 37.
——— Alicia [or Adeliza] de, benefaction of, 37.
Venice, 48.
Venus, Temple of, 4, 6.
Verona, 51.
Vexin, The, 12.
Viker, Hugh, benefaction of, 112.
Villanes, 13, 14.
Viollet-le-Duc, 188.
Virgin, The Blessed, 3.
Viterbo, 73.

Vitric, Andrew of, 54.
Vlnestowe: see Elstow.

Walden Regis: see King's Walden.
Wallingford, 66.
Walpole, 128, 165.
Waltheof, Earl, 1; his death and epitaph, 2; 11, 22, 148.
Wanton, Edward, Receiver to Abbey, 126.
Wardon, Abbot of, 35, 125.
Warpeny, 16.
Warwick, Henry, Earl of, 12.
———— Richard, Earl of, 183.
Welbury, 164.
Wemyngton: see Wymington.
Weng: see Wing.
Wentworth, Mary, 143, 180.
Wescota: see Westcott.
Westbury, acquisition of Church of by Abbey, 64; 72, 77, 88, 90, 123, 125.
———— William of, 64.
Westcott, 40.
    Wescota, gift of land at to Abbey, 29; 40.
Westminster, 65, 84, 92, 95, 105, 114, 177.
Weston, 18, 28, 53.
    Westune, gift of Church to Abbey, 15.
Westoning, 119, 123, 125, 126, 163, 164, 165.
Weyf, 82, 84, 102.
Whitbread, Mr., purchases Abbey, 185, 186; endows Vicarage, 187.
Whithed, Henry, Bailiff of Elstow, 126.
Whytebred, Thomas, 160, 161.
Wilbarston, 90, 91, 123, 126, 165.
Wilden, 164, 166.
Wilhamstede and Willamste: see Willshamstead.
William I., 1, 11, 19, 20, 28, 39, 53, 54.
———— II., 12, 20.
———— Medicus, 15, 22, 24, 27, 43.
———— son of Richard, 29.
Willshamstead, 20, 90; gifts of property at to Abbey, 110, 111, 112; 123, 124, 126, 156, 158, 163, 164, 183.
    Wilhamstede, 101.
    Willamste, 87.
    Willeshampsted, 174.
    Wilsamested, 15.
    Wilshamstude, 82, 83.
    Wilshamstudia, 26.
    Winnessamstede, gift Abbey, 13.
    Wylshamsted, 116.

Wiment: see Wymington.
Wimundesle: see Wymondley.
Winchester, 2, 17, 44.
────── Bishops of:—
  De Pontissara, commissioner for Tax. Pap. Nic., 86.
  Sendale, sig. 100.
Wing, 89.
  Weng, 88, 89.
Wingate, Katherine, Chaplain to Abbess, 133, 135, 141.
Winnessamestede: see Willshamstead.
Witney, Deanery of, 87.
Woburn, 32.
  Woborna, gift of tithe at to Abbey, 27.
  Wooborn, 124.
  Wouborn, 87.
Woburnia, Richard, Abbot of, 70.
Wotton, 117, 127.
Wycumbe, Deanery of, 87.

Wyldole, 124, 128.
Wymington, 36, 117, 165.
  Wiment, gift of land at to Abbey, 28; 36.
  Wyrmington, 87.
Wymondley, 20; suit v. Abbess, re Church of, 52—55; 90, 126, 163, 164, 166, 182, 191.
  Wimundesle, 54, 55.
  Wymundele, 88.
────── William, Prior of, 60, 62, 63.
────── Prior of, 125.
Wyrmington: see Wymington.

Yelden, 87, 89, 117, 166.
  Gynelden, 87.
York, 10.
── Archbishops of:—
  Giffard, 74 n.
  Murdac, 35.
  Thurstan, sig. 17.

ADDENDA AND CORRIGENDA.

P. 3, *l.* 4. With regard to the vexed question of the dedication of the Church, to which, it will be observed, repeated allusion is made in these pages, the writer of an article contributed to the 'Saturday Review' of 17th September, 1881, makes the following valuable remarks:—

"Elstow . . . takes its designation, the *stow* or place of S. Helen, from the original dedication of the Church in Saxon times to S. Helena, the mother of the Emperor Constantine. The Church of Rome, with her all-absorbing centralization, has ever shewn herself as unfriendly to local saints, as to provincial liturgies or national uses. Thus S. Guthlac was almost buried in his own Crowland beneath the later names of S. Mary and S. Bartholomew; S. Peter took precedence of S. Wilfrid at Ripon, and of S. Etheldreda at Ely, while his brother Apostle, S. Andrew, was placed before S. David, in his own cathedral of Menevia. In this way the old Saxon chapel of S. Helen became the Church of S. Mary of Elstow, which, in due course, had to give way at the Reformation to the Holy and Undivided Trinity."

p. 9, *l.* 11. For the "Iron crown of *Hungary*," read "*Lombardy*."

p. 12, *l.* 21. The statement, that Henry of Beaumont was "created Earl of Warwick, 1068," cannot be substantiated. It is probable that he was placed in charge of Warwick Castle about that year, but his promotion to the Earldom did not, apparently, take place until after the reign of William I.

p. 34, *l.* 3. For "§ 25," read "§ 26."

p. 52 et seq. Reginald of Argentain *v.* the Abbess, *re* the advowson of Wymondley. Since these pages have been in type, additional, and almost contemporary, evidence has been found, to prove that the Abbess was successful in her defence, in a memorandum of Bishop Wells [1209—35], printed by Clutterbuck in his History of Hertfordshire [ii. 545]:—

ADDENDA AND CORRIGENDA.

"The Vicarage of the Church of Great Wymondley, which belongs to the Abbess and Convent of Aunestowe, consists in the whole altarage [i.e. offerings laid upon the altar] with a suitable residence, and in one acre in one field, and another in another. And the Vicar pays to the said nuns half a mark per annum, and is responsible for the synodals, but the Nuns are to provide entertainment for the Archdeacon."

From the last clause of this it seems pretty evident that Wymondley *was* included in the original grant of Hitchin. See p. 15.

The advowson of Great Wymondley appears to have been granted, at the dissolution, with that of Hitchin, to Trinity College, Cambridge. That of Little Wymondley, which was the joint property of the Abbess of Elstow and the Prior of Wymondley, passed into private hands, and is now held by Mr. Unwin Heathcote, of Shephalbury, Stevenage.

p. 57, *l.* 16. For "1293," read "1203."

p. 58, *l.* 18. The story commencing at this line belongs to the time when Falk de Breauté was placed in the custody of the Bishop of London. See p. 68.

p. 60. Covenant between the Templars and the Abbess. Here, again, the memoranda of Bishop Wells supply confirmatory evidence, one relating to Hitchin being as follows:—

"The Vicarage of the Church of Hycche, which belongs to the Abbess and Convent of Aunestowe, consists in the whole altarage of the same Church, and in one acre in one field and another in another, with a suitable residence. And the Vicar pays to the said Nuns thirteen marks per annum, from which they are to pay one mark per annum to the brothers of the Temple. And the Vicar is responsible for the synodals, but the Nuns are to provide entertainment for the Archdeacon. Two Chaplains are needed." [*Clutterbuck*, iii. 35.]

The spelling of the name, "Aunestowe," adopted in the above extracts, and which is found again in the record of the suit *re* Goddington [p. 65] is somewhat remarkable; and Bishop Wells is credited with having been the first to remark in it the curious fact that "Aune" is the French term for an "Ell."

p. 64, *l.* 29. After the word "property," insert "he."

BX 2596 .E48 W53 1885 IMST
Wigram, Spencer Robert,
Chronicles of the Abbey of
Elstow 47229569

www.ingramcontent.com/pod-product-compliance
Lightning Source LLC
Chambersburg PA
CBHW021938240426
43669CB00047B/341